Real-Time Concepts for Embedded Systems

Qing Li

with Caroline Yao

CRC Press
Taylor & Francis Group
Boca Raton London New York

CRC Press is an imprint of the
Taylor & Francis Group, an **informa** business

CRC Press
Taylor & Francis Group
6000 Broken Sound Parkway NW, Suite 300
Boca Raton, FL 33487-2742

First issued in hardback 2017

ISBN-13: 978-1-57820-124-2 (pbk)
ISBN-13: 978-1-138-43647-3 (hbk)

Cover art design: Damien Castaneda

Library of Congress Cataloging-in-Publication Data
Li, Qing, 1971-
  Real-time concepts for embedded systems / Qing Li ; with Caroline Yao.
        p. cm.
Includes bibliographical references and index.
    ISBN-13: 978-1-57820-124-2 ISBN-10: 1-57820-124-1 (alk. paper)
1. Embedded computer systems. 2. Real-time programming. I. Yao, Caroline. II. Title.
Tk7895.E42L494 2003   2003008483
004'.33—dc21

Visit the Taylor & Francis Web site at
http://www.taylorandfrancis.com

and the CRC Press Web site at
http://www.crcpress.com

To my wife, Huaying, and my daughter, Jane, for their love, understanding, and support.

To my parents, Dr. Y. H. and Dr. N. H. Li, and my brother, Dr. Yang Li,
for being the exemplification of academic excellence.

TABLE OF CONTENTS

FOREWORD IX

PREFACE XI
    Audience for this Book xii
    Acknowledgments xii

CHAPTER 1   INTRODUCTION 1
    1.1 Real Life Examples of Embedded Systems 2
    1.2 Real-Time Embedded Systems 10
    1.3 The Future of Embedded Systems 16
    1.4 Points to Remember. 17

CHAPTER 2   BASICS OF DEVELOPING FOR EMBEDDED SYSTEMS. . . . 19
    2.1 Introduction. 19
    2.2 Overview of Linkers and the Linking Process 20
    2.3 Executable and Linking Format. 23
    2.4 Mapping Executable Images into Target Embedded Systems 27
    2.5 Points to Remember. 34

CHAPTER 3   EMBEDDED SYSTEM INITIALIZATION 35
    3.1 Introduction. 35
    3.2 Target System Tools and Image Transfer. 36
    3.3 Target Boot Scenarios 39

3.4 Target System Software Initialization Sequence 46
3.5 On-Chip Debugging. 51
3.6 Points to Remember. 52

CHAPTER 4   INTRODUCTION TO REAL-TIME OPERATING SYSTEMS . . .53
4.1 Introduction. 53
4.2 A Brief History of Operating Systems. 54
4.3 Defining an RTOS 55
4.4 The Scheduler. 57
4.5 Objects. 61
4.6 Services 62
4.7 Key Characteristics of an RTOS. 62
4.8 Points to Remember. 64

CHAPTER 5   TASKS. 65
5.1 Introduction. 65
5.2 Defining a Task 65
5.3 Task States and Scheduling 67
5.4 Typical Task Operations 72
5.5 Typical Task Structure. 76
5.6 Synchronization, Communication, and Concurrency 77
5.7 Points to Remember. 77

CHAPTER 6   SEMAPHORES. 79
6.1 Introduction. 79
6.2 Defining Semaphores 79
6.3 Typical Semaphore Operations 84
6.4 Typical Semaphore Use 87
6.5 Points to Remember. 95

CHAPTER 7   MESSAGE QUEUES. 97
7.1 Introduction. 97
7.2 Defining Message Queues 97
7.3 Message Queue States 99
7.4 Message Queue Content. 100
7.5 Message Queue Storage 101
7.6 Typical Message Queue Operations 101
7.7 Typical Message Queue Use. 105
7.8 Points to Remember. 110

CHAPTER 8 OTHER KERNEL OBJECTS **111**

8.1 Introduction. 111

8.2 Pipes 111

8.3 Event Registers 118

8.4 Signals 121

8.5 Condition Variables. 126

8.6 Points to Remember. 130

CHAPTER 9 OTHER RTOS SERVICES **133**

9.1 Introduction. 133

9.2 Other Building Blocks 133

9.3 Component Configuration. 139

9.4 Points to Remember. 141

CHAPTER 10 EXCEPTIONS AND INTERRUPTS **143**

10.1 Introduction. 143

10.2 What are Exceptions and Interrupts?. 144

10.3 Applications of Exceptions and Interrupts. 145

10.4 A Closer Look at Exceptions and Interrupts 146

10.5 Processing General Exceptions 150

10.6 The Nature of Spurious Interrupts. 163

10.7 Points to Remember. 165

CHAPTER 11 TIMER AND TIMER SERVICES **167**

11.1 Introduction. 167

11.2 Real-Time Clocks and System Clocks .168

11.3 Programmable Interval Timers. 169

11.4 Timer Interrupt Service Routines. 171

11.5 A Model for Implementing the Soft-Timer Handling Facility. 171

11.6 Timing Wheels. 176

11.7 Soft Timers and Timer Related Operations 182

11.8 Points to Remember. 185

CHAPTER 12 I/O SUBSYSTEM **187**

12.1 Introduction. 187

12.2 Basic I/O Concepts. 188

12.3 The I/O Subsystem. 192

12.4 Points to Remember. 197

CHAPTER 13   MEMORY MANAGEMENT **199**
   13.1 Introduction 199
   13.2 Dynamic Memory Allocation in Embedded Systems 200
   13.3 Fixed-Size Memory Management in Embedded Systems 208
   13.4 Blocking vs. Non-Blocking Memory Functions 209
   13.5 Hardware Memory Management Units 211
   13.6 Points to Remember 212

CHAPTER 14   MODULARIZING AN APPLICATION FOR CONCURRENCY .**213**
   14.1 Introduction 213
   14.2 An Outside-In Approach to Decomposing Applications 214
   14.3 Guidelines and Recommendations for Identifying Concurrency 217
   14.4 Schedulability Analysis—Rate Monotonic Analysis 225
   14.5 Points to Remember 229

CHAPTER 15   SYNCHRONIZATION AND COMMUNICATION **231**
   15.1 Introduction 231
   15.2 Synchronization 231
   15.3 Communication 236
   15.4 Resource Synchronization Methods 238
   15.5 Critical Section Revisited 240
   15.6 Common Practical Design Patterns 241
   15.7 Specific Solution Design Patterns 247
   15.8 Points to Remember 258

CHAPTER 16   COMMON DESIGN PROBLEMS **259**
   16.1 Introduction 259
   16.2 Resource Classification 260
   16.3 Deadlocks 260
   16.4 Priority Inversion 273
   16.5 Points to Remember 280

APPENDIX A   REFERENCES **281**

ABOUT THE AUTHORS **285**

INDEX **287**

FOREWORD

We live in a world today in which software plays a critical part. The most critical software is not running on large systems and PCs. Rather, it runs inside the infrastructure and in the devices that we use every day. Our transportation, communications, and energy systems won't work if the embedded software contained in our cars, phones, routers and power plants crashes.

The design of this invisible, embedded software is crucial to all of us. Yet, there has been a real shortage of good information as to effective design and implementation practices specific to this very different world. Make no mistake, it is indeed different and often more difficult to design embedded software than more traditional programs. Time, and the interaction of multiple tasks in real-time, must be managed. Seemingly esoteric concepts, such as priority inversion, can become concrete in a hurry when they bring a device to its knees. Efficiency—a small memory footprint and the ability to run on lower cost hardware—become key design considerations because they directly affect cost, power usage, size, and battery life. Of course, reliability is paramount when so much is at stake—company and product reputations, critical infrastructure functions, and, sometimes, even lives.

Mr. Li has done a marvelous job of pulling together the relevant information. He lays out the issues, the decision and design process, and the available tools and methods. The latter part of the book provides valuable insights and practical experiences in understanding application development, common design problems, and solutions. The book will be helpful to anyone embarking on an embedded design project, but will be of particular help to engineers who are experienced in software development but not yet in real-time and embedded software development. It is also a wonderful text or reference volume for academic use.

The quality of the pervasive, invisible software surrounding us will determine much about the world being created today. This book will have a positive effect on that quality and is a welcome addition to the engineering bookshelf.

Jerry Fiddler
Chairman and Co-Founder, Wind River

PREFACE

Embedded systems are omnipresent and play significant roles in modern-day life. Embedded systems are also diverse and can be found in consumer electronics, such as digital cameras, DVD players and printers; in industrial robots; in advanced avionics, such as missile guidance systems and flight control systems; in medical equipment, such as cardiac arrhythmia monitors and cardiac pacemakers; in automotive designs, such as fuel injection systems and auto-braking systems. Embedded systems have significantly improved the way we live today—and will continue to change the way we live tomorrow.

Programming embedded systems is a special discipline and demands that embedded systems developers have working knowledge of a multitude of technology areas. These areas range from low-level hardware devices, compiler technology, and debugging techniques, to the inner workings of real-time operating systems and multithreaded application design. These requirements can be overwhelming to programmers new to the embedded world. The learning process can be long and stressful. As such, I felt compelled to share my knowledge and experiences through practical discussions and illustrations in jumpstarting your embedded systems projects.

Some books use a more traditional approach, focusing solely on programming low-level drivers and software that control the underlying hardware devices. Other books provide a high-level abstract approach using object-oriented methodologies and modeling languages. This book, however, concentrates on bridging the gap between the higher-level abstract modeling concepts and the lower-level fundamental programming aspects of embedded systems development. The discussions carried throughout this book are based on years of experience gained from design and implementation of commercial embedded systems, lessons learnt from previous mistakes, wisdom passed down from others, and results obtained from academic research. These elements join together to form useful insights, guidelines, and recommendations that you can actually use in your real-time embedded systems projects.

This book provides a solid understanding of real-time embedded systems with detailed practical examples and industry knowledge on key concepts, design issues, and solutions. This book supplies a rich set of ready-to-use embedded design building blocks that can accelerate your development efforts and increase your productivity.

I hope that *Real-Time Concepts for Embedded Systems* will become a key reference for you as you embark upon your development endeavors.

If you would like to sign up for e-mail news updates, please send a blank e-mail to: rtconcepts@news.cmpbooks.com. If you have a suggestion, correction, or addition to make to the book, e-mail me at qingli@speakeasy.net

---

Audience for this Book

This book is oriented primarily toward *junior* to *intermediate* software developers working in the realm of embedded computing.

If you are an *experienced* developer but new to real-time embedded systems development, you will also find the approach to design in this book quite useful. If you are a *technical manager* who is active in software design reviews of real-time systems, you can refer to this book to become better informed regarding the design and implementation phases. This book can also be used as complementary reference material if you are an engineering or computer science *student*.

Before using this book, you should be proficient in at least one programming language and should have some exposure to the software-development process.

Acknowledgments

We would like to thank the team at CMP Books and especially Paul Temme, Michelle O'Neal, Marc Briand, Brandy Ernzen, and Robert Ward.

We wish to express our thanks to the reviewers Jerry Krasner, Shin Miyakawa, Jun-ichiro itojun Hagino, and Liliana Britvic for their contributions.

We would like to thank Nauman Arshad for his initial participation on this project.

We would also like to thank Anne-Marie Eileraas, Salvatore LiRosi, Loren Shade, and numerous other individuals at Wind River for their support.

Finally, thanks go to our individual families for their love and support, Huaying and Jane Lee, Maya and William Yao.

In this chapter...

- Real Life Examples of Embedded
  Systems 2
- Real-Time Embedded Systems. 10
- The Future of Embedded Systems. . .16
- Points to Remember 17

CHAPTER 1

INTRODUCTION

In ways virtually unimaginable just a few decades ago, embedded systems are reshaping the way people live, work, and play. Embedded systems come in an endless variety of types, each exhibiting unique characteristics. For example, most vehicles driven today embed intelligent computer chips that perform value-added tasks, which make the vehicles easier, cleaner, and more fun to drive. Telephone systems rely on multiple integrated hardware and software systems to connect people around the world. Even private homes are being filled with intelligent appliances and integrated systems built around embedded systems, which facilitate and enhance everyday life.

Often referred to as *pervasive* or *ubiquitous* computers, embedded systems represent a class of dedicated computer systems designed for specific purposes. Many of these embedded systems are reliable and predictable. The devices that embed them are convenient, user-friendly, and dependable.

One special class of embedded systems is distinguished from the rest by its requirement to respond to external events in real time. This category is classified as the *real-time embedded system*.

As an introduction to embedded systems and real-time embedded systems, this chapter focuses on:

- examples of embedded systems,
- defining embedded systems,
- defining embedded systems with real-time behavior, and
- current trends in embedded systems.

1

1.1 Real Life Examples of Embedded Systems

Even though often nearly invisible, embedded systems are ubiquitous. Embedded systems are present in many industries, including industrial automation, defense, transportation, and aerospace. For example, NASA's Mars Path Finder, Lockheed Martin's missile guidance system, and the Ford automobile all contain numerous embedded systems.

Every day, people throughout the world use embedded systems without even knowing it. In fact, the embedded system's invisibility is its very beauty: users reap the advantages without having to understand the intricacies of the technology.

Remarkably adaptable and versatile, embedded systems can be found at home, at work, and even in recreational devices. Indeed, it is difficult to find a segment of daily life that does not involve embedded systems in some way. Some of the more visible examples of embedded systems are provided in the next sections.

1.1.1 Embedded Systems in the Home Environment

Hidden conveniently within numerous household appliances, embedded systems are found all over the house. Consumers enjoy the effort-saving advanced features and benefits provided by these embedded technologies.

As shown in Figure 1.1 embedded systems in the home assume many forms, including security systems, cable and satellite boxes for televisions, home theater systems, and telephone answering machines. As advances in microprocessors continue to improve the functionality of ordinary products, embedded systems are helping drive the development of additional home-based innovations.

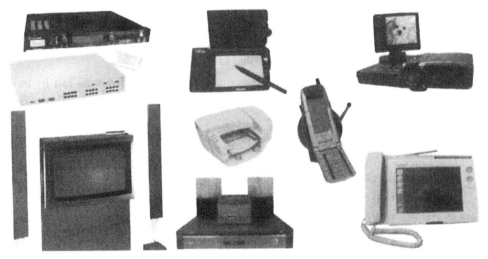

Figure 1.1   Embedded systems at home.

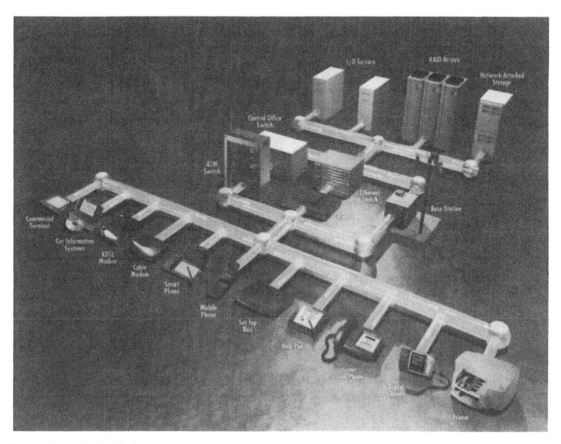

Figure 1.2   Embedded systems at work.

1.1.2   Embedded Systems in the Work Environment

Embedded systems have also changed the way people conduct business. Perhaps the most significant example is the Internet, which is really just a very large collection of embedded systems that are interconnected using various networking technologies. Figure 1.2 illustrates what a small segment of the Internet might look like.

From various individual network end-points (for example, printers, cable modems, and enterprise network routers) to the backbone gigabit switches, embedded technology has helped make use of the Internet necessary to any business model. The network routers and the backbone gigabit switches are examples of real-time embedded systems. Advancements in real-time embedded technology are making Internet connectivity both reliable and responsive, despite the enormous amount of voice and data traffic carried over the network.

1.1.3 Embedded Systems in Leisure Activities

At home, at work, even at play, embedded systems are flourishing. A child's toy unexpectedly springs to life with unabashed liveliness. Automobiles equipped with in-car navigation systems transport people to destinations safely and efficiently. Listening to favorite tunes with anytime-anywhere freedom is readily achievable, thanks to embedded systems buried deep within sophisticated portable music players, as shown in Figure 1.3.

Figure 1.3   Navigation system and portable music player.

Even the portable computing device, called a *web tablet*, shown in Figure 1.4, is an embedded system.

Embedded systems also have teamed with other technologies to deliver benefits to the traditionally low-tech world. GPS technology, for example, uses satellites to pinpoint locations to centimeter-level accuracy, which allows hikers, cyclists, and other outdoor enthusiasts to use GPS handheld devices to enjoy vast spaces without getting lost. Even fishermen use GPS devices to store the locations of their favorite fishing holes.

Figure 1.4   A web tablet.

Embedded systems also have taken traditional radio-controlled airplanes, racecars, and boats to new heights...and speeds. As complex embedded systems in disguise, these devices take command inputs from joysticks and pass them wirelessly to the device's receiver, enabling the model airplane, racecar, or boat to engage in speedy and complex maneuvers. In fact, the introduction of embedded technology has rendered these sports safer and more enjoyable for model owners by virtually eliminating the once-common threat of crashing due to signal interference.

1.1.4 Defining the Embedded System

Some texts define embedded systems as computing systems or devices without a keyboard, display, or mouse. These texts use the "look" characteristic as the differentiating factor by saying, "embedded systems do not look like ordinary personal computers; they look like digital cameras or smart toasters." These statements are all misleading.

A general definition of *embedded systems* is: embedded systems are computing systems with tightly coupled hardware and software integration, that are designed to perform a dedicated function. The word embedded reflects the fact that these systems are usually an integral part of a larger system, known as the embedding system. Multiple embedded systems can coexist in an embedding system.

This definition is good but subjective. In the majority of cases, embedded systems are truly embedded, i.e., they are "systems within systems." They either cannot or do not function on their own. Take, for example, the digital set-top box (DST) found in many home entertainment systems nowadays. The digital audio/video decoding system, called the *A/V decoder*, which is an integral part of the DST, is an embedded system. The A/V decoder accepts a single multimedia stream and produces sound and video frames as output. The signals received from the satellite by the DST contain multiple streams or channels. Therefore, the A/V decoder works in conjunction with the transport stream decoder, which is yet another embedded system. The transport stream decoder de-multiplexes the incoming multimedia streams into separate channels and feeds only the selected channel to the A/V decoder.

In some cases, embedded systems can function as standalone systems. The network router illustrated in Figure 1.2 is a standalone embedded system. It is built using a specialized communication processor, memory, a number of network access interfaces (known as network ports), and special software that implements packet routing algorithms. In other words, the network router is a standalone embedded system that routes packets coming from one port to another, based on a programmed routing algorithm.

The definition also does not necessarily provide answers to some often-asked questions. For example: "Can a personal computer be classified as an embedded system? Why? Can an Apple iBook that is used only as a DVD player be called an embedded system?"

A single comprehensive definition does not exist. Therefore, we need to focus on the characteristics of embedded systems from many different perspectives to gain a real understanding of what embedded systems are and what makes embedded systems special.

1.1.5   Embedded Processor and Application Awareness

The processors found in common personal computers (PC) are general-purpose or universal processors. They are complex in design because these processors provide a full scale of features and a wide spectrum of functionalities. They are designed to be suitable for a variety of applications. The systems using these universal processors are programmed with a multitude of applications. For example, modern processors have a built-in memory management unit (MMU) to provide memory protection and virtual memory for multitasking-capable, general-purpose operating systems. These universal processors have advanced cache logic. Many of these processors have a built-in math co-processor capable of performing fast floating-point operations. These processors provide interfaces to support a variety of external peripheral devices. These processors result in large power consumption, heat production, and size. The complexity means these processors are also expensive to fabricate. In the early days, embedded systems were commonly built using general-purpose processors.

Because of the quantum leap in advancements made in microprocessor technology in recent years, embedded systems are increasingly being built using embedded processors instead of general-purpose processors. These embedded processors are special-purpose processors designed for a specific class of applications. The key is application awareness, i.e., knowing the nature of the applications and meeting the requirement for those applications that it is designed to run.

One class of embedded processors focuses on size, power consumption, and price. Therefore, some embedded processors are limited in functionality, i.e., a processor is good enough for the class of applications for which it was designed but is likely inadequate for other classes of applications. This is one reason why many embedded processors do not have fast CPU speeds. For example, the processor chosen for a personal digital assistant (PDA) device does not have a floating-point co-processor because floating-point operations are either not needed or software emulation is sufficient. The processor might have a 16-bit addressing architecture instead of 32-bit, due to its limited memory storage capacity. It might have a 200MHz CPU speed because the majority of the applications are interactive and display-intensive, rather than computation-intensive. This class of embedded processors is small because the overall PDA device is slim and fits in the palm of your hand. The limited functionality means reduced power consumption and long-lasting battery life. The smaller size reduces the overall cost of processor fabrication.

On the other hand, another class of embedded processors focuses on performance. These embedded processors are powerful and packed with advanced chip-design technologies, such as advanced pipeline and parallel processing architecture. These processors are designed to satisfy those applications with intensive computing requirements not achievable with general-purpose processors. An emerging class of highly specialized and high-performance embedded processors includes network processors developed for the network equipment and telecommunications industry. Overall, system and application speeds are the main concerns.

Yet another class of embedded processors focuses on all four requirements—performance, size, power consumption, and price. Take, for example, the embedded digital signal processor (DSP) used in cell phones. Real-time voice communication involves digital signal processing and cannot tolerate delays. A DSP has specialized arithmetic units, optimized design in the memory, and addressing and bus architectures with multiprocessing capability that allow the DSP to perform complex calculations extremely fast in real time. A DSP outperforms a general-purpose processor running at the same clock speed many times over comes to digital signal processing. These reasons are why DSPs, instead of general-purpose processors, are chosen for cell phone designs. Even though

DSPs are incredibly fast and powerful embedded processors, they are reasonably priced, which keeps the overall prices of cell phones competitive. The battery from which the DSP draws power lasts for hours and hours. A cell phone under $100 fits in half the palm-size of an average person at the time this book was written.

System-on-a-chip (SoC) processors are especially attractive for embedded systems. The SoC processor is comprised of a CPU core with built-in peripheral modules, such as a programmable general-purpose timer, programmable interrupt controller, DMA controller, and possibly Ethernet interfaces. Such a self-contained design allows these embedded processors to be used to build a variety of embedded applications without needing additional external peripheral devices, again reducing the overall cost and size of the final product.

Sometimes a gray area exists when using processor type to differentiate between embedded and non-embedded systems. It is worth noting that, in large-scale, high-performance embedded systems, the choice between embedded processors and universal microprocessors is a difficult one.

In high-end embedded systems, system performance in a predefined context outweighs power consumption and cost. The choice of a high-end, general purpose processor is as good as the choice of a high-end, specialized embedded processor in some designs. Therefore, using processor type alone to classify embedded systems may result in wrong classifications.

1.1.6 Hardware and Software Co-Design Model

Commonly both the hardware and the software for an embedded system are developed in parallel. Constant design feedback between the two design teams should occur in this development model. The result is that each side can take advantage of what the other can do. The software component can take advantage of special hardware features to gain performance. The hardware component can simplify module design if functionality can be achieved in software that reduces overall hardware complexity and cost. Often design flaws, in both the hardware and software, are uncovered during this close collaboration.

The hardware and software co-design model reemphasizes the fundamental characteristic of embedded systems—they are application-specific. An embedded system is usually built on custom hardware and software. Therefore, using this development model is both permissible and beneficial.

1.1.7 Cross-Platform Development

Another typical characteristic of embedded systems is its method of software development, called *cross-platform development*, for both system and application software. Software for an embedded system is developed on one platform but runs on another. In this context, the *platform* is the combination of hardware (such as particular type of processor), operating system, and software development tools used for further development.

The *host system* is the system on which the embedded software is developed. The *target system* is the embedded system under development.

The main software tool that makes cross-platform development possible is a cross compiler. A *cross compiler* is a compiler that runs on one type of processor architecture but produces object code for a different type of processor architecture. A cross compiler is used because the target system cannot host its own compiler. For example, the DIAB compiler from Wind River Systems is such a cross compiler. The DIAB compiler runs on the Microsoft Windows operating system (OS) on the IA-32 architecture and runs on various UNIX operating systems, such as the Solaris OS on the SPARC architecture. The compiler can produce object code for numerous processor types, such as Motorola's 68000, MIPS, and ARM. We discuss more cross-development tools in Chapter 2.

1.1.8 Software Storage and Upgradeability

Code for embedded systems (such as the real-time embedded operating system, the system software, and the application software) is commonly stored in ROM and NVRAM memory devices. In Chapter 3, we discuss the embedded system booting process and the steps involved in extracting code from these storage devices. Upgrading an embedded system can mean building new PROM, deploying special equipment and/or a special method to reprogram the EPROM, or reprogramming the flash memory.

The choice of software storage device has an impact on development. The process to reprogram an EPROM when small changes are made in the software can be tedious and time-consuming, and this occurrence is common during development. Removing an EPROM device from its socket can damage the EPROM; worse yet, the system itself can be damaged if careful handling is not exercised.

The choice of the storage device can also have an impact on the overall cost of maintenance. Although PROM and EPROM devices are inexpensive, the cost can add up if a large volume of shipped systems is in the field. Upgrading an embedded system in these cases means shipping replacement PROM and EPROM chips. The embedded system can be upgraded without the need for chip replacement and can be upgraded dynamically over a network if flash memory or EEPROM is used as the code storage device (see the following sidebar).

Armed with the information presented in the previous sections, we can now attempt to answer the questions raised earlier. A personal computer is not an embedded system because it is built using a general-purpose processor and is built independently from the software that runs on it. The software applications developed for personal computers, which run operating systems such as FreeBSD or Windows, are developed natively (as opposed to cross-developed) on those operating systems. For the same reasons, an Apple iBook used only as a DVD player is used like an embedded system but is not an embedded system.

Read Only Memory (ROM)

With non-volatile content and without the need for an external power source.

- **Mask Programmed ROM**—the memory content is programmed during the manufacturing process. Once programmed, the content cannot be changed. It cannot be reprogrammed.

- **Field Programmable ROM (PROM)**—the memory content can be custom-programmed one time. The memory content cannot change once programmed.

- **Erasable Programmable ROM (EPROM)**—an EPROM device can be custom-programmed, erased, and reprogrammed as often as required within its lifetime (hundreds or even thousands of times). The memory content is non-volatile once programmed. Traditional EPROM devices are erased by exposure to ultraviolet (UV) light. An EPROM device must be removed from its housing unit first. It is then reprogrammed using a special hardware device called an EPROM programmer.

- **Electrically Erasable Programmable ROM (EEPROM or E²PROM)**—modern EPROM devices are erased electrically and are thus called EEPROM. One important difference between an EPROM and an EEPROM device is that with the EEPROM device, memory content of a single byte can be selectively erased and reprogrammed. Therefore, with an EEPROM device, incremental changes can be made. Another difference is the EEPROM can be reprogrammed without a special programmer and can stay in the device while being reprogrammed. The versatility of byte-level programmability of the EEPROM comes at a price, however, as programming an EEPROM device is a slow process.

- **Flash Memory**—the flash memory is a variation of EEPROM, which allows for block-level (e.g., 512-byte) programmability that is much faster than EEPROM.

Random Access Memory (RAM)

Also called Read/Write Memory, requires external power to maintain memory content. The term random access refers to the ability to access any memory cell directly. RAM is much faster than ROM. Two types of RAM that are of interest:

- **Dynamic RAM (DRAM)**—DRAM is a RAM device that requires periodic refreshing to retain its content.

- **Static RAM (SRAM)**—SRAM is a RAM device that retains its content as long as power is supplied by an external power source. SRAM does not require periodic refreshing and it is faster than DRAM.

- **Non-Volatile RAM (NVRAM)**—NVRAM is a special type of SRAM that has backup battery power so it can retain its content after the main system power is shut off. Another variation of NVARM combines SRAM and EEPROM so that its content is written into the EEPROM when power is shut off and is read back from the EEPROM when power is restored.

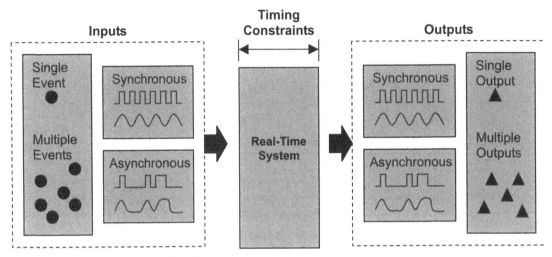

Figure 1.5   A simple view of real-time systems.

1.2 Real-Time Embedded Systems

In the simplest form, real-time systems can be defined as those systems that respond to external events in a timely fashion, as shown in Figure 1.5. The response time is guaranteed. We revisit this definition after presenting some examples of real-time systems.

External events can have synchronous or asynchronous characteristics. Responding to external events includes recognizing when an event occurs, performing the required processing as a result of the event, and outputting the necessary results within a given time constraint. Timing constraints include finish time, or both start time and finish time.

A good way to understand the relationship between real-time systems and embedded systems is to view them as two intersecting circles, as shown in Figure 1.6. It can be seen that not all embedded systems exhibit real-time behaviors nor are all real-time systems embedded. However, the two systems are not mutu-

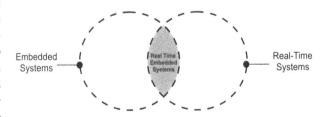

Figure 1.6   Real-time embedded systems.

ally exclusive, and the area in which they overlap creates the combination of systems known as *real-time embedded systems*.

Knowing this fact and because we have covered the various aspects of embedded systems in the previous sections, we can now focus our attention on real-time systems.

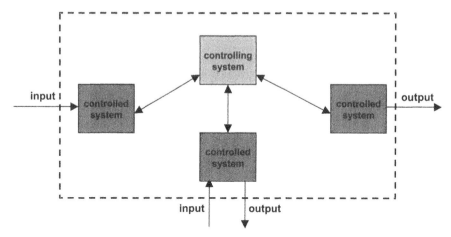

Figure 1.7   Structure of real-time systems.

1.2.1   Real-Time Systems

The environment of the real-time system creates the external events. These events are received by one or more components of the real-time system. The response of the real-time system is then injected into its environment through one or more of its components. Decomposition of the real-time system, as shown in Figure 1.5, leads to the general structure of real-time systems.

The structure of a real-time system, as shown in Figure 1.7, is a controlling system and at least one controlled system. The controlling system interacts with the controlled system in various ways. First, the interaction can be *periodic*, in which communication is initiated from the controlling system to the controlled system. In this case, the communication is predictable and occurs at predefined intervals. Second, the interaction can be *aperiodic*, in which communication is initiated from the controlled system to the controlling system. In this case, the communication is unpredictable and is determined by the random occurrences of external events in the environment of the controlled system. Finally, the communication can be a combination of both types. The controlling system must process and respond to the events and information generated by the controlled system in a guaranteed time frame.

Imagine a real-time weapons defense system whose role is to protect a naval destroyer by shooting down incoming missiles. The idea is to shred an incoming missile into pieces with bullets before it reaches the ship. The weapons system is comprised of a radar system, a command-and-decision (C&D) system, and weapons firing control system. The controlling system is the C&D system, whereas the controlled systems are the radar system and the weapons firing control system.

- The radar system scans and searches for potential targets. Coordinates of a potential target are sent to the C&D system periodically with high frequency after the target is acquired.
- The C&D system must first determine the threat level by threat classification and evaluation, based on the target information provided by the radar system. If a threat is imminent, the C&D system must, at a minimum, calculate the speed and flight path or trajectory, as well as estimate the impact location. Because a missile tends to drift off its flight path with the degree of drift dependent on the precision of its guidance system, the C&D system calculates an area (a box) around the flight path.
- The C&D system then activates the weapons firing control system closest to the anticipated impact location and guides the weapons system to fire continuously within the moving area or box until the target is destroyed. The weapons firing control system is comprised of large-caliber, multi-barrel, high-muzzle velocity, high-power machine guns.

In this weapons defense system example, the communication between the radar system and the C&D system is aperiodic, because the occurrence of a potential target is unpredictable and the potential target can appear at any time. The communication between the C&D system and the weapons firing control system is, however, periodic because the C&D system feeds the firing coordinates into the weapons control system periodically (with an extremely high frequency). Initial firing coordinates are based on a pre-computed flight path but are updated in real-time according to the actual location of the incoming missile.

Consider another example of a real-time system—the cruise missile guidance system. A cruise missile flies at subsonic speed. It can travel at about 10 meters above water, 30 meters above flat ground, and 100 meters above mountain terrains. A modern cruise missile can hit a target within a 50-meter range. All these capabilities are due to the high-precision, real-time guidance system built into the nose of a cruise missile. In a simplified view, the guidance system is comprised of the radar system (both forward-looking and look-down radars), the navigation system, and the divert-and-altitude-control system. The navigation system contains digital maps covering the missile flight path. The forward-looking radar scans and maps out the approaching terrains. This information is fed to the navigation system in real time. The navigation system must then recalculate flight coordinates to avoid terrain obstacles. The new coordinates are immediately fed to the divert-and-altitude-control system to adjust the flight path. The look-down radar periodically scans the ground terrain along its flight path. The scanned data is compared with the estimated section of the pre-recorded maps. Corrective adjustments are made to the flight coordinates and sent to the divert-and-altitude-control system if data comparison indicates that the missile has drifted off the intended flight path.

In this example, the controlling system is the navigation system. The controlled systems are the radar system and the divert-and-altitude-control system. We can observe both periodic and aperiodic communications in this example. The communication between the radars and the navigation system is aperiodic. The communication between the navigation system and the diver-and-altitude-control system is periodic.

Let us consider one more example of a real-time system—a DVD player. The DVD player must decode both the video and the audio streams from the disc simultaneously. While a movie is being played, the viewer can activate the on-screen display using a remote control. On-screen display is a user menu that allows the user to change parameters, such as the audio output format and language options. The DVD player is the controlling system, and the remote control is the controlled system. In this case, the remote control is viewed as a sensor because it feeds events, such as pause and language selection, into the DVD player.

1.2.2   Characteristics of Real-Time Systems

The C&D system in the weapons defense system must calculate the anticipated flight path of the incoming missile quickly and guide the firing system to shoot the missile down before it reaches the destroyer. Assume T1 is the time the missile takes to reach the ship and is a function of the missile's distance and velocity. Assume T2 is the time the C&D system takes to activate the weapons firing control system and includes transmitting the firing coordinates plus the firing delay. The difference between T1 and T2 is how long the computation may take. The missile would reach its intended target if the C&D system took too long in computing the flight path. The missile would still reach its target if the computation produced by the C&D system was inaccurate. The navigation system in the cruise missile must respond to the changing terrain fast enough so that it can re-compute coordinates and guide the altitude control system to a new flight path. The missile might collide with a mountain if the navigation system cannot compute new flight coordinates fast enough, or if the new coordinates do not steer the missile out of the collision course.

Therefore, we can extract two essential characteristics of real-time systems from the examples given earlier. These characteristics are that real-time systems must produce correct computational results, called *logical or functional correctness*, and that these computations must conclude within a predefined period, called *timing correctness*.

Real-time systems are defined as those systems in which the overall correctness of the system depends on both the functional correctness and the timing correctness. The timing correctness is at least as important as the functional correctness.

It is important to note that we said the timing correctness is at least as important as the functional correctness. In some real-time systems, functional correctness is sometimes sacrificed for timing correctness. We address this point shortly after we introduce the classifications of real-time systems.

Similar to embedded systems, real-time systems also have substantial knowledge of the environment of the controlled system and the applications running on it. This reason is one why many real-time systems are said to be deterministic, because in those real-time systems, the response time to a detected event is bounded. The action (or actions) taken in response to an event is known a priori. A deterministic real-time system implies that each component of the system must have a deterministic behavior that contributes to the overall determinism of the system. As can be seen, a deterministic real-time system can be less adaptable to the changing environment. The lack of adaptability can result in a less robust system. The levels of determinism and of robustness must be balanced. The method of balancing between the two is system- and application-specific. This discussion, however, is beyond the scope of this book. Consult the reference material for additional coverage on this topic.

1.2.3 Hard and Soft Real-Time Systems

In the previous section, we said computation must complete before reaching a given deadline. In other words, real-time systems have timing constraints and are deadline-driven. Real-time systems can be classified, therefore, as either hard real-time systems or soft real-time systems.

What differentiates hard real-time systems and soft real-time systems are the degree of tolerance of missed deadlines, usefulness of computed results after missed deadlines, and severity of the penalty incurred for failing to meet deadlines.

For hard real-time systems, the level of tolerance for a missed deadline is extremely small or zero tolerance. The computed results after the missed deadline are likely useless for many of these systems. The penalty incurred for a missed deadline is catastrophe. For soft real-time systems, however, the level of tolerance is non-zero. The computed results after the missed deadline have a rate of depreciation. The usefulness of the results does not reach zero immediately passing the deadline, as in the case of many hard real-time systems. The physical impact of a missed deadline is non-catastrophic.

A *hard real-time system* is a real-time system that must meet its deadlines with a near-zero degree of flexibility. The deadlines must be met, or catastrophes occur. The cost of such catastrophe is extremely high and can involve human lives. The computation results obtained after the deadline have either a zero-level of usefulness or have a high rate of depreciation as time moves further from the missed deadline before the system produces a response.

A *soft real-time system* is a real-time system that must meet its deadlines but with a degree of flexibility. The deadlines can contain varying levels of tolerance, average timing deadlines, and even statistical distribution of response times with different degrees of acceptability. In a soft real-time system, a missed deadline does not result in system failure, but costs can rise in proportion to the delay, depending on the application.

Penalty is an important aspect of hard real-time systems for several reasons.

- What is meant by "must meet the deadline"?

  It means something catastrophic occurs if the deadline is not met. It is the penalty that sets the requirement.

- Missing the deadline means a system failure, and no recovery is possible other than a reset, so the deadline must be met. Is this a hard real-time system?

  That depends. If a system failure means the system must be reset but no cost is associated with the failure, the deadline is not a hard deadline, and the system is not a hard real-time system. On the other hand, if a cost is associated, either in human lives or financial penalty such as a $50 million lawsuit, the deadline is a hard deadline, and it is a hard real-time system. It is the penalty that makes this determination.

- What defines the deadline for a hard real-time system?

  It is the penalty. For a hard real-time system, the deadline is a deterministic value, and, for a soft real-time system, the value can be estimation.

One thing worth noting is that the length of the deadline does not make a real-time system hard or soft, but it is the requirement for meeting it within that time.

The weapons defense and the missile guidance systems are hard real-time systems. Using the missile guidance system for an example, if the navigation system cannot compute the new coordinates in response to approaching mountain terrain before or at the deadline, not enough distance is left for the missile to change altitude. This system has zero tolerance for a missed deadline. The new coordinates obtained after the deadline are no longer useful because at subsonic speed the distance is too short for the altitude control system to navigate the missile into the new flight path in time. The penalty is a catastrophic event in which the missile collides with the mountain. Similarly, the weapons defense system is also a zero-tolerance system. The missed deadline results in the missile sinking the destroyer, and human lives potentially being lost. Again, the penalty incurred is catastrophic.

On the other hand, the DVD player is a soft real-time system. The DVD player decodes the video and the audio streams while responding to user commands in real time. The user might send a series of commands to the DVD player rapidly causing the decoder to miss its deadline or deadlines. The result or penalty is momentary but visible video distortion or audible audio distortion. The DVD player has a high level of tolerance because it continues to function. The decoded data obtained after the deadline is still useful.

Timing correctness is critical to most hard real-time systems. Therefore, hard real-time systems make every effort possible in predicting if a pending deadline might be missed.

Returning to the weapons defense system, let us discuss how a hard real-time system takes corrective actions when it anticipates a deadline might be missed. In the weapons defense system example, the C&D system calculates a firing box around the projected missile flight path. The missile must be destroyed a certain distance away from the ship or the shrapnel can still cause damage. If the C&D system anticipates a missed deadline (for example, if by the time the precise firing coordinates are computed, the missile would have flown past the safe zone), the C&D system must take corrective action immediately. The C&D system enlarges the firing box and computes imprecise firing coordinates by methods of estimation instead of computing for precise values. The C&D system then activates additional weapons firing systems to compensate for this imprecision. The result is that additional guns are brought online to cover the larger firing box. The idea is that it is better to waste bullets than sink a destroyer.

This example shows why sometimes functional correctness might be sacrificed for timing correctness for many real-time systems.

Because one or a few missed deadlines do not have a detrimental impact on the operations of soft real-time systems, a soft real-time system might not need to predict if a pending deadline might be missed. Instead, the soft real-time system can begin a recovery process after a missed deadline is detected.

For example, using the real-time DVD player, after a missed deadline is detected, the decoders in the DVD player use the computed results obtained after the deadline and use the data to make a decision on what future video frames and audio data must be discarded to re-synchronize the two streams. In other words, the decoders find ways to catch up.

So far, we have focused on meeting the deadline or the finish time of some work or job, e.g., a computation. At times, meeting the start time of the job is just as important. The lack of required resources for the job, such as CPU or memory, can prevent a job from starting and can lead to missing the job completion deadline. Ultimately this problem becomes a resource-scheduling problem. The scheduling algorithms of a real-time system must schedule system resources so that jobs created in response to both periodic and aperiodic events can obtain the resources at the appropriate time. This process affords each job the ability to meet its specific timing constraints. This topic is addressed in detail in Chapter 14.

1.3 The Future of Embedded Systems

Until the early 1990s, embedded systems were generally simple, autonomous devices with long product lifecycles. In recent years, however, the embedded industry has experienced dramatic transformation, as reported by the Gartner Group, an independent research and advisory firm, as well as by other sources:

- Product market windows now dictate feverish six- to nine-month turnaround cycles.
- Globalization is redefining market opportunities and expanding application space.

- Connectivity is now a requirement rather than a bonus in both wired and emerging wireless technologies.
- Electronics-based products are more complex.
- Interconnecting embedded systems are yielding new applications that are dependent on networking infrastructures.
- The processing power of microprocessors is increasing at a rate predicted by Moore's Law, which states that the number of transistors per integrated circuit doubles every 18 months.

If past trends give any indication of the future, then as technology evolves, embedded software will continue to proliferate into new applications and lead to smarter classes of products. With an ever-expanding marketplace fortified by growing consumer demand for devices that can virtually run themselves as well as the seemingly limitless opportunities created by the Internet, embedded systems will continue to reshape the world for years to come.

1.4 Points to Remember

- An embedded system is built for a specific application. As such, the hardware and software components are highly integrated, and the development model is the hardware and software co-design model.
- Embedded systems are generally built using embedded processors.
- An embedded processor is a specialized processor, such as a DSP, that is cheaper to design and produce, can have built-in integrated devices, is limited in functionality, produces low heat, consumes low power, and does not necessarily have the fastest clock speed but meets the requirements of the specific applications for which it is designed.
- Real-time systems are characterized by the fact that timing correctness is just as important as functional or logical correctness.
- The severity of the penalty incurred for not satisfying timing constraints differentiates hard real-time systems from soft real-time systems.
- Real-time systems have a significant amount of application awareness similar to embedded systems.
- Real-time embedded systems are those embedded system with real-time behaviors.

In this chapter...

- Overview of Linkers and the Linking
  Process 20
- Executable and Linking Format 23
- Mapping Executable Images into Target
  Embedded Systems 27
- Points to Remember. 34

CHAPTER 2

BASICS OF DEVELOPING FOR EMBEDDED SYSTEMS

2.1 Introduction

Chapter 1 states that one characteristic of embedded systems is the cross-platform development methodology. The primary components in the development environment are the host system, the target embedded system, and potentially many connectivity solutions available between the host and the target embedded system, as shown in Figure 2.1.

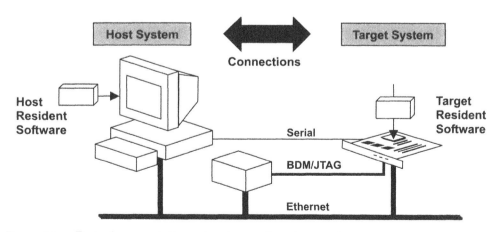

Figure 2.1   Typical cross-platform development environment.

The essential development tools offered by the host system are the cross compiler, linker, and source-level debugger. The target embedded system might offer a dynamic loader, a link loader, a monitor, and a debug agent. A set of connections might be available between the host and the target system. These connections are used for downloading program images from the host system to the target system. These connections can also be used for transmitting debugger information between the host debugger and the target debug agent.

Programs including the system software, the real-time operating system (RTOS), the kernel, and the application code must be developed first, compiled into object code, and linked together into an executable image. Programmers writing applications that execute in the same environment as used for development, called *native development,* do not need to be concerned with how an executable image is loaded into memory and how execution control is transferred to the application. Embedded developers doing cross-platform development, however, are required to understand the target system fully, how to store the program image on the target embedded system, how and where to load the program image during runtime, and how to develop and debug the system iteratively. Each of these aspects can impact how the code is developed, compiled, and most importantly linked.

The areas of focus in this chapter are

- the ELF object file format,
- the linker and linker command file, and
- mapping the executable image onto the target embedded system.

This chapter does not provide full coverage on each tool, such as the compiler and the linker, nor does this chapter fully describe a specific object file format. Instead, this chapter focuses on providing in-depth coverage on the aspects of each tool and the object file format that are most relevant to embedded system development. The goal is to offer the embedded developer practical insights on how the components relate to one another. Knowing the big picture allows an embedded developer to put it all together and ask the specific questions if and when necessary.

2.2 Overview of Linkers and the Linking Process

Figure 2.2 illustrates how different tools take various input files and generate appropriate output files to ultimately be used in building an executable image.

The developer writes the program in the C/C++ source files and header files. Some parts of the program can be written in assembly language and are produced in the corresponding assembly source files. The developer creates a `makefile` for the `make` utility to facilitate an environment that can easily track the file modifications and invoke the compiler and the assembler to rebuild the source files when necessary. From these source files, the compiler and the assembler produce object files that contain both machine binary code and program data. The archive utility concatenates a collection of object files to form a

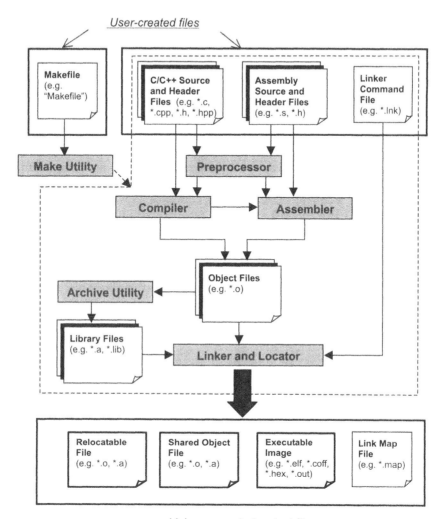

Figure 2.2   Creating an image file for the target system.

library. The linker takes these object files as input and produces either an executable image or an object file that can be used for additional linking with other object files. The linker command file instructs the linker on how to combine the object files and where to place the binary code and data in the target embedded system.

The main function of the linker is to combine multiple object files into a larger relocatable object file, a shared object file, or a final executable image. In a typical program, a section of code in one source file can reference variables defined in another source file. A function in one source file can call a function in another source file. The global variables and non-static functions are commonly referred to as *global symbols*. In source files, these symbols have various names, for example, a global variable called foo_bar or a global function called func_a. In the final executable binary image, a symbol refers to an address location in memory. The content of this memory location is either data for variables or executable code for functions.

The compiler creates a symbol table containing the symbol name to address mappings as part of the object file it produces. When creating relocatable output, the compiler generates the address that, for each symbol, is relative to the file being compiled. Consequently, these addresses are generated with respect to offset 0. The symbol table contains the global symbols defined in the file being compiled, as well as the external symbols referenced in the file that the linker needs to resolve. The linking process performed by the linker involves symbol resolution and symbol relocation.

Symbol resolution is the process in which the linker goes through each object file and determines, for the object file, in which (other) object file or files the external symbols are defined. Sometimes the linker must process the list of object files multiple times while trying to resolve all of the external symbols. When external symbols are defined in a static library, the linker copies the object files from the library and writes them into the final image.

Symbol relocation is the process in which the linker maps a symbol reference to its definition. The linker modifies the machine code of the linked object files so that code references to the symbols reflect the actual addresses assigned to these symbols. For many symbols, the relative offsets change after multiple object files are merged. Symbol relocation requires code modification because the linker adjusts the machine code referencing these symbols to reflect their finalized addresses. The relocation table tells the linker where in the program code to apply the relocation action. Each entry in the relocation table contains a reference to the symbol table. Using this reference, the linker can retrieve the actual address of the symbol and apply it to the program location as specified by the relocation entry. It is possible for the relocation table to contain both the address of the symbol and the information on the relocation entry. In this case, there is no reference between the relocation table and the symbol table.

Figure 2.3 illustrates these two concepts in a simplified view and serves as an example for the following discussions.

For an executable image, all external symbols must be resolved so that each symbol has an absolute memory address because an executable image is ready for execution. The exception to this rule is that those symbols defined in shared libraries may still contain relative addresses, which are resolved at runtime (dynamic linking).

A relocatable object file may contain unresolved external symbols. Similar to a library, a linker-reproduced relocatable object file is a concatenation of multiple object files with

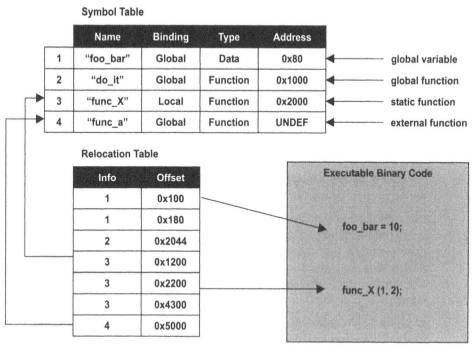

Symbol Table

	Name	Binding	Type	Address	
1	"foo_bar"	Global	Data	0x80	global variable
2	"do_it"	Global	Function	0x1000	global function
3	"func_X"	Local	Function	0x2000	static function
4	"func_a"	Global	Function	UNDEF	external function

Relocation Table

Info	Offset
1	0x100
1	0x180
2	0x2044
3	0x1200
3	0x2200
3	0x4300
4	0x5000

Executable Binary Code

foo_bar = 10;

func_X (1, 2);

Figure 2.3   Relationship between the symbol table and the relocation table.

one main difference—the file is partially resolved and is used for further linking with other object files to create an executable image or a shared object file. A shared object file has dual purposes. It can be used to link with other shared object files or relocatable object modules, or it can be used as an executable image with dynamic linking.

2.3 Executable and Linking Format

Typically an object file contains

- general information about the object file, such as file size, binary code and data size, and source file name from which it was created,
- machine-architecture-specific binary instructions and data,
- symbol table and the symbol relocation table, and
- debug information, which the debugger uses.

The manner in which this information is organized in the object file is the *object file format*. The idea behind a standard object file format is to allow development tools which might be produced by different vendors—such as a compiler, assembler, linker, and debugger that conform to the well-defined standard—to interoperate with each other.

This interoperability means a developer can choose a compiler from vendor A to produce object code used to form a final executable image by a linker from vendor B. This concept gives the end developer great flexibility in choice for development tools because the developer can select a tool based on its functional strength rather than its vendor.

Two common object file formats are the common object file format (COFF) and the executable and linking format (ELF). These file formats are incompatible with each other; therefore, be sure to select the tools, including the debugger, that recognize the format chosen for development.

We focus our discussion on ELF because it supersedes COFF. Understanding the object file format allows the embedded developer to map an executable image into the target embedded system for static storage, as well as for runtime loading and execution. To do so, we need to discuss the specifics of ELF, as well as how it relates to the linker.

Using the ELF object file format, the compiler organizes the compiled program into various system-defined, as well as user-defined, content groupings called *sections*. The program's binary instructions, binary data, symbol table, relocation table, and debug information are organized and contained in various sections. Each section has a type. Content is placed into a section if the section type matches the type of the content being stored.

A section also contains important information such as the load address and the run address. The concept of load address versus run address is important because the run address and the load address can be different in embedded systems. This knowledge can also be helpful in understanding embedded system loader and link loader concepts introduced in Chapter 3.

Chapter 1 discusses the idea that embedded systems typically have some form of ROM for non-volatile storage and that the software for an embedded system can be stored in ROM. Modifiable data must reside in RAM. Programs that require fast execution speed also execute out of RAM. Commonly therefore, a small program in ROM, called a *loader*, copies the initialized variables into RAM, transfers the program code into RAM, and begins program execution out of RAM. This physical ROM storage address is referred to as the section's *load address*. The section's *run address* refers to the location where the section is at the time of execution. For example, if a section is copied into RAM for execution, the section's run address refers to an address in RAM, which is the destination address of the loader copy operation. The linker uses the program's run address for symbol resolutions.

The ELF file format has two different interpretations, as shown in Figure 2.4. The linker interprets the file as a linkable module described by the section header table, while the loader interprets the file as an executable module described by the program header table.

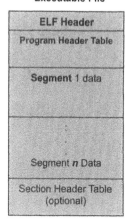

Figure 2.4   Executable and linking format.

Listing 2.1 shows both the section header and the program header, as represented in C programming structures. We describe the relevant fields during the course of this discussion.

Listing 2.1   Section header and program header.

Section header	Program header
`typedef struct {`	`typedef struct {`
`    Elf32_Word sh_name;`	`    Elf32_Word p_type;`
`    Elf32_Word sh_type;`	`    Elf32_Off  p_offset;`
`    Elf32_Word sh_flags;`	`    Elf32_Addr p_vaddr;`
`    Elf32_Addr sh_addr;`	`    Elf32_Addr p_paddr;`
`    Elf32_Off  sh_offset;`	`    Elf32_Word p_filesz;`
`    Elf32_Word sh_size;`	`    Elf32_Word p_memsz;`
`    Elf32_Word sh_link;`	`    Elf32_Word p_flags;`
`    Elf32_Word sh_info;`	`    Elf32_Word p_align;`
`    Elf32_Word sh_addralign;`	`} Elf32_Phdr;`
`    Elf32_Word sh_entsize;`	
`} Elf32_Shdr;`	

A *section header table* is an array of section header structures describing the sections of an object file. A *program header table* is an array of program header structures describing a loadable segment of an image that allows the loader to prepare the image for execution. Program headers are applied only to executable images and shared object files.

One of the fields in the section header structure is sh_type, which specifies the type of a section. Table 2.1 lists some section types.

Table 2.1   Section types.

NULL	Inactive header without a section.
PROGBITS	Code or initialized data.
SYMTAB	Symbol table for static linking.
STRTAB	String table.
RELA/REL	Relocation entries.
HASH	Run-time symbol hash table.
DYNAMIC	Information used for dynamic linking.
NOBITS	Uninitialized data.
DYNSYM	Symbol table for dynamic linking.

The sh_flags field in the section header specifies the attribute of a section. Table 2.2 lists some of these attributes.

Table 2.2   Section attributes.

WRITE	Section contains writeable data.
ALLOC	Section contains allocated data.
EXECINSTR	Section contains executable instructions.

Some common system-created default sections with predefined names for the PROGBITS are .text, .sdata, .data, .sbss, and .bss. Program code and constant data are contained in the .text section. This section is read-only because code and constant data are not expected to change during the lifetime of the program execution. The .sbss and .bss sections contain uninitialized data. The .sbss section stores *small data*, which is the data such as variables with sizes that fit into a specific size. This size limit is architecture-dependent. The result is that the compiler and the assembler can generate smaller and more efficient code to access these data items. The .sdata and .data sections contain initialized data items. The small data concept described for .sbss applies to .sdata. A .text section with executable code has the EXECINSTR attribute. The .sdata and .data sections have the WRITE attribute. The .sbss and .bss sections have both the WRITE and the ALLOC attributes.

Other common system-defined sections are .symtab containing the symbol table, .strtab containing the string table for the program symbols, .shstrtab containing the string table for the section names, and .relaname containing the relocation information for the section named *name*. We have discussed the role of the symbol table (SYMTAB) previously. In Figure 2.3, the symbol name is shown as part of the symbol table. In practice, each entry in the symbol table contains a reference to the string table (STRTAB) where the character representation of the name is stored.

The developer can define custom sections by invoking the linker command .section. For example, where the source files states

    .section my_section

the linker creates a new section called my_section. The reasons for creating custom named sections are explained shortly.

The sh_addr is the address where the program section should reside in the target memory. The p_paddr is the address where the program segment should reside in the target memory. The sh_addr and the p_paddr fields refer to the load addresses. The loader uses the load address field from the section header as the starting address for the image transfer from non-volatile memory to RAM.

For many embedded applications, the run address is the same as the load address. These embedded applications are directly downloaded into the target system memory for immediate execution without the need for any code or data transfer from one memory type or location to another. This practice is common during the development phase. We revisit this topic in Chapter 3, which covers the topic of image transfer from the host system to the target system.

2.4 Mapping Executable Images into Target Embedded Systems

After multiple source files (C/C++ and assembly files) have been compiled and assembled into ELF object files, the linker must combine these object files and merge the sections from the different object files into program segments. This process creates a single executable image for the target embedded system. The embedded developer uses linker commands (called *linker directives*) to control how the linker combines the sections and allocates the segments into the target system. The linker directives are kept in the *linker command file*. The ultimate goal of creating a linker command file is for the embedded developer to map the executable image into the target system accurately and efficiently.

2.4.1   Linker Command File

The format of the linker command file, as well as the linker directives, vary from linker to linker. It is best to consult the programmer's reference manual from the vendor for specific linker commands, syntaxes, and extensions. Some common directives, however,

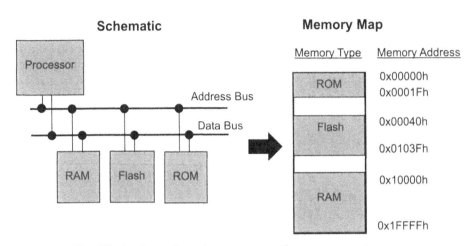

Figure 2.5   Simplified schematic and memory map for a target system.

are found among the majority of the available linkers used for building embedded applications. Two of the more common directives supported by most linkers are MEMORY and SECTION.

The MEMORY directive can be used to describe the target system's *memory map*. The memory map lists the different types of memory (such as RAM, ROM, and flash) that are present on the target system, along with the ranges of addresses that can be accessed for storing and running an executable image. An embedded developer needs to be familiar with the addressable physical memory on a target system before creating a linker command file. One of the best ways to do this process, other than having direct access to the hardware engineering team that built the target system, is to look at the target system's *schematics*, as shown in Figure 2.5, and the hardware documentation. Typically, the hardware documentation describes the target system's memory map.

The linker combines input sections having the same name into a single output section with that name by default. The developer-created, custom-named sections appear in the object file as independent sections. Sometimes developers might want to change this default linker behavior of only coalescing sections with the same name. The embedded developer might also need to instruct the linker on where to map the sections, in other words, what addresses should the linker use when performing symbol resolutions. The embedded developer can use the SECTION directive to achieve these goals.

The MEMORY directive defines the types of physical memory present on the target system and the address range occupied by each physical memory block, as specified in the following generalized syntax

```
MEMORY {
    area-name : org = start-address, len = number-of-bytes
    ...
}
```

In the example shown in Figure 2.5, three physical blocks of memory are present:

- a ROM chip mapped to address space location 0, with 32 bytes,
- some flash memory mapped to address space location 0x40, with 4,096 bytes, and
- a block of RAM that starts at origin 0x10000, with 65,536 bytes.

Translating this memory map into the MEMORY directive is shown in Listing 2.2. The named areas are ROM, FLASH, and RAM.

Listing 2.2   Memory map.

```
MEMORY {
      ROM:    origin = 0x0000h,   length = 0x0020h
      FLASH:  origin = 0x0040h,   length = 0x1000h
      RAM:    origin = 0x1000h,   length = 0x10000h
}
```

The SECTION directive tells the linker which input sections are to be combined into which output section, which output sections are to be grouped together and allocated in contiguous memory, and where to place each section, as well as other information. A general notation of the SECTION command is shown in Listing 2.3.

Listing 2.3   SECTION command.

```
SECTION {
      output-section-name : { contents } > area-name
      ...
      GROUP {
            [ALIGN(expression)]
            section-definition
            ...
      } > area-name
}
```

Figure 2.6   Combining input sections into an executable image.

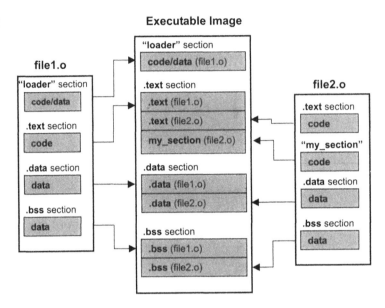

The example shown in Figure 2.6 contains three default sections (.text, .data, and .bss), as well as two developer-specified sections (loader and my_section), contained in two object files generated by a compiler or assembler (file1.o and file2.o). Translating this example into the MEMORY directive is shown in Listing 2.4.

Listing 2.4   Example code.

```
SECTION {
        .text   :
        {
                my_section
                *(.text)

        }
        loader : > FLASH
        GROUP ALIGN (4) :
        {
                .text,
                .data  : {}
                .bss   : {}
        } >RAM

}
```

The SECTION command in the linker command file instructs the linker to combine the input section named my_section and the default .text sections from all object files into the final output .text section. The loader section is placed into flash memory. The sections .text, .data, and .bss are grouped together and allocated in contiguous physical RAM memory aligned on the 4-byte boundary, as shown in Figure 2.7.

Tips on section allocation include the following:

- allocate sections according to size to fully use available memory, and
- examine the nature of the underlying physical memory, the attributes, and the purpose of a section to determine which physical memory is best suited for allocation.

2.4.2 Mapping Executable Images

Various reasons exist why an embedded developer might want to define custom sections, as well as to map these sections into different target memory areas as shown in the last example. The following sections list some of these reasons.

Module Upgradeability

Chapter 1 discusses the storage options and upgradability of software on embedded systems. Software can be easily upgraded when stored in non-volatile memory devices, such as flash devices. It is possible to upgrade the software dynamically while the system is still running. Upgrading the software can involve downloading the new program image over either a serial line or a network and then re-programming the flash memory. The

Figure 2.7   Mapping an executable image into the target system.

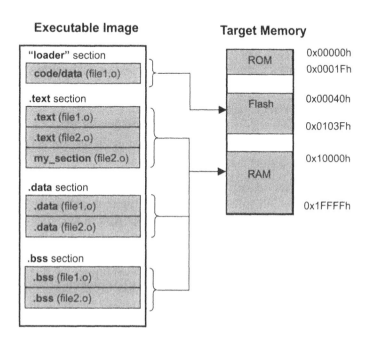

loader in the example could be such an application. The initial version of the loader might be capable of transferring an image from ROM to RAM. A newer version of the loader might be capable of transferring an image from the host over the serial connection to RAM. Therefore, the loader code and data section would be created in a custom loader section. The entire section then would be programmed into the flash memory for easy upgradeability in the future.

Memory Size Limitation

The target system usually has different types of physical memory, but each is limited in size. At times, it is impossible to fit all of the code and data into one type of memory, for example, the SDRAM. Because SDRAM has faster access time than DRAM, it is always desirable to map code and data into it. The available physical SDRAM might not be large enough to fit everything, but plenty of DRAM is available in the system. Therefore, the strategy is to divide the program into multiple sections and have some sections allocated into the SDARM, while the rest is mapped into the DRAM. For example, an often-used function along with a frequently searched lookup table might be mapped to the SDRAM. The remaining code and data is allocated into the DRAM.

Data Protection

Programs usually have various types of constants, such as integer constants and string constants. Sometimes these constants are kept in ROM to avoid accidental modification. In this case, these constants are part of a special data section, which is allocated into ROM.

2.4.3 Example in Practice

Consider an example system containing 256 bytes of ROM, 16KB of flash memory, and two blocks of RAM. RAMB0 is 128KB of SDRAM, and RAMB1 is 2MB of DRAM. An embedded application with a number of sections, as listed in Table 2.3, needs to be mapped into this target system.

One possible allocation is shown in Listing 2.5; it considers why an embedded engineer might want greater section allocation control.

This program allocation is shown in Figure 2.8 (page 34). The section allocation strategies applied include the following:

- The .rodata section contains system initialization parameters. Most likely these default values never change; therefore, allocate this section to ROM.
- The loader program is usually part of the system program that executes at startup. The _loader and the _wflash sections are allocated into flash memory because the loader code can be updated with new versions that understand more object formats. You need the flash memory programmer for this purpose, which can also be updated. Therefore, section _wflash is allocated into the flash memory as well.
- The embedded programmer interacts with the monitor program to probe system execution states and help debug application code; therefore, it should be responsive to

Table 2.3 **Example embedded application with sections**.

Sections	Size	Attribute[1]	Description
_loader	10KB	RD	Contains the loader code
_wflash	2KB	RD	Contains the flash memory programmer
.rodata	128 bytes	RD	Contains non-volatile default initialization parameters and data, such as copyright information
.sbss	10KB	R/W	Contains uninitialized data less than 64KB (e.g., global variables)
.sdata	2KB	R/W	Contains initialized data less than 64KB
.bss	128KB	R/W	Contains uninitialized data larger than 64KB
.data	512KB	R/W	Contains initialized data larger than 64KB
_monitor	54KB	RD	Contains the monitor code
.text	512KB	RD	Contains other program code

1. RD = read only; R/W = readable and writeable

Listing 2.5 **Possible section allocation**.

```
MEMORY {
        ROM:    origin = 0x00000h,   length = 0x000100h
        FLASH:  origin = 0x00110h,   length = 0x004000h
        RAMB0:  origin = 0x05000h,   length = 0x020000h
        RAMB1:  origin = 0x25000h,   length = 0x200000h
}
SECTION {
        .rodata  : > ROM
        _loader  : > FLASH
        _wflash  : > FLASH
        _monitor : > RAMB0
        .sbss  (ALIGN 4)  : > RAMB0
        .sdata (ALIGN 4)  : > RAMB0
        .text    : > RAMB1
        .bss  (ALIGN 4) : > RAMB1
        .data (ALIGN 4) : > RAMB1
}
```

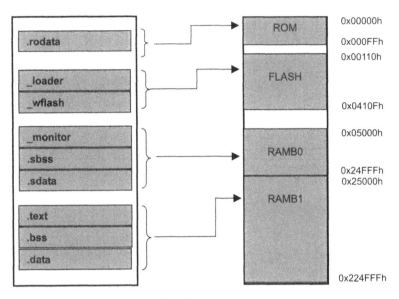

Figure 2.8   Mapping an executable image into the target system.

user commands. SDRAM is faster than DRAM, with shorter access time. Therefore, section _monitor is allocated into RAMB0.

- RAMB0 still has space left to accommodate both sections .sbss and .sdata. The allocation strategy for these two sections is to use the leftover fast memory fully.
- The remaining sections (.text, .bss, and .data) are allocated into RAMB1, which is the only memory that can accommodate all of these large sections.

2.5 **Points to Remember**

Some points to remember include the following:

- The linker performs symbol resolution and symbol relocation.
- An embedded programmer must understand the exact memory layout of the target system towards which development is aimed.
- An executable target image is comprised of multiple program sections.
- The programmer can describe the physical memory, such as its size and its mapping address, to the linker using the linker command file. The programmer can also instruct the linker on combining input sections into output sections and placing the output program sections using the linker command file.
- Each program section can reside in different types of physical memory, based on how the section is used. Program code (or .text section) can stay in ROM, flash, and RAM during execution. Program data (or .data section) must stay in RAM during execution.

In this chapter...

- Target System Tools and Image Transfer 36
- Target Boot Scenarios 39
- Target System Software Initialization
  Sequence 46
- On-Chip Debugging 51
- Points to Remember 52

CHAPTER 3

EMBEDDED SYSTEM INITIALIZATION

3.1 Introduction

It takes just minutes for a developer to compile and run a "Hello World!" application on a non-embedded system. On the other hand, for an embedded developer, the task is not so trivial. It might take days before seeing a successful result. This process can be a frustrating experience for a developer new to embedded system development.

Booting the target system, whether a third-party evaluation board or a custom design, can be a mystery to many newcomers. Indeed, it is daunting to pick up a programmer's reference manual for the target board and pore over tables of memory addresses and registers or to review the hardware component interconnection diagrams, wondering what it all means, what to do with the information (some of which makes little sense), and how to relate the information to running an image on the target system.

Questions to resolve at this stage are

- how to load the image onto the target system,
- where in memory to load the image,
- how to initiate program execution, and
- how the program produces recognizable output.

We answer these questions in this chapter and hopefully reduce frustration by demystifying the booting and initialization process of embedded systems.

Chapter 2 discusses constructing an executable image with multiple program sections according to the target system memory layout. After the final image is successfully built and residing on the host system, the next step is to execute it on the target.

The focus of this chapter is

- image transfer from the host to the target system,
- the embedded monitor and debug agent,
- the target system loader,
- the embedded system booting process,
- various initialization procedures, and
- an introduction to BDM and JTAG interfaces.

3.2 Target System Tools and Image Transfer

An executable image built for a target embedded system can be transferred from the host development system onto the target, which is called *loading the image*, by:

- Programming the entire image into the EEPROM or flash memory.
- Downloading the image over either a serial (typically RS-232) or network connection. This process requires the presence of a data transfer utility program on the host system, as well as the presence of a target loader, an embedded monitor, or a target debug agent on the target system.
- Downloading the image through either a JTAG or BDM interface (discussed in section 3.5).

These approaches are the most common, and this list is by no means comprehensive. Some of the possible host-to-target connectivity solutions are shown in Figure 2.1. Figure 3.1 exemplifies a target embedded system. We refer to the ELF image format (introduced in Chapter 2) exclusively throughout this chapter.

The embedded software for the final product is commonly stored in either ROM or the flash memory. The entire executable image is burned into the ROM or flash memory using special equipment. If ROM is used, the ROM chip is set into its socket on the target board. For embedded system boards that have both ROM and flash memory, the next step is to set the necessary jumpers. Jumpers are the part of the target board's wiring that controls which memory chip the processor uses to start executing its first set of instructions upon reboot. For example, if the image is stored in the flash memory and the jumpers are set to use the flash memory, the processor fetches its first instruction from the starting address where the flash is mapped. Therefore, set the jumpers appropriately according to the image storage.

This final production method, however, is impractical during the development stage because developers construct software in incremental steps with high frequency. The process is interactive in that a portion of the code is written, debugged, and tested, and the entire process then repeats for the new code. Reprogramming the EEPROM or the flash memory each time the code changes due to bugs or code addition is time consuming. The methods for downloading the image over a serial or a network connection or

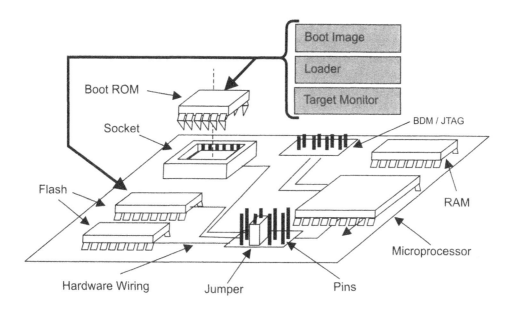

Figure 3.1   View of the target embedded system.

for downloading the image through a JTAG or BDM interface solve this problem by transferring the image directly into the target system's RAM memory.

3.2.1   Embedded Loader

A common approach taken at the early development phase is to write a loader program for the target side, which is called the *loader*, and use the loader to download the image from the host system. In the scenario shown in Figure 3.1, the loader has a small memory footprint, so it typically can be programmed into a ROM chip. A data transfer utility resides on the host system side. The loader works in conjunction with its host utility counterpart to perform the image transfer.

After the loader is written, it is programmed into the ROM. Part of the same ROM chip is occupied by the boot image. At a minimum, this boot image (typically written by a hardware engineer) consists of the code that executes on system power up. This code initializes the target hardware, such as the memory system and the physical RAM, into a known state. In other words, the boot image prepares the system to execute the loader. The loader begins execution after this boot image completes the necessary initialization work.

For this transfer method to work, a data transfer protocol, as well as the communication parameters, must be agreed upon between the host utility and the target loader. The data transfer protocol refers to the transfer rules. For example, a transfer protocol might be that the image transfer request should be initiated from the loader to the host utility; in which case, the host utility sends out the image file size followed by the actual image, and the loader sends an acknowledgement to the host utility upon completion. Data transfer rate, such as the baud rate for the serial connection, and per packet size are examples of communication parameters. The loader and the utility program operate as a unit, which is often capable of using more than one type of connection. At a minimum, the transfer takes place over the serial connection. More sophisticated loaders can download images over the network, for example, over the Ethernet using protocols such as the Trivial File Transfer Protocol (TFTP) or the File Transfer Protocol (FTP). In this case, the host utility program is either the TFTP server or the FTP server respectively. Both proprietary and well-known transfer protocols can be applied in either the serial or the network connection, but more commonly proprietary protocols are used with a serial connection.

The loader downloads the image directly into the RAM memory. The loader needs to understand the object file format (for example, the ELF format) because, as discussed in Chapter 2, the object file contains information such as the load address, which the loader uses for section placement.

The loader transfers control to the downloaded image after the transfer completes. A loader with flash programming capability can also transfer the image into the flash memory. In that case, the board jumpers must be set appropriately so that the processor executes out of flash memory after the image download completes.

A loader can be part of the final application program, and it can perform other functions in addition to downloading images, as discussed in more detail later in this chapter.

3.2.2 Embedded Monitor

An alternative to the boot image plus loader approach is to use an embedded monitor. A *monitor* is an embedded software application commonly provided by the target system manufacturer for its evaluation boards. The monitor enables developers to examine and debug the target system at run time. Similar to the boot image, the monitor is executed on power up and performs system initialization such as

- initializing the required peripheral devices, for example, the serial interface and the system timer chip for memory refresh, at a minimum,
- initializing the memory system for downloading the image, and
- initializing the interrupt controller and installing default interrupt handlers.

The monitor has a well-defined user interface accessible through a terminal emulation program over the serial interface. The monitor defines a set of commands allowing the developer to

- download the image,
- read from and write to system memory locations,
- read and write system registers,

- set and clear different types of breakpoints,
- single-step instructions, and
- reset the system.

The way in which the monitor downloads the image from the host system over the serial or network connection is similar to how the loader does it. The monitor is capable of downloading the image into either the RAM memory or the flash memory. In essence, the monitor has both the boot image and the loader functionalities incorporated but with the added interactive debug capability. The monitor is still present while the newly downloaded image executes. A special keystroke on the host system, for example, CTRL+D, interrupts the program execution and reactivates the monitor user interface so the developer can conduct interactive debugging activities.

The monitor is generally developed by the hardware engineers and is also used by the hardware engineers to perform both system device diagnostics and low-level code debugging. Some manufactures give the monitor source code to their customers. In that case, the code can be extracted and modified to work with a custom-designed target board.

3.2.3   Target Debug Agent

The target debug agent functions much like the monitor does but with one added feature: the target agent gives the host debugger enough information to provide visual source-level debug capability. Again, an agreed-upon communication protocol must be established between the host debugger and the target agent. The host debugger is something that the host tools vendor offers. Sometimes a RTOS vendor offers a host-based debugger simply because the debug agent is an integral part of the RTOS. The host debugger vendor works closely with the RTOS vendor to provide a fully compatible tool. The debug agent has built-in knowledge of the RTOS objects and services, which allows the developer to explore such objects and services fully and visually.

3.3 Target Boot Scenarios

We have described the software components involved in transferring images from the host to the target. In this section, we describe the details of the loading process itself and how control is transferred to the newly acquired image.

Embedded processors, after they are powered on, fetch and execute code from a pre-defined and hard-wired address offset. The code contained at this memory location is called the *reset vector*. The reset vector is usually a jump instruction into another part of the memory space where the real initialization code is found. The reason for jumping to another part of memory is to keep the reset vector small. The reset vector belongs to a small range of memory space reserved by the system for special purposes. The reset vector, as well as the system boot startup code, must be in permanent storage. Because of this issue, the system startup code, called the *bootstrap code,* resides in the system ROM, the on-board flash memory, or other types of non-volatile memory devices. We

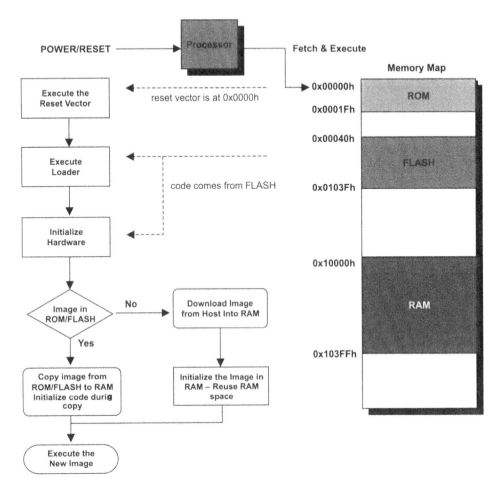

Figure 3.2   Example bootstrap overview.

will revisit the loader program from the system-bootstrapping perspective. In the discussions to follow, the loader refers to the code that performs system bootstrapping, image downloading, and initialization.

The concepts are best explained through an example. In this example, assume an embedded loader has been developed and programmed into the on-board flash memory. Also, assume that the target image contains various program sections. Each section has a designated location in the memory map. The reset vector is contained in a small ROM, which is mapped to location 0x0h of the address space. The ROM contains some essential initial values required by the processor on reset. These values are the reset vector, the initial stack pointer, and the usable RAM address.

In the example shown in Figure 3.2, the reset vector is a jump instruction to memory location 0x00040h; the reset vector transfers program control to the instruction at this address. Startup initialization code begins at this flash memory address. This system initialization code contains, among other things, the target image loader program and the default system exception vectors. The system exception vectors point to instructions that reside in the flash memory. See Chapter 10 for detailed discussions on interrupts, exceptions, and exception vectors and handlers.

The first part of the system bootstrap process is putting the system into a known state. The processor registers are set with appropriate default values. The stack pointer is set with the value found in the ROM. The loader disables the system interrupts because the system is not yet prepared to handle the interrupts. The loader also initializes the RAM memory and possibly the on-processor caches. At this point, the loader performs limited hardware diagnostics on those devices needed for its operation.

As discussed in Chapter 2, program execution is faster in RAM than if the executable code runs directly out of the flash memory. To this end, the loader optionally can copy the code from the flash memory into the RAM. Because of this capability, a program section can have both a load address and a run address. The load address is the address in which the program sections reside, while the run address is the address to which the loader program copies the program sections and prepares it for execution. Enabling runtime debugging is another main reason for a program to execute out of the RAM. For example, the debugger must be able to modify the runtime code in order to insert breakpoints.

An executable image contains initialized and uninitialized data sections. These sections are both readable and writeable. These sections must reside in RAM and therefore are copied out of the flash memory into RAM as part of system initialization. The initialized data sections (.data and .sdata) contain the initial values for the global and static variables. The content of these sections, therefore, is part of the final executable image and is transferred verbatim by the loader. On the other hand, the content for the uninitialized data sections .bss and.sbss) is empty. The linker reserves space for these sections in the memory map. The allocation information for these sections, such as the section size and the section run address, is part of the section header. It is the loader's job to retrieve this information from the section header and allocate the same amount of memory in RAM during the loading process. The loader places these sections into RAM according to the section's run address.

An executable image is likely to have constants. Constant data is part of the .const section, which is read-only. Therefore, it is possible to keep the .const section in read-only memory during program execution. Frequently accessed constants, such as lookup tables, should be transferred into RAM for performance gain.

The next step in the boot process is for the loader program to initialize the system devices. Only the necessary devices that the loader requires are initialized at this stage. In other words, a needed device is initialized to the extent that a required subset of the

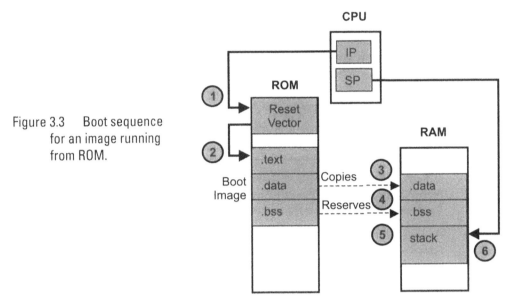

Figure 3.3 Boot sequence for an image running from ROM.

device capabilities and features are enabled and operational. In the majority of cases, these devices are part of the I/O system; therefore, these devices are fully initialized when the downloaded image performs I/O system initialization as part of the startup sequence.

Now the loader program is ready to transfer the application image to the target system. The application image contains the RTOS, the kernel, and the application code written by the embedded developer. The application image can come from two places:

- the read-only memory devices on the target, or
- the host development system.

We describe three common image execution scenarios:

- execute from ROM while using RAM for data,
- execute from RAM after being copied from ROM, and
- execute from RAM after being downloaded from a host system.

In the discussions to follow, the term ROM refers to read-only memory devices in general.

3.3.1 Executing from ROM Using RAM for Data

Some embedded devices have such limited memory resources that the program image executes directly out of the ROM. Sometimes the board vendor provides the boot ROM, and the code in the boot ROM does not copy instructions out to RAM for execution. In these cases, however, the data sections must still reside in RAM. Figure 3.3 shows this boot scenario.

Two CPU registers are of concern: the Instruction Pointer (IP) register and the Stack Pointer (SP) register. The IP points to the next instruction (code in the .text section) that the CPU must execute, while the SP points to the next free address in the stack. The C programming language uses the stack to pass function parameters during function invocation. The stack is created from a space in RAM, and the system stack pointer registers must be set appropriately at start up.

The boot sequence for an image running from ROM is as follows:

1. The CPU's IP is hardwired to execute the first instruction in memory (the reset vector).
2. The reset vector jumps to the first instruction of the .text section of the boot image. The .text section remains in ROM; the CPU uses the IP to execute .text. The code initializes the memory system, including the RAM.
3. The .data section of the boot image is copied into RAM because it is both readable and writeable.
4. Space is reserved in RAM for the .bss section of the boot image because it is both readable and writeable. There is nothing to transfer because the content for the .bss section is empty.
5. Stack space is reserved in RAM.
6. The CPU's SP register is set to point to the beginning of the newly created stack.

At this point, the boot completes. The CPU continues to execute the code in the .text section until it is complete or until the system is shut down.

Note that the boot image is not in the ELF format but contains binary machine code ready for execution. The boot image is created in the ELF format. The EEPROM programmer software, however, removes the ELF-specific data, such as the program header table and the section header table, when programming the boot image into the ROM, so that it is ready for execution upon processor reset.

The boot image needs to keep internal information in its program, which is critical to initializing the data sections, because the section header table is not present. As shown in Figure 3.3, the .data section is copied into RAM in its entirety. Therefore, the boot image must know the starting address of its data section and how big the data section is. One approach to this issue is to insert two special labels into the .data section: one label placed at the section's beginning and the other placed at the end. Special assembly code is written to retrieve the addresses of these labels. These are the load addresses of the labels. The linker reference manual should contain the specific program code syntax and link commander file syntax used for retrieving the load address of a symbol. The difference between these two addresses is the size of the section. A similar approach is taken for the .bss section.

If the .text section is copied into RAM, two dummy functions can be defined. These dummy functions do nothing other than return from function. One function is placed at the beginning of the .text section, while the other is placed at the end. This reason is one why an embedded developer might create custom sections and instruct the linker on where to place a section, as well as how to combine the various sections into a single output section through the linker command file.

3.3.2 Executing from RAM after Image Transfer from ROM

In the second boot scenario, the boot loader transfers an application image from ROM to RAM for execution. The large application image is stored in ROM in a compressed form to reduce the storage space required. The loader must decompress this image before it can initialize the sections of that image. Depending on the compression algorithm used and whether enough space is left in the ROM, some state information produced from the compression work can be stored to simplify image decompression. The loader needs a work area in RAM for the decompression process. It is common and good practice to perform checksum calculations over the boot image to ensure the image integrity before loading and execution.

The first six steps are identical to the previous boot scenario. After completing those steps, the process continues as follows:

7. The compressed application image is copied from ROM to RAM.

8–10. Initialization steps that are part of the decompression procedure are completed.

11. The loader transfers control to the image. This is done by "jumping" to the beginning address of the initialized image using a processor-specific "jump" instruction. This "jump" instruction effectively sets a new value into the instruction pointer.

12. As shown in Figure 3.4, the memory area that the loader program occupies is recycled. Specifically, the stack pointer is reinitialized (see the dotted line) to point to this area, so it can be used as the stack for the new program. The decompression work area is also recycled into the available memory space implicitly.

Note that the loader program is still available for use because it is stored in ROM. Making the loader available for later use is often intentional on the designer's part. Imagine a situation in which the loader program has a built-in monitor. As mentioned earlier, part of the monitor startup sequence is to install default interrupt handlers. This issue is extremely important because during the development phase the program under construction is incomplete and is being constantly updated. As such, this program might not be able to handle certain system interrupts and exceptions. It is beneficial to have the monitor conduct default processing in such cases. For example, a program avoids processing memory access exceptions by not installing an exception handler for it. In this case, the monitor takes control of the system when the program execution triggers such an exception, for example, when the program crashes. The developer then gets the opportunity to debug and back-trace the execution sequence through the monitor interface. As indicated earlier, a monitor allows the developer to modify the processor registers. Therefore, as soon as the bug is uncovered and a new program image is built, the developer can set the instruction pointer register to the starting address of the loader program in ROM, effectively transferring control to the loader. The result is that the

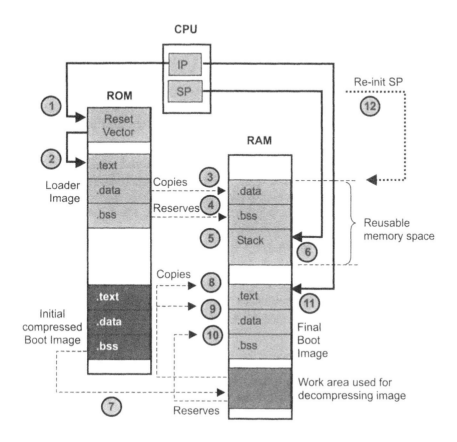

Figure 3.4   Boot sequence for an image executing from RAM after transfer from ROM.

loader begins to download the new image and reinitializes the entire system without having to power cycle on the system.

Similarly, another benefit of running the loader out of the ROM is to prevent a program that is behaving badly from corrupting its code in systems without protection from the MMU.

In this example, the loader image is in an executable machine code format. The application image is in the ELF format but has been compressed through an algorithm that works independently of the object file format. The application image is in the ELF format so that the loader can be written as a generic utility, able to load many application program images. If the application image is in the ELF format, the loader program can extract the necessary information from the image for initialization.

3.3.3　Executing from RAM after Image Transfer from Host

In the third boot scenario, the target debug agent transfers an application image from the host system into RAM for execution. This practice is typical during the later development phases when the majority of the device drivers have been fully implemented and debugged. The system can handle interrupts and exceptions correctly. At this stage, the target system facilitates a stable environment for further application development, allowing the embedded developer to focus on application design and implementation rather than the low-level hardware details.

The debug agent is RTOS-aware and understands RTOS objects and services. The debug agent can communicate with a host debugger and transfer target images through the host debugger. The debug agent can also function as a standalone monitor. The developer can access the command line interface for the target debug agent through a simple terminal program over the serial link. The developer can issue commands over the command line interface to instruct the debug agent on the target image's location on the host system and to initiate the transfer.

The debug agent downloads the image into a temporary area in RAM first. After the download is complete and the image integrity verified, the debug agent initializes the image according to the information presented in the program section header table. This boot scenario is shown in Figure 3.5.

The first six steps are identical to the initial boot scenario. After completing those steps, the process continues as follows:

7.　The application image is downloaded from the host development system.
8.　The image integrity is verified.
9.　The image is decompressed if necessary.
10–12. The debug agent loads the image sections into their respective run addresses in RAM.
13.　The debug agent transfers control to the download image.

There is a good reason why the memory area used by the debug agent is not recycled. In this example, the downloaded image contains an RTOS, which is introduced in Chapter 4. One of the core components of a RTOS is a scheduler, which facilitates the simultaneous existence and execution of multiple programs, called tasks or threads. The scheduler can save the execution state information of the debug agent and revive the agent later. Thus, the debug agent can continue to communicate with the host debugger while the downloaded image executes, providing interactive, visual, source-level debugging.

3.4 Target System Software Initialization Sequence

The target image referred to repeatedly in the last section is a combination of sophisticated software components and modules as shown in Figure 3.6. The software components include the following: the board support package (BSP), which contains a full

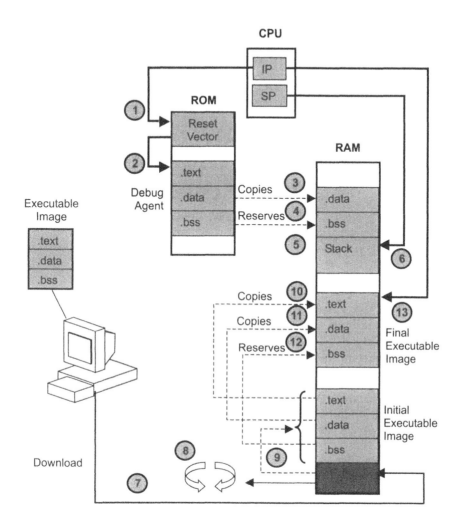

Figure 3.5   Boot sequence for an image executing from RAM after transfer from the host system.

spectrum of drivers for the system hardware components and devices; the RTOS, which provides basic services, such as resource synchronization services, I/O services, and scheduling services needed by the embedded applications; and the other components, which provide additional services, such as file system services and network services.

Figure 3.6   Software
components of a target
image.

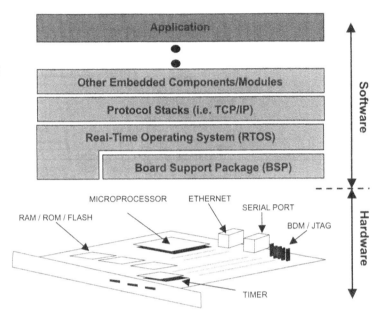

These software components perform full system initialization after the target image gains control from the loading program.

Assuming the target image is structured as shown in Figure 3.6, then Figure 3.7 illustrates the steps required to initialize most target systems. The main stages are

- hardware initialization,
- RTOS initialization, and
- application initialization.

Note that these steps are not all that are required to initialize the target system. Rather, this summary provides a high-level example from which to learn. Each stage is discussed more thoroughly in the following sections.

3.4.1   Hardware Initialization

The previous sections described aspects of steps 1 and 2 in Figure 3.7 in which a boot image executes after the CPU begins executing instructions from the reset vector. Typically at this stage, the minimum hardware initialization required to get the boot image to execute is performed, which includes:

1. starting execution at the reset vector
2. putting the processor into a known state by setting the appropriate registers:
    - getting the processor type
    - getting or setting the CPU's clock speed

Figure 3.7   The software
initialization process.

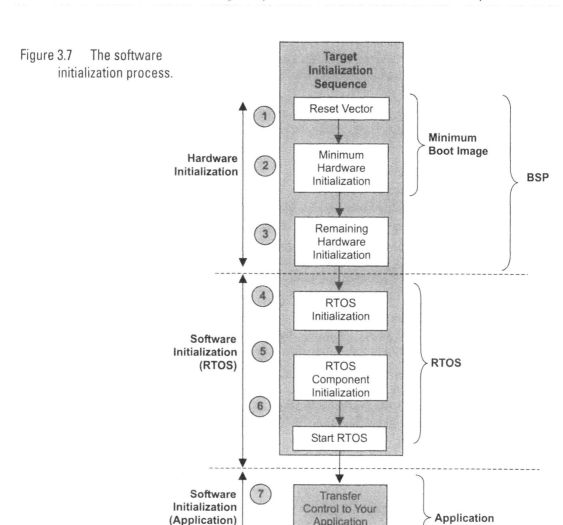

3.   disabling interrupts and caches
4.   initializing memory controller, memory chips, and cache units:
   • getting the start addresses for memory
   • getting the size of memory
   • performing preliminary memory tests, if required

After the boot sequence initializes the CPU and memory, the boot sequence copies and decompresses, if necessary, the sections of code that need to run. It also copies and decompresses its data into RAM.

Most of the early initialization code is in low-level assembly language that is specific to the target system's CPU architecture. Later-stage initialization code might be written in a higher-level programming language, such as C.

As the boot code executes, the code calls the appropriate functions to initialize other hardware components, if present, on the target system. Eventually, all devices on the target board are initialized (as shown in step 3 of Figure 3.7). These might include the following:

- setting up execution handlers;
- initializing interrupt handlers;
- initializing bus interfaces, such as VME, PCI, and USB; and
- initializing board peripherals such as serial, LAN, and SCSI.

Most embedded systems developers consider steps 1 and 2 in Figure 3.7 as the initial boot sequence, and steps 1 to 3 as the BSP initialization phase. Steps 1 to 3 are also called the hardware initialization stage.

Writing a BSP for a particular target system is not trivial. The developer must have a good understanding of the underlying hardware components. Along with understanding the target system's block diagrams, data flow, memory map, and interrupt map, the developer must also know the assembly language for the target system's microprocessor.

Developers can save a great deal of time and effort by using sample BSPs if they come with the target evaluation board or from the RTOS vendor. Typically, the microprocessor registers that a developer needs to program are listed in these BSPs, along with the sequence in which to work with them to properly initialize target-system hardware.

A completed BSP initialization phase has initialized all of the target-system hardware and has provided a set of function calls that upper layers of software (for example, the RTOS) can use to communicate with the hardware components of the target system.

3.4.2 RTOS Initialization

Step 4 of Figure 3.7 begins the RTOS software initialization. Key things that can happen in steps 4 to 6 include:

1. initializing the RTOS
2. initializing different RTOS objects and services, if present (usually controlled with a user-configurable header file):
    - task objects
    - semaphore objects
    - message-queue objects
    - timer services
    - interrupt services
    - memory-management services

3. creating necessary stacks for RTOS

4. initializing additional RTOS extensions, such as:
   - TCP/IP stack
   - file systems

5. starting the RTOS and its initial tasks

The components of an RTOS (for example, tasks, semaphores, and message queues) are discussed in more detail in later chapters of this book. For now, note that the RTOS abstracts the application code from the hardware and provides software objects and services that facilitate embedded-systems application development.

3.4.3 Application Software Initialization

After the RTOS is initialized and running with the required components, control is transferred to a user-defined application. This transfer takes place when the RTOS code calls a predefined function (that is RTOS dependent) which is implemented by the user-defined application. At this point, the RTOS services are available. This application also goes through initialization, during which all necessary objects, services, data structures, variables, and other constructs are declared and implemented. For a simple, user application such as the "hello world" application, all the work can be done in this function. This user-defined application (maybe the "hello world" application) might finally produce its impressive output. On the other hand, for a complex application, it will create task or tasks to perform the work. These application-created tasks will execute once the kernel scheduler runs. The kernel scheduler runs when this control-transfer function exits.

3.5 On-Chip Debugging

Many silicon vendors recognize the need for built-in microprocessor debugging, called on-chip debugging (OCD). BDM and JTAG are two types of OCD solutions that allow direct access and control over the microprocessor and system resources without needing software debug agents on the target or expensive in-circuit emulators. As shown in Figure 3.1, the embedded processor with OCD capability provides an external interface. The developer can use the external interface to download code, read or write processor registers, modify system memory, and command the processor to execute one instruction and halt, thus facilitating single-step debugging. Depending on the selected processor, it might be possible to disable the on-chip peripherals while OCD is in effect. It might also be possible to gain a near real-time view of the executing system state. OCD is used to solve the chicken-and-egg problem often encountered at the beginning development stage—if the monitor is the tool for debugging a running program, what debugs the monitor while it's developed? The powerful debug capabilities offered by the OCD combined with the quick turnaround time required to set up the connection means that software engineers find OCD solutions invaluable when writing hardware initialization code, low-level drivers, and even applications.

JTAG stands for Joint Test Action Group, which was founded by electronics manufacturers to develop a new and cost-effective test solution. The result, produced by the JTAG consortium, is sanctioned by the IEEE1149.1 standard.

BDM stands for background debug mode. It refers to the microprocessor debug interface introduced by Motorola and found on its processor chips. The term also describes the non-intrusive nature (on the executing system) of the debug method provided by the OCD solutions.

An OCD solution is comprised of both hardware and software. Special hardware devices, called personality modules, are built for the specific processor type and are required to connect between the OCD interface on the target system and the host development system. The interface on the target system is usually an 8- or 10-pin connector. The host side of the connection can be the parallel port, the serial port, or the network interface. The OCD-aware host debugger displays system state information, such as the contents of the processor registers, the system memory dump, and the current executing instruction. The host debugger provides the interface between the embedded software developer and the target processor and its resources.

3.6 Points to Remember

Some points to remember include the following:

- Developers have many choices for downloading an executable image to a target system. They can use target-monitor-based, debug-agent-based, or hardware-assisted connections.
- The boot ROM can contain a boot image, loader image, monitor image, debug agent, or even executable image.
- Hardware-assisted connections are ideal, both when first initializing a physical target system as well as later, for programming the final executable image into ROM or flash memory.
- Some of the different ways to boot a target system include running an image out of ROM, running an image out of RAM after copying it from ROM, and running an image out of RAM after downloading it from a host.
- A system typically undergoes three distinct initialization stages: hardware initialization, OS initialization (RTOS), and application initialization.
- After the target system is initialized, application developers can use this platform to download, test, and debug applications that use an underlying RTOS.

In this chapter...

- A Brief History of Operating Systems . 54
- Defining an RTOS 55
- The Scheduler 57
- Objects 61
- Services 62
- Key Characteristics of an RTOS 62
- Points to Remember 64

CHAPTER 4

INTRODUCTION TO REAL-TIME OPERATING SYSTEMS

4.1 Introduction

A real-time operating system (RTOS) is key to many embedded systems today and, provides a software platform upon which to build applications. Not all embedded systems, however, are designed with an RTOS. Some embedded systems with relatively simple hardware or a small amount of software application code might not require an RTOS. Many embedded systems, however, with moderate-to-large software applications require some form of scheduling, and these systems require an RTOS.

This chapter sets the stage for all subsequent chapters in this section. It describes the key concepts upon which most real-time operating systems are based. Specifically, this chapter provides

- a brief history of operating systems,
- a definition of an RTOS,
- a description of the scheduler,
- a discussion of objects,
- a discussion of services, and
- the key characteristics of an RTOS.

53

4.2 A Brief History of Operating Systems

In the early days of computing, developers created software applications that included low-level machine code to initialize and interact with the system's hardware directly. This tight integration between the software and hardware resulted in non-portable applications. A small change in the hardware might result in rewriting much of the application itself. Obviously, these systems were difficult and costly to maintain.

As the software industry progressed, operating systems that provided the basic software foundation for computing systems evolved and facilitated the abstraction of the underlying hardware from the application code. In addition, the evolution of operating systems helped shift the design of software applications from large, monolithic applications to more modular, interconnected applications that could run on top of the operating system environment.

Over the years, many versions of operating systems evolved. These ranged from general-purpose operating systems (GPOS), such as UNIX and Microsoft Windows, to smaller and more compact real-time operating systems, such as VxWorks. Each is briefly discussed next.

In the 60s and 70s, when mid-sized and mainframe computing was in its prime, UNIX was developed to facilitate multi-user access to expensive, limited-availability computing systems. UNIX allowed many users performing a variety of tasks to share these large and costly computers. multi-user access was very efficient: one user could print files, for example, while another wrote programs. Eventually, UNIX was ported to all types of machines, from microcomputers to supercomputers.

In the 80s, Microsoft introduced the Windows operating system, which emphasized the personal computing environment. Targeted for residential and business users interacting with PCs through a graphical user interface, the Microsoft Windows operating system helped drive the personal-computing era.

Later in the decade, momentum started building for the next generation of computing: the post-PC, embedded-computing era. To meet the needs of embedded computing, commercial RTOSes, such as VxWorks, were developed. Although some functional similarities exist between RTOSes and GPOSes, many important differences occur as well. These differences help explain why RTOSes are better suited for real-time embedded systems.

Some core functional similarities between a typical RTOS and GPOS include:

- some level of multitasking,
- software and hardware resource management,
- provision of underlying OS services to applications, and
- abstracting the hardware from the software application.

On the other hand, some key functional differences that set RTOSes apart from GPOSes include:

- better reliability in embedded application contexts,
- the ability to scale up or down to meet application needs,
- faster performance,
- reduced memory requirements,
- scheduling policies tailored for real-time embedded systems,
- support for diskless embedded systems by allowing executables to boot and run from ROM or RAM, and
- better portability to different hardware platforms.

Today, GPOSes target general-purpose computing and run predominantly on systems such as personal computers, workstations, and mainframes. In some cases, GPOSes run on embedded devices that have ample memory and very soft real-time requirements. GPOSes typically require a lot more memory, however, and are not well suited to real-time embedded devices with limited memory and high performance requirements.

RTOSes, on the other hand, can meet these requirements. They are reliable, compact, and scalable, and they perform well in real-time embedded systems. In addition, RTOSes can be easily tailored to use only those components required for a particular application.

Again, remember that today many smaller embedded devices are still built without an RTOS. These simple devices typically contain a small-to-moderate amount of application code. The focus of this book, however, remains on embedded devices that use an RTOS.

4.3 Defining an RTOS

A real-time operating system (RTOS) is a program that schedules execution in a timely manner, manages system resources, and provides a consistent foundation for developing application code. Application code designed on an RTOS can be quite diverse, ranging from a simple application for a digital stopwatch to a much more complex application for aircraft navigation. Good RTOSes, therefore, are scalable in order to meet different sets of requirements for different applications.

For example, in some applications, an RTOS comprises only a kernel, which is the core supervisory software that provides minimal logic, scheduling, and resource-management algorithms. Every RTOS has a kernel. On the other hand, an RTOS can be a combination of various modules, including the kernel, a file system, networking protocol stacks, and other components required for a particular application, as illustrated at a high level in Figure 4.1.

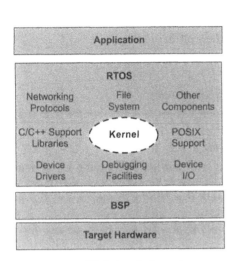

Figure 4.1   High-level view of an RTOS, its kernel, and other components found in embedded systems.

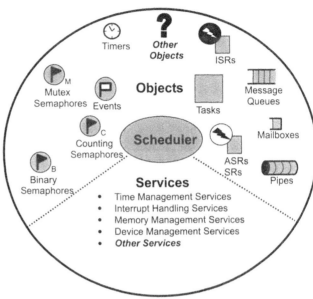

Figure 4.2   Common components in an RTOS kernel that including objects, the scheduler, and some services.

Although many RTOSes can scale up or down to meet application requirements, this book focuses on the common element at the heart of all RTOSes—the kernel. Most RTOS kernels contain the following components:

- **Scheduler**—is contained within each kernel and follows a set of algorithms that determines which task executes when. Some common examples of scheduling algorithms include round-robin and preemptive scheduling.
- **Objects**—are special kernel constructs that help developers create applications for real-time embedded systems. Common kernel objects include tasks, semaphores, and message queues.
- **Services**—are operations that the kernel performs on an object or, generally operations such as timing, interrupt handling, and resource management.

Figure 4.2 illustrates these components, each of which is described next.

This diagram is highly simplified; remember that not all RTOS kernels conform to this exact set of objects, scheduling algorithms, and services.

4.4 The Scheduler

The scheduler is at the heart of every kernel. A scheduler provides the algorithms needed to determine which task executes when. To understand how scheduling works, this section describes the following topics:

- schedulable entities,
- multitasking,
- context switching,
- dispatcher, and
- scheduling algorithms.

4.4.1 Schedulable Entities

A schedulable entity is a kernel object that can compete for execution time on a system, based on a predefined scheduling algorithm. Tasks and processes are all examples of schedulable entities found in most kernels.

A task is an independent thread of execution that contains a sequence of independently schedulable instructions. Some kernels provide another type of a schedulable object called a process. Processes are similar to tasks in that they can independently compete for CPU execution time. Processes differ from tasks in that they provide better memory protection features, at the expense of performance and memory overhead. Despite these differences, for the sake of simplicity, this book uses task to mean either a task or a process.

Note that message queues and semaphores are not schedulable entities. These items are inter-task communication objects used for synchronization and communication. Chapter 6 discusses semaphores, and Chapter 7 discusses message queues in more detail.

So, how exactly does a scheduler handle multiple schedulable entities that need to run simultaneously? The answer is by multitasking. The multitasking discussions are carried out in the context of uniprocessor environments.

4.4.2 Multitasking

Multitasking is the ability of the operating system to handle multiple activities within set deadlines. A real-time kernel might have multiple tasks that it has to schedule to run. One such multitasking scenario is illustrated in Figure 4.3.

In this scenario, the kernel multitasks in such a way that many threads of execution appear to be running concurrently; however, the kernel is actually interleaving executions sequentially, based on a preset scheduling algorithm (see "Scheduling Algorithms" on page 59). The scheduler must ensure that the appropriate task runs at the right time.

An important point to note here is that the tasks follow the kernel's scheduling algorithm, while interrupt service routines (ISR) are triggered to run because of hardware interrupts and their established priorities.

As the number of tasks to schedule increases, so do CPU performance requirements. This fact is due to increased switching between the contexts of the different threads of execution.

4.4.3   The Context Switch

Each task has its own context, which is the state of the CPU registers required each time it is scheduled to run. A context switch occurs when the scheduler switches from one task to another. To better understand what happens during a context switch, let's examine further what a typical kernel does in this scenario.

Every time a new task is created, the kernel also creates and maintains an associated task control block (TCB). TCBs are system data structures that the kernel uses to maintain task-specific information. TCBs contain everything a kernel needs to know about a particular task. When a task is running, its context is highly dynamic. This dynamic context is maintained in the TCB. When the task is not running, its context is frozen within the TCB, to be restored the next time the task runs. A typical context switch scenario is illustrated in Figure 4.3.

As shown in Figure 4.3, when the kernel's scheduler determines that it needs to stop running task 1 and start running task 2, it takes the following steps:

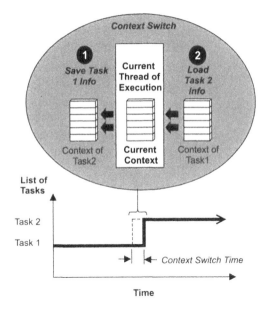

Figure 4.3   Multitasking using a context switch.

1. The kernel saves task 1's context information in its TCB.
2. It loads task 2's context information from its TCB, which becomes the current thread of execution.
3. The context of task 1 is frozen while task 2 executes, but if the scheduler needs to run task 1 again, task 1 continues from where it left off just before the context switch.

The time it takes for the scheduler to switch from one task to another is the context switch time. It is relatively insignificant compared to most operations that a task performs. If an application's design includes frequent context switching, however, the application can incur unnecessary performance overhead. Therefore, design applications in a way that does not involve excess context switching.

Every time an application makes a system call, the scheduler has an opportunity to determine if it needs to switch contexts. When the scheduler determines a context switch is necessary, it relies on an associated module, called the dispatcher, to make that switch happen.

4.4.4   The Dispatcher

The dispatcher is the part of the scheduler that performs context switching and changes the flow of execution. At any time an RTOS is running, the flow of execution, also known as flow of control, is passing through one of three areas: through an application task, through an ISR, or through the kernel. When a task or ISR makes a system call, the flow of control passes to the kernel to execute one of the system routines provided by the kernel. When it is time to leave the kernel, the dispatcher is responsible for passing control to one of the tasks in the user's application. It will not necessarily be the same task that made the system call. It is the scheduling algorithms (to be discussed shortly) of the scheduler that determines which task executes next. It is the dispatcher that does the actual work of context switching and passing execution control.

Depending on how the kernel is first entered, dispatching can happen differently. When a task makes system calls, the dispatcher is used to exit the kernel after every system call completes. In this case, the dispatcher is used on a call-by-call basis so that it can coordinate task-state transitions that any of the system calls might have caused. (One or more tasks may have become ready to run, for example.)

On the other hand, if an ISR makes system calls, the dispatcher is bypassed until the ISR fully completes its execution. This process is true even if some resources have been freed that would normally trigger a context switch between tasks. These context switches do not take place because the ISR must complete without being interrupted by tasks. After the ISR completes execution, the kernel exits through the dispatcher so that it can then dispatch the correct task.

4.4.5   Scheduling Algorithms

As mentioned earlier, the scheduler determines which task runs by following a scheduling algorithm (also known as scheduling policy). Most kernels today support two common scheduling algorithms:

- preemptive priority-based scheduling, and
- round-robin scheduling.

The RTOS manufacturer typically predefines these algorithms; however, in some cases, developers can create and define their own scheduling algorithms. Each algorithm is described next.

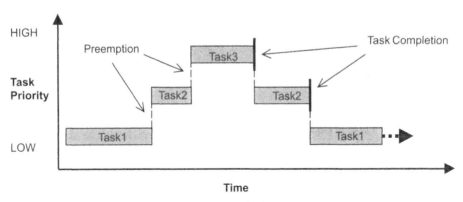

Figure 4.4   Preemptive priority-based scheduling.

Preemptive Priority-Based Scheduling

Of the two scheduling algorithms introduced here, most real-time kernels use preemptive priority-based scheduling by default. As shown in Figure 4.4 with this type of scheduling, the task that gets to run at any point is the task with the highest priority among all other tasks ready to run in the system.

Real-time kernels generally support 256 priority levels, in which 0 is the highest and 255 the lowest. Some kernels appoint the priorities in reverse order, where 255 is the highest and 0 the lowest. Regardless, the concepts are basically the same. With a preemptive priority-based scheduler, each task has a priority, and the highest-priority task runs first. If a task with a priority higher than the current task becomes ready to run, the kernel immediately saves the current task's context in its TCB and switches to the higher-priority task. As shown in Figure 4.4 task 1 is preempted by higher-priority task 2, which is then preempted by task 3. When task 3 completes, task 2 resumes; likewise, when task 2 completes, task 1 resumes.

Although tasks are assigned a priority when they are created, a task's priority can be changed dynamically using kernel-provided calls. The ability to change task priorities dynamically allows an embedded application the flexibility to adjust to external events as they occur, creating a true real-time, responsive system. Note, however, that misuse of this capability can lead to priority inversions, deadlock, and eventual system failure.

Round-Robin Scheduling

Round-robin scheduling provides each task an equal share of the CPU execution time. Pure round-robin scheduling cannot satisfy real-time system requirements because in real-time systems, tasks perform work of varying degrees of importance. Instead, preemptive, priority-based scheduling can be augmented with round-robin scheduling which uses time slicing to achieve equal allocation of the CPU for tasks of the same priority as shown in Figure 4.5.

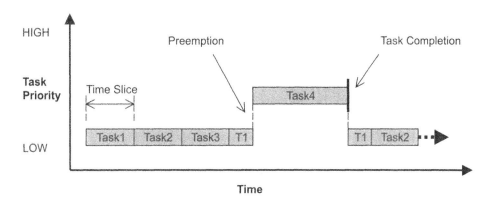

Figure 4.5   Round-robin and preemptive scheduling.

With time slicing, each task executes for a defined interval, or time slice, in an ongoing cycle, which is the round robin. A run-time counter tracks the time slice for each task, incrementing on every clock tick. When one task's time slice completes, the counter is cleared, and the task is placed at the end of the cycle. Newly added tasks of the same priority are placed at the end of the cycle, with their run-time counters initialized to 0.

If a task in a round-robin cycle is preempted by a higher-priority task, its run-time count is saved and then restored when the interrupted task is again eligible for execution. This idea is illustrated in Figure 4.5, in which task 1 is preempted by a higher-priority task 4 but resumes where it left off when task 4 completes.

4.5 Objects

Kernel objects are special constructs that are the building blocks for application development for real-time embedded systems. The most common RTOS kernel objects are

- **Tasks**—are concurrent and independent threads of execution that can compete for CPU execution time.
- **Semaphores**—are token-like objects that can be incremented or decremented by tasks for synchronization or mutual exclusion.
- **Message Queues**—are buffer-like data structures that can be used for synchronization, mutual exclusion, and data exchange by passing messages between tasks.

Developers creating real-time embedded applications can combine these basic kernel objects (as well as others not mentioned here) to solve common real-time design problems, such as concurrency, activity synchronization, and data communication. These design problems and the kernel objects used to solve them are discussed in more detail in later chapters.

4.6 Services

Along with objects, most kernels provide services that help developers create applications for real-time embedded systems. These services comprise sets of API calls that can be used to perform operations on kernel objects or can be used in general to facilitate timer management, interrupt handling, device I/O, and memory management. Again, other services might be provided; these services are those most commonly found in RTOS kernels.

4.7 Key Characteristics of an RTOS

An application's requirements define the requirements of its underlying RTOS. Some of the more common attributes are

- reliability,
- predictability,
- performance,
- compactness, and
- scalability.

These attributes are discussed next; however, the RTOS attribute an application needs depends on the type of application being built.

4.7.1 Reliability

Embedded systems must be reliable. Depending on the application, the system might need to operate for long periods without human intervention.

Different degrees of reliability may be required. For example, a digital solar-powered calculator might reset itself if it does not get enough light, yet the calculator might still be considered acceptable. On the other hand, a telecom switch cannot reset during operation without incurring high associated costs for down time. The RTOSes in these applications require different degrees of reliability.

Although different degrees of reliability might be acceptable, in general, a reliable system is one that is available (continues to provide service) and does not fail. A common way that developers categorize highly reliable systems is by quantifying their downtime per year, as shown in Table 4.1. The percentages under the "Number of 9s" column indicate the percent of the total time that a system must be available.

While RTOSes must be reliable, note that the RTOS by itself is not what is measured to determine system reliability. It is the combination of all system elements—including the hardware, BSP, RTOS, and application—that determines the reliability of a system.

Table 4.1   Categorizing highly available systems by allowable downtime.[1]

Number of 9s	Downtime per year	Typical application
3 Nines (99.9%)	~9 hours	Desktop
4 Nines (99.99%)	~1 hour	Enterprise Server
5 Nines (99.999%)	~5 minutes	Carrier-Class Server
6 Nines (99.9999%)	~31 seconds	Carrier Switch Equipment

1   Source: "Providing Open Architecture High Availability Solutions," Revision 1.0, Published by HA Forum, February 2001.

4.7.2   Predictability

Because many embedded systems are also real-time systems, meeting time requirements is key to ensuring proper operation. The RTOS used in this case needs to be predictable to a certain degree. The term deterministic describes RTOSes with predictable behavior, in which the completion of operating system calls occurs within known timeframes.

Developers can write simple benchmark programs to validate the determinism of an RTOS. The result is based on timed responses to specific RTOS calls. In a good deterministic RTOS, the variance of the response times for each type of system call is very small.

4.7.3   Performance

This requirement dictates that an embedded system must perform fast enough to fulfill its timing requirements. Typically, the more deadlines to be met—and the shorter the time between them—the faster the system's CPU must be. Although underlying hardware can dictate a system's processing power, its software can also contribute to system performance. Typically, the processor's performance is expressed in million instructions per second (MIPS).

Throughput also measures the overall performance of a system, with hardware and software combined. One definition of throughput is the rate at which a system can generate output based on the inputs coming in. Throughput also means the amount of data transferred divided by the time taken to transfer it. Data transfer throughput is typically measured in multiples of bits per second (bps).

Sometimes developers measure RTOS performance on a call-by-call basis. Benchmarks are written by producing timestamps when a system call starts and when it completes. Although this step can be helpful in the analysis stages of design, true performance testing is achieved only when the system performance is measured as a whole.

4.7.4   Compactness

Application design constraints and cost constraints help determine how compact an embedded system can be. For example, a cell phone clearly must be small, portable, and low cost. These design requirements limit system memory, which in turn limits the size of the application and operating system.

In such embedded systems, where hardware real estate is limited due to size and costs, the RTOS clearly must be small and efficient. In these cases, the RTOS memory footprint can be an important factor. To meet total system requirements, designers must understand both the static and dynamic memory consumption of the RTOS and the application that will run on it.

4.7.5   Scalability

Because RTOSes can be used in a wide variety of embedded systems, they must be able to scale up or down to meet application-specific requirements. Depending on how much functionality is required, an RTOS should be capable of adding or deleting modular components, including file systems and protocol stacks.

If an RTOS does not scale up well, development teams might have to buy or build the missing pieces. Suppose that a development team wants to use an RTOS for the design of a cellular phone project and a base station project. If an RTOS scales well, the same RTOS can be used in both projects, instead of two different RTOSes, which saves considerable time and money.

4.8 Points to Remember

Some points to remember include the following:

- RTOSes are best suited for real-time, application-specific embedded systems; GPOSes are typically used for general-purpose systems.
- RTOSes are programs that schedule execution in a timely manner, manage system resources, and provide a consistent foundation for developing application code.
- Kernels are the core module of every RTOS and typically contain kernel objects, services, and scheduler.
- Kernels can deploy different algorithms for task scheduling. The most common two algorithms are preemptive priority-based scheduling and round-robin scheduling.
- RTOSes for real-time embedded systems should be reliable, predictable, high performance, compact, and scalable.

In this chapter...

- Defining a Task 65
- Task States and Scheduling 67
- Typical Task Operations 72
- Typical Task Structure 76
- Synchronization, Communication, and
  Concurrency 77
- Points to Remember 77

CHAPTER 5

TASKS

5.1 Introduction

Simple software applications are typically designed to run sequentially, one instruction at a time, in a pre-determined chain of instructions. However, this scheme is inappropriate for real-time embedded applications, which generally handle multiple inputs and outputs within tight time constraints. Real-time embedded software applications must be designed for concurrency.

Concurrent design requires developers to decompose an application into small, schedulable, and sequential program units. When done correctly, concurrent design allows system multitasking to meet performance and timing requirements for a real-time system. Most RTOS kernels provide task objects and task management services to facilitate designing concurrency within an application.

This chapter discusses the following topics:

- task definition,
- task states and scheduling,
- typical task operations,
- typical task structure, and
- task coordination and concurrency.

5.2 Defining a Task

A *task* is an independent thread of execution that can compete with other concurrent tasks for processor execution time. As mentioned earlier, developers decompose applications

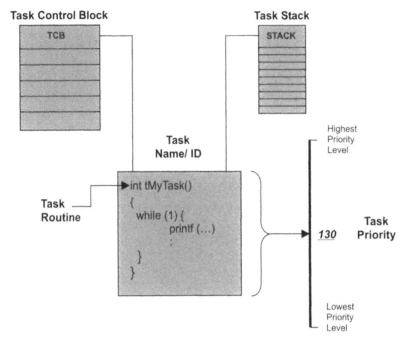

Figure 5.1   A task, its associated parameters, and supporting data structures.

into multiple concurrent tasks to optimize the handling of inputs and outputs within set time constraints.

A task is *schedulable*. As Chapter 4 discusses, the task is able to compete for execution time on a system, based on a predefined scheduling algorithm. A task is defined by its distinct set of parameters and supporting data structures. Specifically, upon creation, each task has an associated name, a unique ID, a priority (if part of a preemptive scheduling plan), a task control block (TCB), a stack, and a task routine, as shown in Figure 5.1). Together, these components make up what is known as the *task object*.

When the kernel first starts, it creates its own set of *system tasks* and allocates the appropriate priority for each from a set of *reserved priority levels*. The reserved priority levels refer to the priorities used internally by the RTOS for its system tasks. An application should avoid using these priority levels for its tasks because running application tasks at such level may affect the overall system performance or behavior. For most RTOSes, these reserved priorities are not enforced. The kernel needs its system tasks and their reserved priority levels to operate. These priorities should not be modified. Examples of system tasks include:

- **initialization or startup task**—initializes the system and creates and starts system tasks,
- **idle task**—uses up processor idle cycles when no other activity is present,
- **logging task**—logs system messages,
- **exception-handling task**—handles exceptions, and
- **debug agent task**—allows debugging with a host debugger.

Note that other system tasks might be created during initialization, depending on what other components are included with the kernel.

The idle task, which is created at kernel startup, is one system task that bears mention and should not be ignored. The idle task is set to the lowest priority, typically executes in an endless loop, and runs when either no other task can run or when no other tasks exist, for the sole purpose of using idle processor cycles. The idle task is necessary because the processor executes the instruction to which the program counter register points while it is running. Unless the processor can be suspended, the program counter must still point to valid instructions even when no tasks exist in the system or when no tasks can run. Therefore, the idle task ensures the processor program counter is always valid when no other tasks are running.

In some cases, however, the kernel might allow a user-configured routine to run instead of the idle task in order to implement special requirements for a particular application. One example of a special requirement is power conservation. When no other tasks can run, the kernel can switch control to the user-supplied routine instead of to the idle task. In this case, the user-supplied routine acts like the idle task but instead initiates power conservation code, such as system suspension, after a period of idle time.

After the kernel has initialized and created all of the required tasks, the kernel jumps to a predefined entry point (such as a predefined function) that serves, in effect, as the beginning of the application. From the entry point, the developer can initialize and create other application tasks, as well as other kernel objects, which the application design might require.

As the developer creates new tasks, the developer must assign each a task name, priority, stack size, and a task routine. The kernel does the rest by assigning each task a unique ID and creating an associated TCB and stack space in memory for it.

5.3 **Task States and Scheduling**

Whether it's a system task or an application task, at any time each task exists in one of a small number of states, including ready, running, or blocked. As the real-time embedded system runs, each task moves from one state to another, according to the logic of a

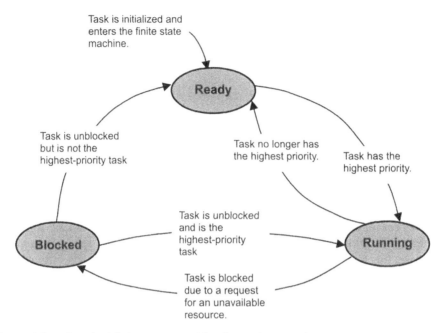

Figure 5.2   A typical finite state machine for task execution states.

simple finite state machine (FSM). Figure 5.2 illustrates a typical FSM for task execution states, with brief descriptions of state transitions.

Although kernels can define task-state groupings differently, generally three main states are used in most typical preemptive-scheduling kernels, including:

- **ready state**—the task is ready to run but cannot because a higher priority task is executing.
- **blocked state**—the task has requested a resource that is not available, has requested to wait until some event occurs, or has delayed itself for some duration.
- **running state**—the task is the highest priority task and is running.

Note some commercial kernels, such as the VxWorks kernel, define other, more granular states, such as suspended, pended, and delayed. In this case, pended and delayed are actually sub-states of the blocked state. A pended task is waiting for a resource that it needs to be freed; a delayed task is waiting for a timing delay to end. The suspended state exists for debugging purposes. For more detailed information on the way a particular RTOS kernel implements its FSM for each task, refer to the kernel's user manual.

Regardless of how a kernel implements a task's FSM, it must maintain the current state of all tasks in a running system. As calls are made into the kernel by executing tasks, the kernel's scheduler first determines which tasks need to change states and then makes those changes.

In some cases, the kernel changes the states of some tasks, but no context switching occurs because the state of the highest priority task is unaffected. In other cases, however, these state changes result in a context switch because the former highest priority task either gets blocked or is no longer the highest priority task. When this process happens, the former running task is put into the blocked or ready state, and the new highest priority task starts to execute.

The following describe the ready, running, and blocked states in more detail. These descriptions are based on a single-processor system and a kernel using a priority-based preemptive scheduling algorithm.

5.3.1 Ready State

When a task is first created and made ready to run, the kernel puts it into the ready state. In this state, the task actively competes with all other ready tasks for the processor's execution time. As Figure 5.2 shows, tasks in the ready state cannot move directly to the blocked state. A task first needs to run so it can make a *blocking call*, which is a call to a function that cannot immediately run to completion, thus putting the task in the blocked state. Ready tasks, therefore, can only move to the running state. Because many tasks might be in the ready state, the kernel's scheduler uses the priority of each task to determine which task to move to the running state.

For a kernel that supports only one task per priority level, the scheduling algorithm is straightforward—the highest priority task that is ready runs next. In this implementation, the kernel limits the number of tasks in an application to the number of priority levels.

However, most kernels support more than one task per priority level, allowing many more tasks in an application. In this case, the scheduling algorithm is more complicated and involves maintaining a *task-ready list*. Some kernels maintain a separate task-ready list for each priority level; others have one combined list.

Figure 5.3 illustrates, in a five-step scenario, how a kernel scheduler might use a task-ready list to move tasks from the ready state to the running state. This example assumes a single-processor system and a priority-based preemptive scheduling algorithm in which 255 is the lowest priority and 0 is the highest. Note that for simplicity this example does not show system tasks, such as the idle task.

In this example, tasks 1, 2, 3, 4, and 5 are ready to run, and the kernel queues them by priority in a task-ready list. Task 1 is the highest priority task (70); tasks 2, 3, and 4 are at the next-highest priority level (80); and task 5 is the lowest priority (90). The

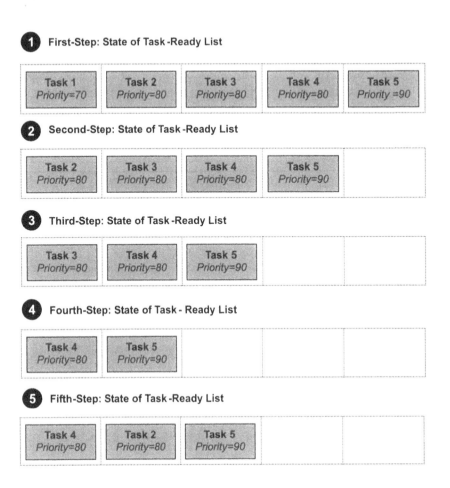

1 First-Step: State of Task-Ready List

Task 1 Priority=70	Task 2 Priority=80	Task 3 Priority=80	Task 4 Priority=80	Task 5 Priority =90

2 Second-Step: State of Task-Ready List

Task 2 Priority=80	Task 3 Priority=80	Task 4 Priority=80	Task 5 Priority=90	

3 Third-Step: State of Task-Ready List

Task 3 Priority=80	Task 4 Priority=80	Task 5 Priority=90		

4 Fourth-Step: State of Task - Ready List

Task 4 Priority=80	Task 5 Priority=90			

5 Fifth-Step: State of Task-Ready List

Task 4 Priority=80	Task 2 Priority=80	Task 5 Priority=90		

Figure 5.3   Five steps showing the way a task-ready list works.

following steps explains how a kernel might use the task-ready list to move tasks to and from the ready state:

1. Tasks 1, 2, 3, 4, and 5 are ready to run and are waiting in the task-ready list.
2. Because task 1 has the highest priority (70), it is the first task ready to run. If nothing higher is running, the kernel removes task 1 from the ready list and moves it to the running state.
3. During execution, task 1 makes a blocking call. As a result, the kernel moves task 1 to the blocked state; takes task 2, which is first in the list of the next-highest priority tasks (80), off the ready list; and moves task 2 to the running state.

4. Next, task 2 makes a blocking call. The kernel moves task 2 to the blocked state; takes task 3, which is next in line of the priority 80 tasks, off the ready list; and moves task 3 to the running state.

5. As task 3 runs, frees the resource that task 2 requested. The kernel returns task 2 to the ready state and inserts it at the end of the list of tasks ready to run at priority level 80. Task 3 continues as the currently running task.

Although not illustrated here, if task 1 became unblocked at this point in the scenario, the kernel would move task 1 to the running state because its priority is higher than the currently running task (task 3). As with task 2 earlier, task 3 at this point would be moved to the ready state and inserted after task 2 (same priority of 80) and before task 5 (next priority of 90).

5.3.2 Running State

On a single-processor system, only one task can run at a time. In this case, when a task is moved to the running state, the processor loads its registers with this task's context. The processor can then execute the task's instructions and manipulate the associated stack.

As discussed in the previous section, a task can move back to the ready state while it is running. When a task moves from the running state to the ready state, it is preempted by a higher priority task. In this case, the preempted task is put in the appropriate, priority-based location in the task-ready list, and the higher priority task is moved from the ready state to the running state.

Unlike a ready task, a running task can move to the blocked state in any of the following ways:

- by making a call that requests an unavailable resource,
- by making a call that requests to wait for an event to occur, and
- by making a call to delay the task for some duration.
- In each of these cases, the task is moved from the running state to the blocked state, as described next.

5.3.3 Blocked State

The possibility of blocked states is extremely important in real-time systems because without blocked states, lower priority tasks could not run. If higher priority tasks are not designed to block, CPU starvation can result.

CPU starvation occurs when higher priority tasks use all of the CPU execution time and lower priority tasks do not get to run.

A task can only move to the blocked state by making a blocking call, requesting that some blocking condition be met. A blocked task remains blocked until the blocking condition is met. (It probably ought to be called the *un*blocking condition, but blocking is the terminology in common use among real-time programmers.) Examples of how blocking conditions are met include the following:

- a semaphore token (described later) for which a task is waiting is released,
- a message, on which the task is waiting, arrives in a message queue, or
- a time delay imposed on the task expires.

When a task becomes unblocked, the task might move from the blocked state to the ready state if it is not the highest priority task. The task is then put into the task-ready list at the appropriate priority-based location, as described earlier.

However, if the unblocked task is the highest priority task, the task moves directly to the running state (without going through the ready state) and preempts the currently running task. The preempted task is then moved to the ready state and put into the appropriate priority-based location in the task-ready list.

5.4 Typical Task Operations

In addition to providing a task object, kernels also provide *task-management services*. Task-management services include the actions that a kernel performs behind the scenes to support tasks, for example, creating and maintaining the TCB and task stacks.

A kernel, however, also provides an API that allows developers to manipulate tasks. Some of the more common operations that developers can perform with a task object from within the application include:

- creating and deleting tasks,
- controlling task scheduling, and
- obtaining task information.

Developers should learn how to perform each of these operations for the kernel selected for the project. Each operation is briefly discussed next.

5.4.1   Task Creation and Deletion

The most fundamental operations that developers must learn are creating and deleting tasks, as shown in Table 5.1.

Table 5.1   Operations for task creation and deletion.

Operation	Description
Create	Creates a task
Delete	Deletes a task

Developers typically create a task using one or two operations, depending on the kernel's API. Some kernels allow developers first to create a task and then start it. In this case, the task is first created and put into a suspended state; then, the task is moved to the ready state when it is started (made ready to run).

Creating tasks in this manner might be useful for debugging or when special initialization needs to occur between the times that a task is created and started. However, in most cases, it is sufficient to create and start a task using one kernel call.

Many kernels also provide *user-configurable hooks*, which are mechanisms that execute programmer-supplied functions, at the time of specific kernel events. The programmer *registers* the function with the kernel by passing a function pointer to a kernel-provided API. The kernel executes this function when the event of interest occurs. Such events can include:

The suspended state is similar to the blocked state, in that the suspended task is neither running nor ready to run. However, a task does not move into or out of the suspended state via the same operations that move a task to or from the blocked state. The exact nature of the suspended state varies between RTOSes. For the present purpose, it is sufficient to know that the task is not yet ready to run.

- when a task is first created,
- when a task is suspended for any reason and a context switch occurs, and
- when a task is deleted.

Hooks are useful when executing special initialization code upon task creation, implementing status tracking or monitoring upon task context switches, or executing clean-up code upon task deletion.

Starting a task does not make it run immediately; it puts the task on the task-ready list.

Carefully consider how tasks are to be deleted in the embedded application. Many kernel implementations allow any task to delete any other task. During the deletion process, a kernel terminates the task and frees memory by deleting the task's TCB and stack.

However, when tasks execute, they can acquire memory or access resources using other kernel objects. If the task is deleted incorrectly, the task might not get to release these resources. For example, assume that a task acquires a semaphore token to get exclusive access to a shared data structure. While the task is operating on this data structure, the task gets deleted. If not handled appropriately, this abrupt deletion of the operating task can result in:

- a corrupt data structure, due to an incomplete write operation,
- an unreleased semaphore, which will not be available for other tasks that might need to acquire it, and
- an inaccessible data structure, due to the unreleased semaphore.

As a result, premature deletion of a task can result in memory or resource leaks.

A *memory leak* occurs when memory is acquired but not released, which causes the system to run out of memory eventually. A *resource leak* occurs when a resource is acquired but never released, which results in a memory leak because each resource takes up space in memory. Many kernels provide *task-deletion locks*, a pair of calls that protect a task from being prematurely deleted during a critical section of code.

This book discusses these concepts in more detail later. At this point, however, note that any tasks to be deleted must have enough time to clean up and release resources or memory before being deleted.

5.4.2 Task Scheduling

From the time a task is created to the time it is deleted, the task can move through various states resulting from program execution and kernel scheduling. Although much of this state changing is automatic, many kernels provide a set of API calls that allow developers to control when a task moves to a different state, as shown in Table 5.2. This capability is called *manual scheduling*.

Table 5.2   Operations for task scheduling.

Operation	Description
Suspend	Suspends a task
Resume	Resumes a task
Delay	Delays a task
Restart	Restarts a task
Get Priority	Gets the current task's priority
Set Priority	Dynamically sets a task's priority
Preemption lock	Locks out higher priority tasks from preempting the current task
Preemption unlock	Unlocks a preemption lock

Using manual scheduling, developers can suspend and resume tasks from within an application. Doing so might be important for debugging purposes or, as discussed earlier, for suspending a high-priority task so that lower priority tasks can execute.

A developer might want to delay (block) a task, for example, to allow manual scheduling or to wait for an external condition that does not have an associated interrupt. Delaying a task causes it to relinquish the CPU and allow another task to execute. After the delay expires, the task is returned to the task-ready list after all other ready tasks at its priority level. A delayed task waiting for an external condition can wake up after a set time to check whether a specified condition or event has occurred, which is called *polling*.

A developer might also want to restart a task, which is not the same as resuming a suspended task. Restarting a task begins the task as if it had not been previously executing. The internal state the task possessed at the time it was suspended (for example, the CPU registers used and the resources acquired) is lost when a task is restarted. By contrast, resuming a task begins the task in the same internal state it possessed when it was suspended.

Restarting a task is useful during debugging or when reinitializing a task after a catastrophic error. During debugging, a developer can restart a task to step through its code again from start to finish. In the case of catastrophic error, the developer can restart a task and ensure that the system continues to operate without having to be completely reinitialized.

Getting and setting a task's priority during execution lets developers control task scheduling manually. This process is helpful during a *priority inversion*, in which a lower priority task has a shared resource that a higher priority task requires and is preempted by an unrelated medium-priority task. (Priority inversion is discussed in more detail in Chapter 16). A simple fix for this problem is to free the shared resource by dynamically increasing the priority of the lower priority task to that of the higher priority task—allowing the task to run and release the resource that the higher priority task requires—and then decreasing the former lower priority task to its original priority.

Finally, the kernel might support *preemption locks*, a pair of calls used to disable and enable preemption in applications. This feature can be useful if a task is executing in a *critical section of code*: one in which the task must not be preempted by other tasks.

5.4.3   Obtaining Task Information

Kernels provide routines that allow developers to access task information within their applications, as shown in Table 5.3. This information is useful for debugging and monitoring.

Table 5.3   Task-information operations.

Operation	Description
Get ID	Get the current task's ID
Get TCB	Get the current task's TCB

One use is to obtain a particular task's ID, which is used to get more information about the task by getting its TCB. Obtaining a TCB, however, only takes a snapshot of the task context. If a task is not dormant (e.g., suspended), its context might be dynamic, and the snapshot information might change by the time it is used. Hence, use this functionality wisely, so that decisions aren't made in the application based on querying a constantly changing task context.

5.5 Typical Task Structure

When writing code for tasks, tasks are structured in one of two ways:

- run to completion, or
- endless loop.

Both task structures are relatively simple. Run-to-completion tasks are most useful for initialization and startup. They typically run once, when the system first powers on. Endless-loop tasks do the majority of the work in the application by handling inputs and outputs. Typically, they run many times while the system is powered on.

5.5.1 Run-to-Completion Tasks

An example of a run-to-completion task is the application-level initialization task, shown in Listing 5.1. The initialization task initializes the application and creates additional services, tasks, and needed kernel objects..

Listing 5.1   Pseudo code for a run-to-completion task.

```
RunToCompletionTask ()
{
        Initialize application
        Create 'endless loop tasks'
        Create kernel objects
        Delete or suspend this task
}
```

The application initialization task typically has a higher priority than the application tasks it creates so that its initialization work is not preempted. In the simplest case, the other tasks are one or more lower priority endless-loop tasks. The application initialization task is written so that it suspends or deletes itself after it completes its work so the newly created tasks can run.

5.5.2 Endless-Loop Tasks

As with the structure of the application initialization task, the structure of an endless loop task can also contain initialization code. The endless loop's initialization code, however, only needs to be executed when the task first runs, after which the task executes in an endless loop, as shown in Listing 5.2.

The critical part of the design of an endless-loop task is the one or more blocking calls within the body of the loop. These blocking calls can result in the blocking of this endless-loop task, allowing lower priority tasks to run.

Listing 5.2   Pseudo code for an endless-loop task.

```
EndlessLoopTask ()
{

        Initialization code
        Loop Forever
        {

                Body of loop
                Make one or more blocking calls

        }

}
```

5.6 Synchronization, Communication, and Concurrency

Tasks synchronize and communicate amongst themselves by using *intertask primitives*, which are kernel objects that facilitate synchronization and communication between two or more threads of execution. Examples of such objects include semaphores, message queues, signals, and pipes, as well as other types of objects. Each of these is discussed in detail in later chapters of this book.

The concept of concurrency and how an application is optimally decomposed into concurrent tasks is also discussed in more detail later in this book. For now, remember that the task object is the fundamental construct of most kernels. Tasks, along with task-management services, allow developers to design applications for concurrency to meet multiple time constraints and to address various design problems inherent to real-time embedded applications.

5.7 Points to Remember

Some points to remember include the following:

- Most real-time kernels provide task objects and task-management services that allow developers to meet the requirements of real-time applications.
- Applications can contain system tasks or user-created tasks, each of which has a name, a unique ID, a priority, a task control block (TCB), a stack, and a task routine.
- A real-time application is composed of multiple concurrent tasks that are independent threads of execution, competing on their own for processor execution time.
- Tasks can be in one of three primary states during their lifetime: ready, running, and blocked.
- Priority-based, preemptive scheduling kernels that allow multiple tasks to be assigned to the same priority use task-ready lists to help scheduled tasks run.

- Tasks can run to completion or can run in an endless loop. For tasks that run in endless loops, structure the code so that the task blocks, which allows lower priority tasks to run.
- Typical task operations that kernels provide for application development include task creation and deletion, manual task scheduling, and dynamic acquisition of task information.

In this chapter...

- *Defining Semaphores* 79
- *Typical Semaphore Operations* 84
- *Typical Semaphore Use* 87
- *Points to Remember* 95

CHAPTER 6

SEMAPHORES

6.1 Introduction

Multiple concurrent threads of execution within an application must be able to synchronize their execution and coordinate mutually exclusive access to shared resources. To address these requirements, RTOS kernels provide a semaphore object and associated semaphore management services.

This chapter discusses the following:

- defining a semaphore,
- typical semaphore operations, and
- common semaphore use.

6.2 Defining Semaphores

A *semaphore* (sometimes called a *semaphore token*) is a kernel object that one or more threads of execution can acquire or release for the purposes of synchronization or mutual exclusion.

When a semaphore is first created, the kernel assigns to it an associated semaphore control block (SCB), a unique ID, a value (binary or a count), and a task-waiting list, as shown in Figure 6.1.

A semaphore is like a key that allows a task to carry out some operation or to access a resource. If the task can acquire the semaphore, it can carry out the intended operation or access the resource. A single semaphore can be acquired a finite number of times. In this sense, acquiring a semaphore is like acquiring the duplicate of a key from an apartment manager—when the apartment manager runs out of duplicates, the manager can give out no more keys. Like-

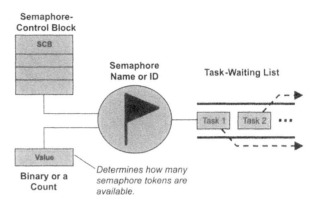

Figure 6.1 A semaphore, its associated parameters, and supporting data structures.

wise, when a semaphore's limit is reached, it can no longer be acquired until someone gives a key back or releases the semaphore.

The kernel tracks the number of times a semaphore has been acquired or released by maintaining a token count, which is initialized to a value when the semaphore is created. As a task acquires the semaphore, the token count is decremented; as a task releases the semaphore, the count is incremented.

If the token count reaches 0, the semaphore has no tokens left. A requesting task, therefore, cannot acquire the semaphore, and the task blocks if it chooses to wait for the semaphore to become available. (This chapter discusses states of different semaphore variants and blocking in more detail in "Typical Semaphore Operations" on page 84, section 6.3.)

The task-waiting list tracks all tasks blocked while waiting on an unavailable semaphore. These blocked tasks are kept in the task-waiting list in either first in/first out (FIFO) order or highest priority first order.

When an unavailable semaphore becomes available, the kernel allows the first task in the task-waiting list to acquire it. The kernel moves this unblocked task either to the running state, if it is the highest priority task, or to the ready state, until it becomes the highest priority task and is able to run. Note that the exact implementation of a task-waiting list can vary from one kernel to another.

A kernel can support many different types of semaphores, including binary, counting, and mutual-exclusion (mutex) semaphores.

Figure 6.2 The state diagram of a binary semaphore.

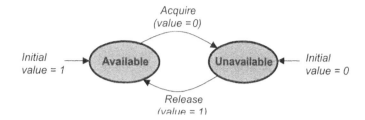

6.2.1 Binary Semaphores

A *binary semaphore* can have a value of either 0 or 1. When a binary semaphore's value is 0, the semaphore is considered *unavailable* (or *empty*); when the value is 1, the binary semaphore is considered *available* (or *full*). Note that when a binary semaphore is first created, it can be initialized to either available or unavailable (1 or 0, respectively). The state diagram of a binary semaphore is shown in Figure 6.2.

Binary semaphores are treated as *global resources*, which means they are shared among all tasks that need them. Making the semaphore a global resource allows any task to release it, even if the task did not initially acquire it.

6.2.2 Counting Semaphores

A *counting semaphore* uses a count to allow it to be acquired or released multiple times. When creating a counting semaphore, assign the semaphore a count that denotes the number of semaphore tokens it has initially. If the initial count is 0, the counting semaphore is created in the unavailable state. If the count is greater than 0, the semaphore is created in the available state, and the number of tokens it has equals its count, as shown in Figure 6.3.

One or more tasks can continue to acquire a token from the counting semaphore until no tokens are left. When all the tokens are gone, the count equals 0, and the counting semaphore moves from the available state to the unavailable state. To move from the unavailable state back to the available state, a semaphore token must be released by any task.

Figure 6.3 The state diagram of a counting semaphore.

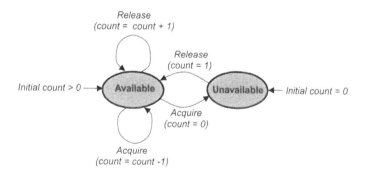

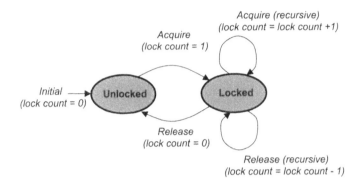

Figure 6.4   The state diagram of a mutual exclusion (mutex) semaphore.

Note that, as with binary semaphores, counting semaphores are global resources that can be shared by all tasks that need them. This feature allows any task to release a counting semaphore token. Each release operation increments the count by one, even if the task making this call did not acquire a token in the first place.

Some implementations of counting semaphores might allow the count to be bounded. A *bounded count* is a count in which the initial count set for the counting semaphore, determined when the semaphore was first created, acts as the maximum count for the semaphore. An *unbounded count* allows the counting semaphore to count beyond the initial count to the maximum value that can be held by the count's data type (e.g., an unsigned integer or an unsigned long value).

6.2.3   Mutual Exclusion (Mutex) Semaphores

A *mutual exclusion (mutex) semaphore* is a special binary semaphore that supports ownership, recursive access, task deletion safety, and one or more protocols for avoiding problems inherent to mutual exclusion. Figure 6.4 illustrates the state diagram of a mutex.

As opposed to the available and unavailable states in binary and counting semaphores, the states of a mutex are *unlocked* or *locked* (0 or 1, respectively). A mutex is initially created in the unlocked state, in which it can be acquired by a task. After being acquired, the mutex moves to the locked state. Conversely, when the task releases the mutex, the mutex returns to the unlocked state. Note that some kernels might use the terms *lock* and *unlock* for a mutex instead of *acquire* and *release*.

Depending on the implementation, a mutex can support additional features not found in binary or counting semaphores. These key differentiating features include ownership, recursive locking, task deletion safety, and priority inversion avoidance protocols.

Mutex Ownership

Ownership of a mutex is gained when a task first locks the mutex by acquiring it. Conversely, a task loses ownership of the mutex when it unlocks it by releasing it. When a task owns the mutex, it is not possible for any other task to lock or unlock that mutex. Contrast this concept with the binary semaphore, which can be released by any task, even a task that did not originally acquire the semaphore.

Recursive Locking

Many mutex implementations also support *recursive locking*, which allows the task that owns the mutex to acquire it multiple times in the locked state. Depending on the implementation, recursion within a mutex can be automatically built into the mutex, or it might need to be enabled explicitly when the mutex is first created.

The mutex with recursive locking is called a *recursive mutex*. This type of mutex is most useful when a task requiring exclusive access to a shared resource calls one or more routines that also require access to the same resource. A recursive mutex allows nested attempts to lock the mutex to succeed, rather than cause *deadlock*, which is a condition in which two or more tasks are blocked and are waiting on mutually locked resources. The problem of recursion and deadlocks is discussed later in this chapter, as well as later in this book.

As shown in Figure 6.4, when a recursive mutex is first locked, the kernel registers the task that locked it as the owner of the mutex. On successive attempts, the kernel uses an internal lock count associated with the mutex to track the number of times that the task currently owning the mutex has recursively acquired it. To properly unlock the mutex, it must be released the same number of times.

In this example, a *lock count* tracks the two states of a mutex (0 for unlocked and 1 for locked), as well as the number of times it has been recursively locked (lock count > 1). In other implementations, a mutex might maintain two counts: a binary value to track its state, and a separate lock count to track the number of times it has been acquired in the lock state by the task that owns it.

Do not confuse the counting facility for a locked mutex with the counting facility for a counting semaphore. The count used for the mutex tracks the number of times that the task owning the mutex has locked or unlocked the mutex. The count used for the counting semaphore tracks the number of tokens that have been acquired or released by any task. Additionally, the count for the mutex is always unbounded, which allows multiple recursive accesses.

Task Deletion Safety

Some mutex implementations also have built-in *task deletion safety*. Premature task deletion is avoided by using *task deletion locks* when a task locks and unlocks a mutex. Enabling this capability within a mutex ensures that while a task owns the mutex, the task cannot be deleted. Typically protection from premature deletion is enabled by setting the appropriate initialization options when creating the mutex.

Priority Inversion Avoidance

Priority inversion commonly happens in poorly designed real-time embedded applications. *Priority inversion* occurs when a higher priority task is blocked and is waiting for a resource being used by a lower priority task, which has itself been preempted by an unrelated medium-priority task. In this situation, the higher priority task's priority level has effectively been inverted to the lower priority task's level.

Enabling certain protocols that are typically built into mutexes can help avoid priority inversion. Two common protocols used for avoiding priority inversion include:

- **priority inheritance protocol**—ensures that the priority level of the lower priority task that has acquired the mutex is raised to that of the higher priority task that has requested the mutex when inversion happens. The priority of the raised task is lowered to its original value after the task releases the mutex that the higher priority task requires.
- **ceiling priority protocol**—ensures that the priority level of the task that acquires the mutex is automatically set to the highest priority of all possible tasks that might request that mutex when it is first acquired until it is released.

When the mutex is released, the priority of the task is lowered to its original value.

Chapter 16 discusses priority inversion and both the priority inheritance and ceiling priority protocols in more detail. For now, remember that a mutex supports ownership, recursive locking, task deletion safety, and priority inversion avoidance protocols; binary and counting semaphores do not.

6.3 Typical Semaphore Operations

Typical operations that developers might want to perform with the semaphores in an application include:

- creating and deleting semaphores,
- acquiring and releasing semaphores,
- clearing a semaphore's task-waiting list, and
- getting semaphore information.

Each operation is discussed next.

6.3.1 Creating and Deleting Semaphores

Table 6.1 identifies the operations used to create and delete semaphores.

Table 6.1   Semaphore creation and deletion operations.

Operation	Description
Create	Creates a semaphore
Delete	Deletes a semaphore

Several things must be considered, however, when creating and deleting semaphores. If a kernel supports different types of semaphores, different calls might be used for creating binary, counting, and mutex semaphores, as follows:

- **binary**—specify the initial semaphore state and the task-waiting order.
- **counting**—specify the initial semaphore count and the task-waiting order.
- **mutex**—specify the task-waiting order and enable task deletion safety, recursion, and priority-inversion avoidance protocols, if supported.

Semaphores can be deleted from within any task by specifying their IDs and making semaphore-deletion calls. Deleting a semaphore is not the same as releasing it. When a semaphore is deleted, blocked tasks in its task-waiting list are unblocked and moved either to the ready state or to the running state (if the unblocked task has the highest priority). Any tasks, however, that try to acquire the deleted semaphore return with an error because the semaphore no longer exists.

Additionally, do not delete a semaphore while it is in use (e.g., acquired). This action might result in data corruption or other serious problems if the semaphore is protecting a shared resource or a critical section of code.

6.3.2   Acquiring and Releasing Semaphores

Table 6.2 identifies the operations used to acquire or release semaphores.

Table 6.2   Semaphore acquire and release operations.

Operation	Description
Acquire	Acquire a semaphore token
Release	Release a semaphore token

The operations for acquiring and releasing a semaphore might have different names, depending on the kernel: for example, *take* and *give*, *sm_p* and *sm_v*, *pend* and *post*, and *lock* and *unlock*. Regardless of the name, they all effectively acquire and release semaphores.

Tasks typically make a request to acquire a semaphore in one of the following ways:

- **Wait forever**—task remains blocked until it is able to acquire a semaphore.
- **Wait with a timeout**—task remains blocked until it is able to acquire a semaphore or until a set interval of time, called the *timeout interval*, passes. At this point, the task is removed from the semaphore's task-waiting list and put in either the ready state or the running state.
- **Do not wait**—task makes a request to acquire a semaphore token, but, if one is not available, the task does not block.

Note that ISRs can also release binary and counting semaphores. Note that most kernels do not support ISRs locking and unlocking mutexes, as it is not meaningful to do so from an ISR. It is also not meaningful to acquire either binary or counting semaphores inside an ISR.

Any task can release a binary or counting semaphore; however, a mutex can only be released (unlocked) by the task that first acquired (locked) it. Note that incorrectly releasing a binary or counting semaphore can result in losing mutually exclusive access to a shared resource or in an I/O device malfunction.

For example, a task can gain access to a shared data structure by acquiring an associated semaphore. If a second task accidentally releases that semaphore, this step can potentially free a third task waiting for that same semaphore, allowing that third task to also gain access to the same data structure. Having multiple tasks trying to modify the same data structure at the same time results in corrupted data.

6.3.3   Clearing Semaphore Task-Waiting Lists

To clear all tasks waiting on a semaphore task-waiting list, some kernels support a *flush* operation, as shown in Table 6.3.

Table 6.3   Semaphore unblock operations.

Operation	Description
Flush	Unblocks all tasks waiting on a semaphore

The flush operation is useful for broadcast signaling to a group of tasks. For example, a developer might design multiple tasks to complete certain activities first and then block while trying to acquire a common semaphore that is made unavailable. After the last task finishes doing what it needs to, the task can execute a semaphore flush operation on the common semaphore. This operation frees all tasks waiting in the semaphore's task waiting list. The synchronization scenario just described is also called *thread rendez-vous*, when multiple tasks' executions need to meet at some point in time to synchronize execution control.

6.3.4   Getting Semaphore Information

At some point in the application design, developers need to obtain semaphore information to perform monitoring or debugging. In these cases, use the operations shown in Table 6.4.

These operations are relatively straightforward but should be used judiciously, as the semaphore information might be dynamic at the time it is requested.

Table 6.4   Semaphore information operations.

Operation	Description
Show info	Show general information about semaphore
Show blocked tasks	Get a list of IDs of tasks that are blocked on a semaphore

6.4 Typical Semaphore Use

Semaphores are useful either for synchronizing execution of multiple tasks or for coordinating access to a shared resource. The following examples and general discussions illustrate using different types of semaphores to address common synchronization design requirements effectively, as listed:

- wait-and-signal synchronization,
- multiple-task wait-and-signal synchronization,
- credit-tracking synchronization,
- single shared-resource-access synchronization,
- recursive shared-resource-access synchronization, and
- multiple shared-resource-access synchronization.

Note that, for the sake of simplicity, not all uses of semaphores are listed here. Also, later chapters of this book contain more advanced discussions on the different ways that mutex semaphores can handle priority inversion.

6.4.1   Wait-and-Signal Synchronization

Two tasks can communicate for the purpose of synchronization without exchanging data. For example, a binary semaphore can be used between two tasks to coordinate the transfer of execution control, as shown in Figure 6.5.

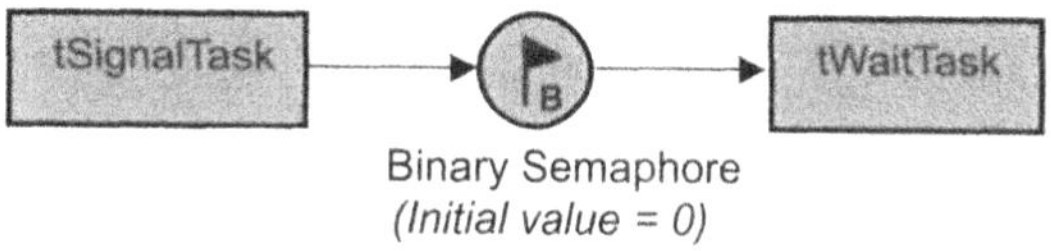

Figure 6.5   Wait-and-signal synchronization between two tasks.

In this situation, the binary semaphore is initially unavailable (value of 0). tWaitTask has higher priority and runs first. The task makes a request to acquire the semaphore but is blocked because the semaphore is unavailable. This step gives the lower priority tSignalTask a chance to run; at some point, tSignalTask releases the binary semaphore and unblocks tWaitTask. The pseudo code for this scenario is shown in Listing 6.1.

Because tWaitTask's priority is higher than tSignalTask's priority, as soon as the semaphore is released, tWaitTask preempts tSignalTask and starts to execute.

Listing 6.1   Pseudo code for wait-and-signal synchronization

```
tWaitTask ( )
{
                :
                Acquire binary semaphore token
                :

}

tSignalTask ( )
{

                :
                Release binary semaphore token
                :

}
```

6.4.2   Multiple-Task Wait-and-Signal Synchronization

When coordinating the synchronization of more than two tasks, use the flush operation on the task-waiting list of a binary semaphore, as shown in Figure 6.6.

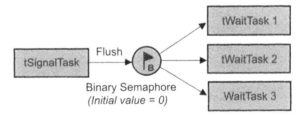

Figure 6.6   Wait-and-signal synchronization between multiple tasks.

As in the previous case, the binary semaphore is initially unavailable (value of 0). The higher priority tWaitTasks 1, 2, and 3 all do some processing; when they are done, they try to acquire the unavailable semaphore and, as a result, block. This action gives tSignalTask a chance to complete its processing and execute a flush command on the semaphore, effectively unblocking the three tWaitTasks, as shown in Listing 6.2. Note that similar code is used for tWaitTask 1, 2, and 3.

Because the tWaitTasks' priorities are higher than tSignalTask's priority, as soon as the semaphore is released, one of the higher priority tWaitTasks preempts tSignalTask and starts to execute.

Note that in the wait-and-signal synchronization shown in Figure 6.6 the value of the binary semaphore after the flush operation is implementation dependent. Therefore, the return value of the acquire operation must be properly checked to see if either a return-from-flush or an error condition has occurred.

Listing 6.2   Pseudo code for wait-and-signal synchronization.

```
tWaitTask ()
{
                  :
         Do some processing specific to task
         Acquire binary semaphore token
                  :
}


tSignalTask ()
{
                  :
         Do some processing
         Flush binary semaphore's task-waiting list
                  :
}
```

6.4.3   Credit-Tracking Synchronization

Sometimes the rate at which the signaling task executes is higher than that of the signaled task. In this case, a mechanism is needed to count each signaling occurrence. The counting semaphore provides just this facility. With a counting semaphore, the signaling task can continue to execute and increment a count at its own pace, while the wait task, when unblocked, executes at its own pace, as shown in Figure 6.7.

Again, the counting semaphore's count is initially 0, making it unavailable. The lower priority tWaitTask tries to acquire this semaphore but blocks until tSignalTask makes the semaphore available by performing a release on it. Even then, tWaitTask will waits in the ready state until the higher priority tSignalTask eventually relinquishes the CPU by making a blocking call or delaying itself, as shown in Listing 6.3.

Because tSignalTask is set to a higher priority and executes at its own rate, it might increment the counting semaphore multiple times before tWaitTask starts processing the first request. Hence, the counting semaphore allows a credit buildup of the number of times that the tWaitTask can execute before the semaphore becomes unavailable.

Figure 6.7   Credit-tracking
synchronization between
two tasks.

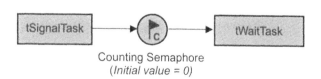

Counting Semaphore
(*Initial value = 0*)

Listing 6.3   Pseudo code for credit-tracking synchronization.

```
tWaitTask ()
{

          :
          Acquire counting semaphore token
          :

}


tSignalTask ()
{

          :
          Release counting semaphore token
          :

}
```

Eventually, when tSignalTask's rate of releasing the semaphore tokens slows, tWaitTask can catch up and eventually deplete the count until the counting semaphore is empty. At this point, tWaitTask blocks again at the counting semaphore, waiting for tSignalTask to release the semaphore again.

Note that this credit-tracking mechanism is useful if tSignalTask releases semaphores in bursts, giving tWaitTask the chance to catch up every once in a while.

Using this mechanism with an ISR that acts in a similar way to the signaling task can be quite useful. Interrupts have higher priorities than tasks. Hence, an interrupt's associated higher priority ISR executes when the hardware interrupt is triggered and typically off-loads some work to a lower priority task waiting on a semaphore.

6.4.4   Single Shared-Resource-Access Synchronization

One of the more common uses of semaphores is to provide for mutually exclusive access to a shared resource. A shared resource might be a memory location, a data structure, or an I/O device—essentially anything that might have to be shared between two or more concurrent threads of execution. A semaphore can be used to serialize access to a shared resource, as shown in Figure 6.8.

In this scenario, a binary semaphore is initially created in the available state (value = 1) and is used to protect the shared resource. To access the shared resource, task 1 or 2 needs to first successfully acquire the binary semaphore before reading from or writing to the shared resource. The pseudo code for both tAccessTask 1 and 2 is similar to Listing 6.4.

Figure 6.8   Single shared-resource-access synchronization.

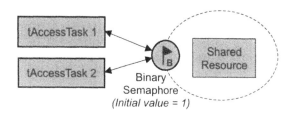

Listing 6.4   Pseudo code for tasks accessing a shared resource.

```
tAccessTask ()
{
            :
       Acquire binary semaphore token
       Read or write to shared resource
       Release binary semaphore token
            :
}
```

This code serializes the access to the shared resource. If tAccessTask 1 executes first, it makes a request to acquire the semaphore and is successful because the semaphore is available. Having acquired the semaphore, this task is granted access to the shared resource and can read and write to it.

Meanwhile, the higher priority tAccessTask 2 wakes up and runs due to a timeout or some external event. It tries to access the same semaphore but is blocked because tAccessTask 1 currently has access to it. After tAccessTask 1 releases the semaphore, tAccessTask 2 is unblocked and starts to execute.

One of the dangers to this design is that any task can accidentally release the binary semaphore, even one that never acquired the semaphore in the first place. If this issue were to happen in this scenario, both tAccessTask 1 and tAccessTask 2 could end up acquiring the semaphore and reading and writing to the shared resource at the same time, which would lead to incorrect program behavior.

To ensure that this problem does not happen, use a mutex semaphore instead. Because a mutex supports the concept of ownership, it ensures that only the task that successfully acquired (locked) the mutex can release (unlock) it.

6.4.5   Recursive Shared-Resource-Access Synchronization

Sometimes a developer might want a task to access a shared resource recursively. This situation might exist if tAccessTask calls Routine A that calls Routine B, and all three need access to the same shared resource, as shown in Figure 6.9.

If a semaphore were used in this scenario, the task would end up blocking, causing a deadlock. When a routine is called from a task, the routine effectively becomes a part of the task. When Routine A runs, therefore, it is running as a part of tAccessTask. Routine A trying to acquire the semaphore is effectively the same as tAccessTask trying to acquire the same semaphore. In this case, tAccessTask would end up blocking while waiting for the unavailable semaphore that it already has.

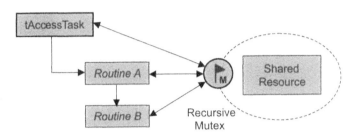

Figure 6.9 Recursive shared- resource-access synchronization.

One solution to this situation is to use a recursive mutex. After tAccessTask locks the mutex, the task owns it. Additional attempts from the task itself or from routines that it calls to lock the mutex succeed. As a result, when Routines A and B attempt to lock the mutex, they succeed without blocking. The pseudo code for tAccessTask, Routine A, and Routine B are similar to Listing 6.5.

Listing 6.5   Pseudo code for recursively accessing a shared resource.

```
tAccessTask ()
{
        :

        Acquire mutex
        Access shared resource
        Call Routine A
        Release mutex

        :

}


Routine A ()
{

        :

        Acquire mutex
        Access shared resource
```

**Listing 6.5   Pseudo code for recursively accessing a shared
             resource. (Continued)**

```
        Call Routine B
        Release mutex
        :
}


Routine B ()
{
        :
        Acquire mutex
        Access shared resource
        Release mutex
        :
}
```

6.4.6   Multiple Shared-Resource-Access Synchronization

For cases in which multiple equivalent shared resources are used, a
counting semaphore comes in
handy, as shown in Figure 6.10.

Note that this scenario does not
work if the shared resources are
not equivalent. The counting
semaphore's count is initially set
to the number of equivalent
shared resources: in this example,
2. As a result, the first two tasks
requesting a semaphore token are
successful. However, the third

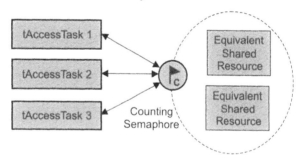

Figure 6.10   Single shared-resource-access
             synchronization.

task ends up blocking until one of the previous two tasks releases a semaphore token, as
shown in Listing 6.6. Note that similar code is used for tAccessTask 1, 2, and 3.

As with the binary semaphores, this design can cause problems if a task releases a semaphore that it did not originally acquire. If the code is relatively simple, this issue might
not be a problem. If the code is more elaborate, however, with many tasks accessing
shared devices using multiple semaphores, mutexes can provide built-in protection in the
application design.

As shown in Figure 6.9, a separate mutex can be assigned for each shared resource.
When trying to lock a mutex, each task tries to acquire the first mutex in a non-blocking
way. If unsuccessful, each task then tries to acquire the second mutex in a blocking way.

Listing 6.6 **Pseudo code for multiple tasks accessing equivalent shared resources.**

```
tAccessTask ()
{
        :
    Acquire a counting semaphore token
    Read or Write to shared resource
    Release a counting semaphore token
        :
}
```

The code is similar to Listing 6.7. Note that similar code is used for tAccessTask 1, 2, and 3.

Listing 6.7 **Pseudo code for multiple tasks accessing equivalent shared resources using mutexes.**

```
tAccessTask ()
{
        :
    Acquire first mutex in non-blocking way
        If not successful then acquire 2nd mutex in a blocking way
    Read or Write to shared resource
    Release the acquired mutex
        :
}
```

Using this scenario, task 1 and 2 each is successful in locking a mutex and therefore having access to a shared resource. When task 3 runs, it tries to lock the first mutex in a non-blocking way (in case task 1 is done with the mutex). If this first mutex is unlocked, task 3 locks it and is granted access to the first shared resource. If the first mutex is still locked, however, task 3 tries to acquire the second mutex, except that this time, it would do so in a blocking way. If the second mutex is also locked, task 3 blocks and waits for the second mutex until it is unlocked.

6.5 Points to Remember

Some points to remember include the following:

- Using semaphores allows multiple tasks, or ISRs to tasks, to synchronize execution to synchronize execution or coordinate mutually exclusive access to a shared resource.

- Semaphores have an associated semaphore control block (SCB), a unique ID, a user-assigned value (binary or a count), and a task-waiting list.

- Three common types of semaphores are binary, counting, and mutual exclusion (mutex), each of which can be acquired or released.

- Binary semaphores are either available (1) or unavailable (0). Counting semaphores are also either available (count ≥ 1) or unavailable (0). Mutexes, however, are either unlocked (0) or locked (lock count ≥ 1).

- Acquiring a binary or counting semaphore results in decrementing its value or count, except when the semaphore's value is already 0. In this case, the requesting task blocks if it chooses to wait for the semaphore.

- Releasing a binary or counting semaphore results in incrementing the value or count, unless it is a binary semaphore with a value of 1 or a bounded semaphore at its maximum count. In this case, the release of additional semaphores is typically ignored.

- Recursive mutexes can be locked and unlocked multiple times by the task that owns them. Acquiring an unlocked recursive mutex increments its lock count, while releasing it decrements the lock count.

- Typical semaphore operations that kernels provide for application development include creating and deleting semaphores, acquiring and releasing semaphores, flushing semaphore's task-waiting list, and providing dynamic access to semaphore information.

In this chapter...

- Defining Message Queues 97
- Message Queue States. 99
- Message Queue Content 100
- Message Queue Storage 101
- Typical Message Queue Operations . . . 101
- Typical Message Queue Use. 105
- Points to Remember. 110

CHAPTER 7

MESSAGE QUEUES

7.1 Introduction

Chapter 6 discusses activity synchronization of two or more threads of execution. Such synchronization helps tasks cooperate in order to produce an efficient real-time system. In many cases, however, task activity synchronization alone does not yield a sufficiently responsive application. Tasks must also be able to exchange messages. To facilitate inter-task data communication, kernels provide a message queue object and message queue management services.

This chapter discusses the following:

- defining message queues,
- message queue states,
- message queue content,
- typical message queue operations, and
- typical message queue use.

7.2 Defining Message Queues

A message queue is a buffer-like object through which tasks and ISRs send and receive messages to communicate and synchronize with data. A message queue is like a pipeline. It temporarily holds messages from a sender until the intended receiver is ready to read them. This temporary buffering decouples a sending and receiving task; that is, it frees the tasks from having to send and receive messages simultaneously.

97

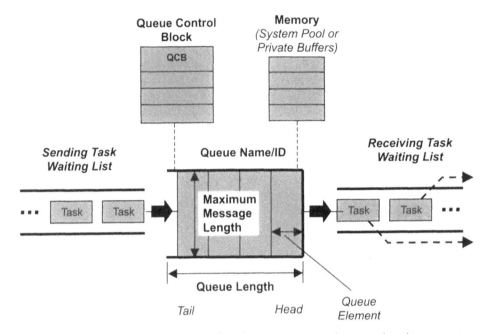

Figure 7.1   A message queue, its associated parameters, and supporting data structures.

As with semaphore introduced in Chapter 6, a message queue has several associated components that the kernel uses to manage the queue. When a message queue is first created, it is assigned an associated queue control block (QCB), a message queue name, a unique ID, memory buffers, a queue length, a maximum message length, and one or more task-waiting lists, as illustrated in Figure 7.1.

It is the kernel's job to assign a unique ID to a message queue and to create its QCB and task-waiting list. The kernel also takes developer-supplied parameters—such as the length of the queue and the maximum message length—to determine how much memory is required for the message queue. After the kernel has this information, it allocates memory for the message queue from either a pool of system memory or some private memory space.

The message queue itself consists of a number of elements, each of which can hold a single message. The elements holding the first and last messages are called the *head* and *tail* respectively. Some elements of the queue may be empty (not containing a message). The total number of elements (empty or not) in the queue is the *total length of the queue*. The developer specified the queue length when the queue was created.

As Figure 7.1 shows, a message queue has two associated task-waiting lists. The receiving task-waiting list consists of tasks that wait on the queue when it is empty. The sending list consists of tasks that wait on the queue when it is full. Empty and full message-queue states, as well as other key concepts, are discussed in more detail next.

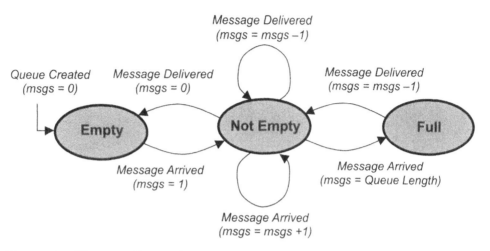

Figure 7.2   The state diagram for a message queue.

7.3 **Message Queue States**

As with other kernel objects, message queues follow the logic of a simple FSM, as shown in Figure 7.2 When a message queue is first created, the FSM is in the empty state. If a task attempts to receive messages from this message queue while the queue is empty, the task blocks and, if it chooses to, is held on the message queue's task-waiting list, in either a FIFO or priority-based order.

In this scenario, if another task sends a message to the message queue, the message is delivered directly to the blocked task. The blocked task is then removed from the task-waiting list and moved to either the ready or the running state. The message queue in this case remains empty because it has successfully delivered the message.

If another message is sent to the same message queue and no tasks are waiting in the message queue's task-waiting list, the message queue's state becomes not empty.

As additional messages arrive at the queue, the queue eventually fills up until it has exhausted its free space. At this point, the number of messages in the queue is equal to the queue's length, and the message queue's state becomes full. While a message queue is in this state, any task sending messages to it will not be successful unless some other task first requests a message from that queue, thus freeing a queue element.

In some kernel implementations when a task attempts to send a message to a full message queue, the sending function returns an error code to that task. Other kernel implementations allow such a task to block, moving the blocked task into the sending task-waiting list, which is separate from the receiving task-waiting list.

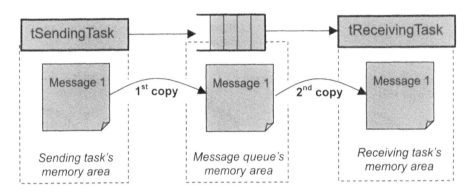

Figure 7.3   Message copying and memory use for sending and receiving messages.

7.4 Message Queue Content

Message queues can be used to send and receive a variety of data. Some examples include:

- a temperature value from a sensor,
- a bitmap to draw on a display,
- a text message to print to an LCD,
- a keyboard event, and
- a data packet to send over the network.

Some of these messages can be quite long and may exceed the maximum message length, which is determined when the queue is created. (Maximum message length should not be confused with total queue length, which is the total number of messages the queue can hold.) One way to overcome the limit on message length is to send a pointer to the data, rather than the data itself. Even if a long message might fit into the queue, it is sometimes better to send a pointer instead in order to improve both performance and memory utilization.

When a task sends a message to another task, the message normally is copied twice, as shown in Figure 7.3 The first time, the message is copied when the message is sent from the sending task's memory area to the message queue's memory area. The second copy occurs when the message is copied from the message queue's memory area to the receiving task's memory area.

An exception to this situation is if the receiving task is already blocked waiting at the message queue. Depending on a kernel's implementation, the message might be copied just once in this case—from the sending task's memory area to the receiving task's memory area, bypassing the copy to the message queue's memory area.

Because copying data can be expensive in terms of performance and memory requirements, keep copying to a minimum in a real-time embedded system by keeping messages small or, if that is not feasible, by using a pointer instead.

7.5 Message Queue Storage

Different kernels store message queues in different locations in memory. One kernel might use a system pool, in which the messages of all queues are stored in one large shared area of memory. Another kernel might use separate memory areas, called private buffers, for each message queue.

7.5.1 System Pools

Using a system pool can be advantageous if it is certain that all message queues will never be filled to capacity at the same time. The advantage occurs because system pools typically save on memory use. The downside is that a message queue with large messages can easily use most of the pooled memory, not leaving enough memory for other message queues. Indications that this problem is occurring include a message queue that is not full that starts rejecting messages sent to it or a full message queue that continues to accept more messages.

7.5.2 Private Buffers

Using private buffers, on the other hand, requires enough reserved memory area for the full capacity of every message queue that will be created. This approach clearly uses up more memory; however, it also ensures that messages do not get overwritten and that room is available for all messages, resulting in better reliability than the pool approach.

7.6 Typical Message Queue Operations

Typical message queue operations include the following:

- creating and deleting message queues,
- sending and receiving messages, and
- obtaining message queue information.

7.6.1 Creating and Deleting Message Queues

Message queues can be created and deleted by using two simple calls, as shown in Table 7.1.

Table 7.1   Message queue creation and deletion operations.

Operation	Description
Create	Creates a message queue
Delete	Deletes a message queue

When created, message queues are treated as global objects and are not owned by any particular task. Typically, the queue to be used by each group of tasks or ISRs is assigned in the design.

When creating a message queue, a developer needs to make some initial decisions about the length of the message queue, the maximum size of the messages it can handle, and the waiting order for tasks when they block on a message queue.

Deleting a message queue automatically unblocks waiting tasks. The blocking call in each of these tasks returns with an error. Messages that were queued are lost when the queue is deleted.

7.6.2 Sending and Receiving Messages

The most common uses for a message queue are sending and receiving messages. These operations are performed in different ways, some of which are listed in Table 7.2.

Table 7.2   Sending and receiving messages.

Operation	Description
Send	Sends a message to a message queue
Receive	Receives a message from a message queue
Broadcast	Broadcasts messages

Sending Messages

When sending messages, a kernel typically fills a message queue from head to tail in FIFO order, as shown in Figure 7.4. Each new message is placed at the end of the queue.

Many message-queue implementations allow urgent messages to go straight to the head of the queue. If all arriving messages are urgent, they all go to the head of the queue, and the queuing order effectively becomes last-in/first-out (LIFO). Many message-queue implementations also allow ISRs to send messages to a message queue. In any case, messages are sent to a message queue in the following ways:

- not block (ISRs and tasks),
- block with a timeout (tasks only), and
- block forever (tasks only).

At times, messages must be sent without blocking the sender. If a message queue is already full, the send call returns with an error, and the task or ISR making the call continues executing. This type of approach to sending messages is the only way to send messages from ISRs, because ISRs cannot block.

Most times, however, the system should be designed so that a task will block if it attempts to send a message to a queue that is full. Setting the task to block either forever or for a specified timeout accomplishes this step. (Figure 7.5). The blocked task is placed

Sending Messages – First-In, First-Out (FIFO) Order

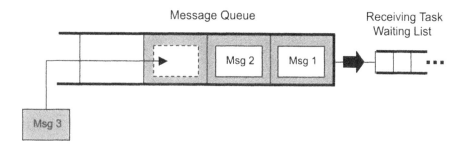

Sending Messages – Last-In, First-Out (LIFO) Order

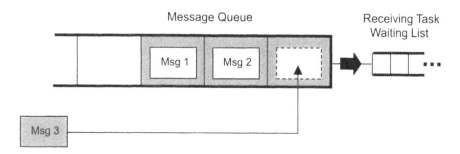

Figure 7.4   Sending messages in FIFO or LIFO order.

in the message queue's task-waiting list, which is set up in either FIFO or priority-based order.

In the case of a task set to block forever when sending a message, the task blocks until a message queue element becomes free (e.g., a receiving task takes a message out of the queue). In the case of a task set to block for a specified time, the task is unblocked if either a queue element becomes free or the timeout expires, in which case an error is returned.

Receiving Messages

As with sending messages, tasks can receive messages with different blocking policies—the same way as they send them—with a policy of not blocking, blocking with a timeout, or blocking forever. Note, however, that in this case, the blocking occurs due to the message queue being empty, and the receiving tasks wait in either a FIFO or priority-based order. The diagram for the receiving tasks is similar to Figure 7.5, except that the blocked receiving tasks are what fills the task list.

Task Waiting List – First-In, First-Out (FIFO) Order

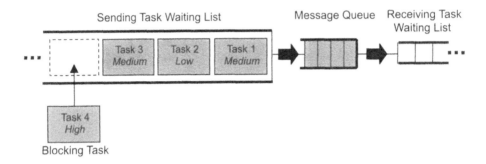

Task Waiting List – Priority-Based Order

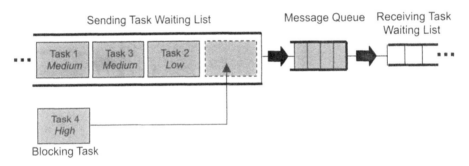

Figure 7.5   FIFO and priority-based task-waiting lists.

For the message queue to become full, either the receiving task list must be empty or the rate at which messages are posted in the message queue must be greater than the rate at which messages are removed. Only when the message queue is full does the task-waiting list for sending tasks start to fill. Conversely, for the task-waiting list for receiving tasks to start to fill, the message queue must be empty.

Messages can be read from the head of a message queue in two different ways:

- destructive read, and
- non-destructive read.

In a destructive read, when a task successfully receives a message from a queue, the task permanently removes the message from the message queue's storage buffer. In a non-destructive read, a receiving task peeks at the message at the head of the queue without removing it. Both ways of reading a message can be useful; however, not all kernel implementations support the non-destructive read.

Some kernels support additional ways of sending and receiving messages. One way is the example of peeking at a message. Other kernels allow broadcast messaging, explained later in this chapter.

7.6.3   Obtaining Message Queue Information

Obtaining message queue information can be done from an application by using the operations listed in Table 7.3.

Table 7.3   Obtaining message queue information operations.

Operation	Description
Show queue info	Gets information on a message queue
Show queue's task-waiting list	Gets a list of tasks in the queue's task-waiting list

Different kernels allow developers to obtain different types of information about a message queue, including the message queue ID, the queuing order used for blocked tasks (FIFO or priority-based), and the number of messages queued. Some calls might even allow developers to get a full list of messages that have been queued up.

As with other calls that get information about a particular kernel object, be careful when using these calls. The information is dynamic and might have changed by the time it's viewed. These types of calls should only be used for debugging purposes.

7.7 Typical Message Queue Use

The following are typical ways to use message queues within an application:

- non-interlocked, one-way data communication,
- interlocked, one-way data communication,
- interlocked, two-way data communication, and
- broadcast communication.

Note that this is not an exhaustive list of the data communication patterns involving message queues. The following sections discuss each of these simple cases.

7.7.1   Non-Interlocked, One-Way Data Communication

One of the simplest scenarios for message-based communications requires a sending task (also called the message source), a message queue, and a receiving task (also called a message sink), as illustrated in Figure 7.6.

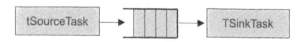

Figure 7.6 Non-interlocked, one-way data communication.

This type of communication is also called non-interlocked (or loosely coupled), one-way data communication. The activities of tSourceTask and tSinkTask are not synchronized. TSourceTask simply sends a message; it does not require acknowledgement from tSinkTask.

The pseudo code for this scenario is provided in Listing 7.1.

Listing 7.1 Pseudo code for non-interlocked, one-way data communication.

```
tSourceTask ()
{
            :
            Send message to message queue
            :
}


tSinkTask ()
{
            :
            Receive message from message queue
            :
}
```

If tSinkTask is set to a higher priority, it runs first until it blocks on an empty message queue. As soon as tSourceTask sends the message to the queue, tSinkTask receives the message and starts to execute again.

If tSinkTask is set to a lower priority, tSourceTask fills the message queue with messages. Eventually, tSourceTask can be made to block when sending a message to a full message queue. This action makes tSinkTask wake up and start taking messages out of the message queue.

ISRs typically use non-interlocked, one-way communication. A task such as tSinkTask runs and waits on the message queue. When the hardware triggers an ISR to run, the ISR puts one or more messages into the message queue. After the ISR completes running, tSinkTask gets an opportunity to run (if it's the highest-priority task) and takes the messages out of the message queue.

Remember, when ISRs send messages to the message queue, they must do so in a non-blocking way. If the message queue becomes full, any additional messages that the ISR sends to the message queue are lost.

7.7.2   Interlocked, One-Way Data Communication

In some designs, a sending task might require a handshake (acknowledgement) that the receiving task has been successful in receiving the message. This process is called interlocked communication, in which the sending task sends a message and waits to see if the message is received.

This requirement can be useful for reliable communications or task synchronization. For example, if the message for some reason is not received correctly, the sending task can resend it. Using interlocked communication can close a synchronization loop. To do so, you can construct a con-

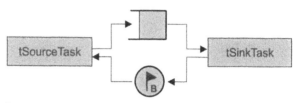

Figure 7.7   Interlocked, one-way data communication.

tinuous loop in which sending and receiving tasks operate in lockstep with each other. An example of one-way, interlocked data communication is illustrated in Figure 7.7.

In this case, tSourceTask and tSinkTask use a binary semaphore initially set to 0 and a message queue with a length of 1 (also called a mailbox). tSourceTask sends the message to the message queue and blocks on the binary semaphore. tSinkTask receives the message and increments the binary semaphore. The semaphore that has just been made available wakes up tSourceTask. tSourceTask, which executes and posts another message into the message queue, blocking again afterward on the binary semaphore.

The pseudo code for interlocked, one-way data communication is provided in Listing 7.2.

The semaphore in this case acts as a simple synchronization object that ensures that tSourceTask and tSinkTask are in lockstep. This synchronization mechanism also acts as a simple acknowledgement to tSourceTask that it's okay to send the next message.

7.7.3   Interlocked, Two-Way Data Communication

Sometimes data must flow bidirectionally   between tasks, which is called interlocked, two-way data communication (also called full-duplex or tightly coupled communication). This form of communication can be useful when designing a client/server-based   system. A diagram is provided in Figure 7.8.

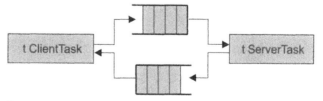

Figure 7.8   Interlocked, two-way data communication.

Listing 7.2   Pseudo code for interlocked, one-way data communication.

```
tSourceTask ()
{
             :
     Send message to message queue
     Acquire binary semaphore
             :
}


tSinkTask ()
{
             :
     Receive message from message queue
     Give binary semaphore
             :
}
```

In this case, tClientTask sends a request to tServerTask via a message queue. tServerTask fulfills that request by sending a message back to tClientTask.

The pseudo code is provided in Listing 7.3.

Listing 7.3   Pseudo code for interlocked, two-way data communication.

```
tClientTask ()
{
             :
     Send a message to the requests queue
     Wait for message from the server queue
             :
}


tServerTask ()
{
             :
     Receive a message from the requests queue
     Send a message to the client queue
             :
}
```

Note that two separate message queues are required for full-duplex communication. If any kind of data needs to be exchanged, message queues are required; otherwise, a simple semaphore can be used to synchronize acknowledgement.

In the simple client/server example, tServerTask is typically set to a higher priority, allowing it to quickly fulfill client requests. If multiple clients need to be set up, all clients can use the client message queue to post requests, while tServerTask uses a separate message queue to fulfill the different clients' requests.

7.7.4   Broadcast Communication

Some message-queue implementations allow developers to broadcast a copy of the same message to multiple tasks, as shown in Figure 7.9.

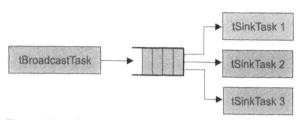

Message broadcasting is a one-to-many-task relationship. tBroadcastTask sends the message on which multiple tSinkTask are waiting.

Figure 7.9   Broadcasting messages.

Pseudo code for broadcasting messages is provided in Listing 7.4.

Listing 7.4   Pseudo code for broadcasting messages.

```
tBroadcastTask ()
{
            :
        Send broadcast message to queue
            :
}


Note: similar code for tSignalTasks 1, 2, and 3.

tSignalTask ()
{
            :
        Receive message on queue
            :
}
```

In this scenario, tSinkTask 1, 2, and 3 have all made calls to block on the broadcast message queue, waiting for a message. When tBroadcastTask executes, it sends one message to the message queue, resulting in all three waiting tasks exiting the blocked state.

Note that not all message queue implementations might support the broadcasting facility. Refer to the RTOS manual to see what types of message-queue-management services and operations are supported.

7.8 Points to Remember

Some points to remember include the following:

- Message queues are buffer-like kernel objects used for data communication and synchronization between two tasks or between an ISR and a task.
- Message queues have an associated message queue control block (QCB), a name, a unique ID, memory buffers, a message queue length, a maximum message length, and one or more task-waiting lists.
- The beginning and end of message queues are called the head and tail, respectively; each buffer that can hold one message is called a message-queue element.
- Message queues are empty when created, full when all message queue elements contain messages, and not empty when some elements are still available for holding new messages.
- Sending messages to full message queues can cause the sending task to block, and receiving messages from an empty message queue can cause a receiving task to block
- Tasks can send to and receive from message queues without blocking, via blocking with a timeout, or via blocking forever. An ISR can only send messages without blocking.
- The task-waiting list associated with a message-queue can release tasks (unblock them) in FIFO or priority-based order. When messages are sent from one task to another, the message is typically copied twice: once from the sending task's memory area to the message queue's and a second time from the message queue's memory area to the task's.
- The data itself can either be sent as the message or as a pointer to the data as the message. The first case is better suited for smaller messages, and the latter case is better suited for large messages.
- Common message-queue operations include creating and deleting message queues, sending to and receiving from message queues, and obtaining message queue information.
- Urgent messages are inserted at the head of the queue if urgent messages are supported by the message-queue implementation.
- Some common ways to use message queues for data based communication include non-interlocked and interlocked queues providing one-way or two-way data communication.

In this chapter...

- Pipes 111
- Event Registers 118
- Signals 121
- Condition Variables 126
- Points to Remember 130

CHAPTER 8

OTHER KERNEL OBJECTS

8.1 Introduction

In addition to the key kernel objects, such as tasks, semaphores, and message queues, kernels provide many other important objects as well. Because every kernel is different, the number of objects a given kernel supports can vary from one to another. This chapter explores additional kernel objects common to embedded systems development, although the list presented here is certainly not all-inclusive. Specifically, this chapter focuses on:

- other kernel objects, including pipes, event registers, signals, and condition variables,
- object definitions and general descriptions,
- associated operations, and
- typical applications of each.

8.2 Pipes

Pipes are kernel objects that provide unstructured data exchange and facilitate synchronization among tasks. In a traditional implementation, a pipe is a unidirectional data exchange facility, as shown in Figure 8.1. Two descriptors, one for each end of the pipe (one end for reading and one for writing), are returned when the pipe is created. Data is written via one descriptor and read via the other. The data remains in the pipe as an unstructured byte stream. Data is read from the pipe in FIFO order.

A pipe provides a simple data flow facility so that the reader becomes blocked when the pipe is empty, and the writer becomes blocked when the pipe is full. Typically, a pipe is used to exchange data between a data-producing task and a data-consuming task, as

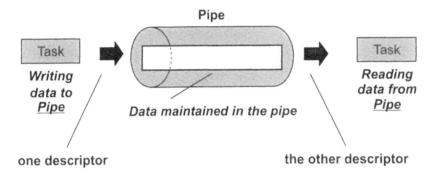

Figure 8.1   A common pipe—unidirectional.

shown in Figure 8.2. It is also permissible to have several writers for the pipe with multiple readers on it.

Note that a pipe is conceptually similar to a message queue but with significant differences. For example, unlike a message queue, a pipe does not store multiple messages. Instead, the data that it stores is not structured, but consists of a stream of bytes. Also, the data in a pipe cannot be prioritized; the data flow is strictly first-in, first-out FIFO. Finally, as is described below, pipes support the powerful select operation, and message queues do not.

8.2.1   Pipe Control Blocks

Pipes can be dynamically created or destroyed. The kernel creates and maintains pipe-specific information in an internal data structure called a *pipe control block*. The structure of the pipe control block varies from one implementation to another. In its general form, a pipe control block contains a kernel-allocated data buffer for the pipe's input and output operation. The size of this buffer is maintained in the control block and is fixed when the pipe is created; it cannot be altered at run time. The current data

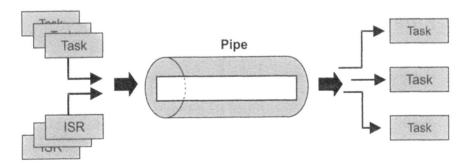

Figure 8.2   Common pipe operation.

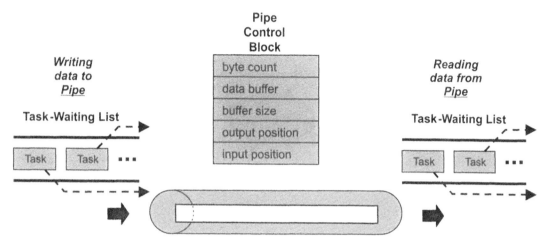

Figure 8.3   Pipe control block.

byte count, along with the current input and output position indicators, are part of the pipe control block. The current data byte count indicates the amount of readable data in the pipe. The input position specifies where the next write operation begins in the buffer. Similarly, the output position specifies where the next read operation begins. The kernel creates two descriptors that are unique within the system I/O space and returns these descriptors to the creating task. These descriptors identify each end of the pipe uniquely.

Two task-waiting lists are associated with each pipe, as shown in Figure 8.3. One waiting list keeps track of tasks that are waiting to write into the pipe while it is full; the other keeps track of tasks that are waiting to read from the pipe while it is empty.

8.2.2   Pipe States

A pipe has a limited number of states associated with it from the time of its creation to its termination. Each state corresponds to the data transfer state between the reader and the writer of the pipe, as illustrated in Figure 8.4.

8.2.3   Named and Unnamed Pipes

A kernel typically supports two kinds of pipe objects: named pipes and unnamed pipes. A *named pipe*, also known as FIFO, has a name similar to a file name and appears in the file system as if it were a file or a device. Any task or ISR that needs to use the named pipe can reference it by name. The *unnamed pipe* does not have a name and does not appear in the file system. It must be referenced by the descriptors that the kernel returns when the pipe is created, as explained in more detail in the following sections.

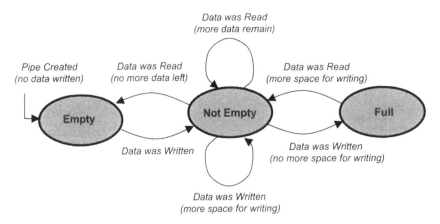

Figure 8.4   States of a pipe.

8.2.4   Typical Pipe Operations

The following set of operations can be performed on a pipe:

- create and destroy a pipe,
- read from or write to a pipe,
- issue control commands on the pipe, and
- select on a pipe.

Create and Destroy

Create and destroy operations are available, as shown in Table 8.1.

Table 8.1   Create and destroy operations.

Operation	Description
Pipe	Creates a pipe
Open	Opens a pipe
Close	Deletes or closes a pipe

The pipe operation creates an unnamed pipe. This operation returns two descriptors to the calling task, and subsequent calls reference these descriptors. One descriptor is used only for writing, and the other descriptor is used only for reading.

Creating a named pipe is similar to creating a file; the specific call is implementation-dependent. Some common names for such a call are mknod and mkfifo. Because a named pipe has a recognizable name in the file system after it is created, the pipe can be opened using the open operation. The calling task must specify whether it is opening the pipe for the read operation or for the write operation; it cannot be both.

The close operation is the counterpart of the open operation. Similar to open, the close operation can only be performed on a named pipe. Some implementations will delete the named pipe permanently once the close operation completes.

Read and Write

Read and write operations are available, as shown in Table 8.2.

Table 8.2   Read and write operations.

Operation	Description
Read	Reads from the pipe
Write	Writes to a pipe

The read operation returns data from the pipe to the calling task. The task specifies how much data to read. The task may choose to block waiting for the remaining data to arrive if the size specified exceeds what is available in the pipe. Remember that a read operation on a pipe is a destructive operation because data is removed from a pipe during this operation, making it unavailable to other readers. Therefore, unlike a message queue, a pipe cannot be used for broadcasting data to multiple reader tasks.

A task, however, can consume a block of data originating from multiple writers during one read operation.

The write operation appends new data to the existing byte stream in the pipe. The calling task specifies the amount of data to write into the pipe. The task may choose to block waiting for additional buffer space to become free when the amount to write exceeds the available space.

No message boundaries exist in a pipe because the data maintained in it is unstructured. This issue represents the main structural difference between a pipe and a message queue. Because there are no message headers, it is impossible to determine the original producer of the data bytes. As mentioned earlier, another important difference between message queues and pipes is that data written to a pipe cannot be prioritized. Because each byte of data in a pipe has the same priority, a pipe should not be used when urgent data must be exchanged between tasks.

Control

Control operations are available, as shown in Table 8.3.

The Fcntl operation provides generic control over a pipe's descriptor using various commands, which control the behavior of the pipe operation. For example, a commonly implemented command is the non-blocking command. The command controls whether

Table 8.3 Control operations.

Operation	Description
Fcntl	Provides control over the pipe descriptor

the calling task is blocked if a read operation is performed on an empty pipe or when a write operation is performed on a full pipe.

Another common command that directly affects the pipe is the flush command. The flush command removes all data from the pipe and clears all other conditions in the pipe to the same state as when the pipe was created. Sometimes a task can be preempted for too long, and when it finally gets to read data from the pipe, the data might no longer be useful. Therefore, the task can flush the data from the pipe and reset its state.

Select

Select operations are available, as shown in Table 8.4.

Table 8.4 Select operations.

Operation	Description
Select	Waits for conditions to occur on a pipe

The select operation allows a task to block and wait for a specified condition to occur on one or more pipes. The wait condition can be waiting for data to become available or waiting for data to be emptied from the pipe(s). Figure 8.5 illustrates a scenario in which a single task is waiting to read from two pipes and write to a third. In this case, the select call returns when data becomes available on either of the top two pipes. The same select call also returns when space for writing becomes available on the bottom pipe. In general, a task reading from multiple pipes can perform a select operation on those pipes, and the select call returns when any one of them has data available. Similarly, a task writing to multiple pipes can perform a select operation on the pipes, and the select call returns when space becomes available on any one of them.

In contrast to pipes, message queues do not support the select operation. Thus, while a task can have access to multiple message queues, it cannot block-wait for data to arrive on any one of a group of empty message queues. The same restriction applies to a writer. In this case, a task can write to multiple message queues, but a task cannot block-wait on a group of full message queues, while waiting for space to become available on any one of them.

It becomes clear then that the main advantage of using a pipe over a message queue for intertask communication is that it allows for the select operation.

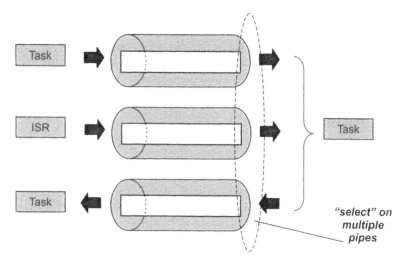

Figure 8.5   The select operation on multiple pipes.

8.2.5   Typical Uses of Pipes

Because a pipe is a simple data channel, it is mainly used for task-to-task or ISR-to-task data transfer, as illustrated in Figure 8.1 and Figure 8.2. Another common use of pipes is for inter-task synchronization.

Inter-task synchronization can be made asynchronous for both tasks by using the select operation.

In Figure 8.6, task A and task B open two pipes for inter-task communication. The first pipe is opened for data transfer from task A to task B. The second pipe is opened for acknowledgement (another data transfer) from task B to task A. Both tasks issue the select operation on the pipes. Task A can wait asynchronously for the data pipe to become writeable (task B has read some data from the pipe). That is, task A can issue a

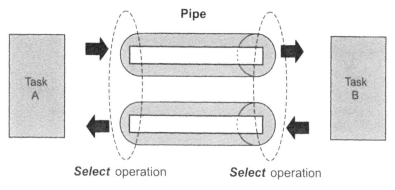

Figure 8.6   Using pipes for inter-task synchronization.

non-blocking call to write to the pipe and perform other operations until the pipe becomes writeable. Task A can also wait asynchronously for the arrival of the transfer acknowledgement from task B on the other pipe. Similarly, task B can wait asynchronously for the arrival of data on the data pipe and wait for the other pipe to become writeable before sending the transfer acknowledgement.

8.3 Event Registers

Some kernels provide a special register as part of each task's control block, as shown in Figure 8.7. This register, called an *event register,* is an object belonging to a task and consists of a group of binary event flags used to track the occurrence of specific events. Depending on a given kernel's implementation of this mechanism, an event register can be 8-, 16-, or 32-bits wide, maybe even more. Each bit in the event register is treated like a binary flag (also called an event flag) and can be either set or cleared.

Through the event register, a task can check for the presence of particular events that can control its execution. An external source, such as another task or an ISR, can set bits in the event register to inform the task that a particular event has occurred.

Applications define the event associated with an event flag. This definition must be agreed upon between the event sender and receiver using the event register.

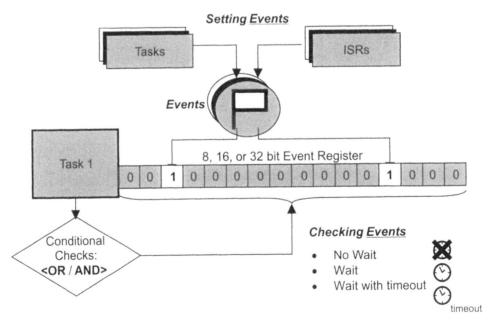

Figure 8.7   Event register.

8.3.1   Event Register Control Blocks

Typically, when the underlying kernel supports the event register mechanism, the kernel creates an event register control block as part of the task control block when creating a task, as shown in Figure 8.8.

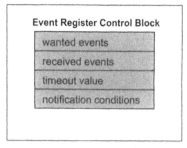

Task Control Block

Figure 8.8   Event register control block.

The task specifies the set of events it wishes to receive. This set of events is maintained in the wanted events register. Similarly, arrived events are kept in the received events register. The task indicates a timeout to specify how long it wishes to wait for the arrival of certain events. The kernel wakes up the task when this timeout has elapsed if no specified events have arrived at the task.

Using the notification conditions, the task directs the kernel as to when it wishes to be notified (awakened) upon event arrivals. For example, the task can specify the notification conditions as "send notification when both event type 1 and event type 3 arrive or when event type 2 arrives." This option provides flexibility in defining complex notification patterns.

8.3.2   Typical Event Register Operations

Two main operations are associated with an event register, the sending and the receiving operations, as shown in Table 8.5.

Table 8.5   Event register operations.

Operation	Description
Send	Sends events to a task
Receive	Receives events

The receive operation allows the calling task to receive events from external sources. The task can specify if it wishes to wait, as well as the length of time to wait for the arrival of desired events before giving up. The task can wait forever or for a specified interval. Specifying a set of events when issuing the receive operation allows a task to block-wait for the arrival of multiple events, although events might not necessarily all arrive simultaneously. The kernel translates this event set into the notification conditions. The receive operation returns either when the notification conditions are satisfied or when the timeout has occurred. Any received events that are not indicated in the receive operation are left pending in the received events register of the event register control block. The receive operation returns immediately if the desired events are already pending.

The event set is constructed using the bit-wise AND/OR operation. With the AND operation, the task resumes execution only after every event bit from the set is on. A task can also block-wait for the arrival of a single event from an event set, which is constructed using the bit-wise OR operation. In this case, the task resumes execution when any one event bit from the set is on.

The send operation allows an external source, either a task or an ISR, to send events to another task. The sender can send multiple events to the designated task through a single send operation. Events that have been sent and are pending on the event bits but have not been chosen for reception by the task remain pending in the received events register of the event register control block.

Events in the event register are not queued. An event register cannot count the occurrences of the same event while it is pending; therefore, subsequent occurrences of the same event are lost. For example, if an ISR sends an event to a task and the event is left pending; and later another task sends the same event again to the same task while it is still pending, the first occurrence of the event is lost.

8.3.3   Typical Uses of Event Registers

Event registers are typically used for unidirectional activity synchronization. It is unidirectional because the issuer of the receive operation determines when activity synchronization should take place. Pending events in the event register do not change the execution state of the receiving task.

In following the diagram, at the time task 1 sends the event X to task 2, no effect occurs to the execution state of task 2 if task 2 has not yet attempted to receive the event.

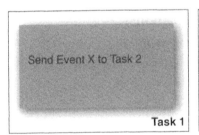
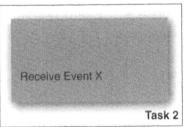

No data is associated with an event when events are sent through the event register. Other mechanisms must be used when data needs to be conveyed along with an event. This lack of associated data can sometimes create difficulties because of the non-cumulative nature of events in the event register. Therefore, the event register by itself is an inefficient mechanism if used beyond simple activity synchronization.

Another difficulty in using an event register is that it does not have a built-in mechanism for identifying the source of an event if multiple sources are possible. One way to overcome this problem is for a task to divide the event bits in the event register into subsets.

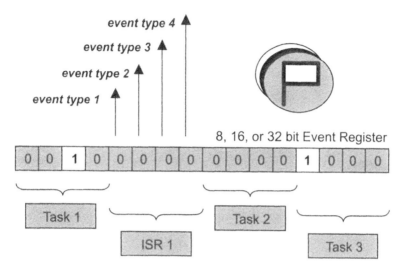

event type 4

event type 3

event type 2

event type 1

8, 16, or 32 bit Event Register

| 0 | 0 | 1 | 0 | 0 | 0 | 0 | 0 | 0 | 0 | 0 | 0 | 1 | 0 | 0 | 0 |

Task 1

ISR 1

Task 2

Task 3

Figure 8.9   Identifying an event source.

The task can then associate each subset with a known source. In this way, the task can identify the source of an event if each relative bit position of each subset is assigned to the same event type.

In Figure 8.9, an event register is divided into 4-bit groups. Each group is assigned to a source, regardless of whether it is a task or an ISR. Each bit of the group is assigned to an event type.

8.4 Signals

A *signal* is a software interrupt that is generated when an event has occurred. It diverts the signal receiver from its normal execution path and triggers the associated asynchronous processing.

Essentially, signals notify tasks of events that occurred during the execution of other tasks or ISRs. As with normal interrupts, these events are asynchronous to the notified task and do not occur at any predetermined point in the task's execution. The difference between a signal and a normal interrupt is that signals are so-called software interrupts, which are generated via the execution of some software within the system. By contrast, normal interrupts are usually generated by the arrival of an interrupt signal on one of the CPU's external pins. They are not generated by software within the system but by external devices. Chapter 10 discusses interrupts and exceptions in detail.

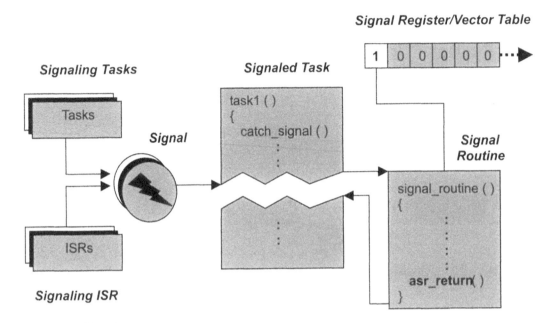

Figure 8.10   Signals.

The number and type of signals defined is both system-dependent and RTOS-dependent. An easy way to understand signals is to remember that each signal is associated with an event. The event can be either unintentional, such as an illegal instruction encountered during program execution, or the event may be intentional, such as a notification to one task from another that it is about to terminate. While a task can specify the particular actions to undertake when a signal arrives, the task has no control over when it receives signals. Consequently, the signal arrivals often appear quite random, as shown in Figure 8.10.

When a signal arrives, the task is diverted from its normal execution path, and the corresponding signal routine is invoked. The terms *signal routine*, *signal handler*, *asynchronous event handler*, and *asynchronous signal routine* are interchangeable. This book uses *asynchronous signal routine* (ASR). Each signal is identified by an integer value, which is the *signal number* or *vector number*.

8.4.1   Signal Control Blocks

If the underlying kernel provides a signal facility, it creates the signal control block as part of the task control block as shown in Figure 8.11.

Signal Control Block

Figure 8.11   Signal control block.

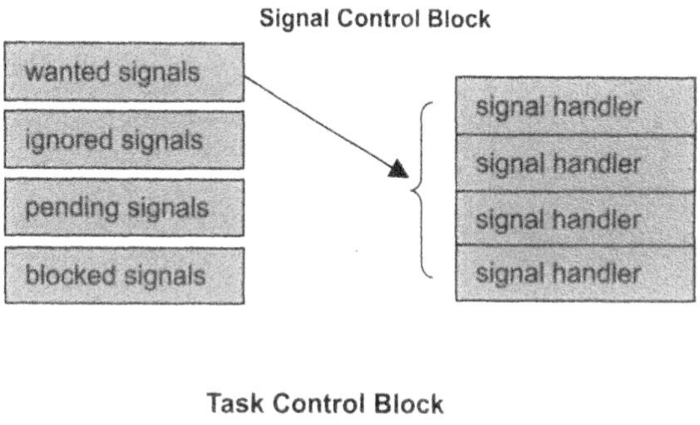

Task Control Block

The signal control block maintains a set of signals—the wanted signals—which the task is prepared to handle. When a task is prepared to handle a signal, it is often said, "the task is *ready to catch* the signal." When a signal interrupts a task, it is often said, "the signal is *raised* to the task." The task can provide a signal handler for each signal to be processed, or it can execute a default handler that the kernel provides. It is possible to have a single handler for multiple types of signals.

Signals can be ignored, made pending, processed (handled), or blocked.

The signals to be ignored by the task are maintained in the ignored signals set. Any signal in this set does not interrupt the task.

Other signals can arrive while the task is in the midst of processing another signal. The additional signal arrivals are kept in the pending signals set. The signals in this set are raised to the task as soon as the task completes processing the previous signal. The pending signals set is a subset of the wanted signals set.

To process a particular signal, either the task-supplied signal handler can be used for signal processing or the default handler supplied by the underlying kernel can be used to process it. It is also possible for the task to process the signal first and then pass it on for additional processing by the default handler.

A fourth kind of response to a signal is possible. In this case, a task does not ignore the signal but blocks the signal from delivery during certain stages of the task's execution when it is critical that the task not be interrupted.

Blocking a signal is similar to the concept of entering a critical section, discussed in Chapter 15. The task can instruct the kernel to block certain signals by setting the blocked signals set. The kernel does not deliver any signal from this set until that signal is cleared from the set.

8.4.2   Typical Signal Operations

Signal operations are available, as shown in Table 8.6.

Table 8.6   Signal operations.

Operation	Description
Catch	Installs a signal handler
Release	Removes a previously installed handler
Send	Sends a signal to another task
Ignore	Prevents a signal from being delivered
Block	Blocks a set of signal from being delivered
Unblock	Unblocks the signals so they can be delivered

A task can catch a signal after the task has specified a handler (ASR) for the signal. The catch operation installs a handler for a particular signal. The kernel interrupts the task's execution upon the arrival of the signal, and the handler is invoked. The task can install the kernel-supplied default handler, the *default actions*, for any signal. The task-installed handler has the options of either processing the signal and returning control to the kernel or processing the signal and passing control to the default handler for additional processing. Handling signals is similar to handling hardware interrupts, and the nature of the ASR is similar to that of the interrupt service routine.

After a handler has been installed for a particular signal, the handler is invoked if the same type of signal is received by any task, not just the one that installed it. In addition, any task can change the handler installed for a particular signal. Therefore, it is good practice for a task to save the previously installed handler before installing its own and then to restore that handler after it finishes catching the handler's corresponding signal.

Figure 8.12 shows the signal vector table, which the kernel maintains. Each element in the vector table is a pointer or offset to an ASR. For signals that don't have handlers assigned, the corresponding elements in the vector table are NULL. The example shows the table after three catch operations have been performed. Each catch operation installs one ASR, by writing a pointer or offset to the ASR into an element of the vector table.

The release operation de-installs a signal handler. It is good practice for a task to restore the previously installed signal handler after calling release.

The send operation allows one task to send a signal to another task. Signals are usually associated with hardware events that occur during execution of a task, such as generation of an unaligned memory address or a floating-point exception. Such signals are generated automatically when their corresponding events occur. The send operation, by contrast, enables a task to explicitly generate a signal.

The ignore operation allows a task to instruct the kernel that a particular set of signals should never be delivered to that task. Some signals, however, cannot be ignored; when these signals are generated, the kernel calls the default handler.

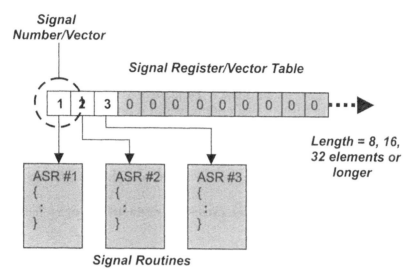

Figure 8.12 The catch operation.

The block operation does not cause signals to be ignored but temporarily prevents them from being delivered to a task. The block operation protects critical sections of code from interruption. Another reason to block a signal is to prevent conflict when the signal handler is already executing and is in the midst of processing the same signal. A signal remains pending while it's blocked.

The unblock operation allows a previously blocked signal to pass. The signal is delivered immediately if it is already pending.

8.4.3 Typical Uses of Signals

Some signals are associated with hardware events and thus are usually sent by hardware ISRs. The ISR is responsible for immediately responding to these events. The ISR, however, might also send a signal so that tasks affected by these hardware events can conduct further, task-specific processing.

As depicted in Figure 8.10, signals can also be used for synchronization between tasks. Signals, however, should be used sparingly for the following reasons:

- Using signals can be expensive due to the complexity of the signal facility when used for inter-task synchronization. A signal alters the execution state of its destination task. Because signals occur asynchronously, the receiving task becomes non-deterministic, which can be undesirable in a real-time system.
- Many implementations do not support queuing or counting of signals. In these implementations, multiple occurrences of the same signal overwrite each other. For

example, a signal delivered to a task multiple times before its handler is invoked has the same effect as a single delivery. The task has no way to determine if a signal has arrived multiple times.

- Many implementations do not support signal delivery that carries information, so data cannot be attached to a signal during its generation.

- Many implementations do not support a signal delivery order, and signals of various types are treated as having equal priority, which is not ideal. For example, a signal triggered by a page fault is obviously more important than a signal generated by a task indicating it is about to exit. On an equal-priority system, the page fault might not be handled first.

- Many implementations do not guarantee when an unblocked pending signal will be delivered to the destination task.

Some kernels do implement real-time extensions to traditional signal handling, which allows

- for the prioritized delivery of a signal based on the signal number,

- each signal to carry additional information, and

- multiple occurrences of the same signal to be queued.

8.5 Condition Variables

Tasks often use shared resources, such as files and communication channels. When a task needs to use such a resource, it might need to wait for the resource to be in a particular state. The way the resource reaches that state can be through the action of another task. In such a scenario, a task needs some way to determine the condition of the resource. One way for tasks to communicate and determine the condition of a shared resource is through a condition variable. A *condition variable* is a kernel object that is associated with a shared resource, which allows one task to wait for other task(s) to create a desired condition in the shared resource. A condition variable can be associated with multiple conditions.

As shown in Figure 8.13, a condition variable implements a predicate. The predicate is a set of logical expressions concerning the conditions of the shared resource. The predicate evaluates to either true or false. A task evaluates the predicate. If the evaluation is true, the task assumes that the conditions are satisfied, and it continues execution. Otherwise, the task must wait for other tasks to create the desired conditions.

When a task examines a condition variable, the task must have exclusive access to that condition variable. Without exclusive access, another task could alter the condition variable's conditions at the same time, which could cause the first task to get an erroneous indication of the variable's state. Therefore, a mutex is always used in conjunction with a condition variable. The mutex ensures that one task has exclusive access to the condition variable until that task is finished with it. For example, if a task acquires the mutex

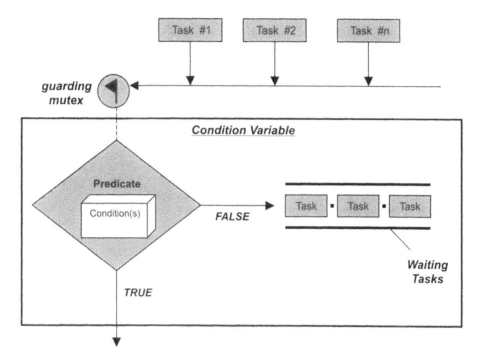

Figure 8.13   Condition variable.

to examine the condition variable, no other task can simultaneously modify the condition variable of the shared resource.

A task must first acquire the mutex before evaluating the predicate. This task must subsequently release the mutex and then, if the predicate evaluates to false, wait for the creation of the desired conditions. Using the condition variable, the kernel guarantees that the task can release the mutex and then block-wait for the condition in one atomic operation, which is the essence of the condition variable. An *atomic operation* is an operation that cannot be interrupted.

Remember, however, that condition variables are not mechanisms for synchronizing access to a shared resource. Rather, most developers use them to allow tasks waiting on a shared resource to reach a desired value or state.

8.5.1 Condition Variable Control Blocks

The kernel maintains a set of information associated with the condition variable when the variable is first created. As stated previously, tasks must block and wait when a condition variable's predicate evaluates to false. These waiting tasks are maintained in the task-waiting list. The kernel guarantees for each task that the combined operation of releasing the associated mutex and performing a block-wait on the condition will be atomic. After the desired conditions have been created, one of the waiting tasks is awakened and resumes execution. The criteria for selecting which task to awaken can be priority-based or FIFO-based, but it is kernel-defined. The kernel guarantees that the selected task is removed from the task-waiting list, reacquires the guarding mutex, and resumes its operation in one atomic operation. The essence of the condition variable is the atomicity of the unlock-and-wait and the resume-and-lock operations provided by the kernel. Figure 8.14 illustrates a condition variable control block.

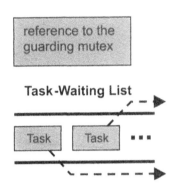

Figure 8.14   Condition variable control block.

The cooperating tasks define which conditions apply to which shared resources. This information is not part of the condition variable because each task has a different predicate or condition for which the task looks. The condition is specific to the task. Chapter 15 presents a detailed example on the usage of the condition variable, which further illustrates this issue.

8.5.2 Typical Condition Variable Operations

A set of operations is allowed for a condition variable, as shown in Table 8.7.

Table 8.7   Condition variable operations.

Operation	Description
Create	Creates and initializes a condition variable
Wait	Waits on a condition variable
Signal	Signals the condition variable on the presence of a condition
Broadcast	Signals to all waiting tasks the presence of a condition

The create operation creates a condition variable and initializes its internal control block.

The wait operation allows a task to block and wait for the desired conditions to occur in the shared resource. To invoke this operation, the task must first successfully acquire the guarding mutex. The wait operation puts the calling task into the task-waiting queue and releases the associated mutex in a single atomic operation.

The signal operation allows a task to modify the condition variable to indicate that a particular condition has been created in the shared resource. To invoke this operation, the signaling task must first successfully acquire the guarding mutex. The signal operation unblocks one of the tasks waiting on the condition variable. The selection of the task is based on predefined criteria, such as execution priority or system-defined scheduling attributes. At the completion of the signal operation, the kernel reacquires the mutex associated with the condition variable on behalf of the selected task and unblocks the task in one atomic operation.

The broadcast operation wakes up every task on the task-waiting list of the condition variable. One of these tasks is chosen by the kernel and is given the guarding mutex. Every other task is removed from the task-waiting list of the condition variable, and instead, those tasks are put on the task-waiting list of the guarding mutex.

8.5.3   Typical Uses of Condition Variables

Listing 8.1 illustrates the usage of the wait and the signal operations.

Listing 8.1   Pseudo code for wait and the signal operations.

```
Task 1
Lock mutex
        Examine shared resource
        While (shared resource is Busy)
                WAIT (condition variable)
        Mark shared resource as Busy
Unlock mutex


Task 2
Lock mutex
        Mark shared resource as Free
        SIGNAL (condition variable)
Unlock mutex
```

Task 1 on the left locks the guarding mutex as its first step. It then examines the state of the shared resource and finds that the resource is busy. It issues the wait operation to wait for the resource to become available, or free. The free condition must be created by task 2 on the right after it is done using the resource. To create the free condition, task 2

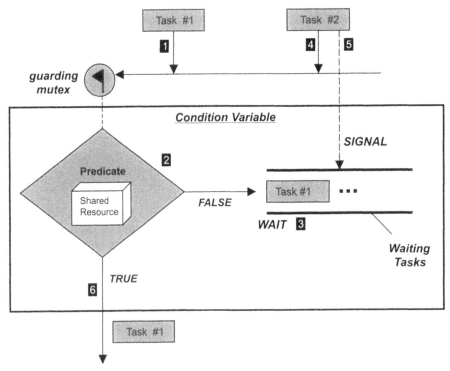

Figure 8.15   Execution sequence of wait and signal operations.

first locks the mutex; creates the condition by marking the resource as free, and finally, invokes the signal operation, which informs task 1 that the free condition is now present.

A signal on the condition variable is lost when nothing is waiting on it. Therefore, a task should always check for the presence of the desired condition before waiting on it. A task should also always check for the presence of the desired condition after a wakeup as a safeguard against improperly generated signals on the condition variable. This issue is the reason that the pseudo code includes a while loop to check for the presence of the desired condition. This example is shown in Figure 8.15.

8.6 Points to Remember

Some points to remember include the following:

- Pipes provide unstructured data exchange between tasks.
- The select operation is allowed on pipes.

- Event registers can be used to communicate application-defined events between tasks.
- Events of the same type are not accumulated in the event register.
- The occurrence of an event in the event register does not change the execution state of the receiving task, unless the task is already waiting on that event.
- Tasks receive signals synchronously.
- The occurrence of a signal changes the execution state of the receiving task.
- Signals can be handled by user-defined actions or by system-defined default actions.
- Multiple occurrences of the same signal are not cumulative.
- A condition variable allows one task to wait until another task has placed a shared resource in a desired state or condition.
- A condition variable is used to synchronize between tasks but is not used as a mechanism to synchronize access to shared resources.

In this chapter...

• Other Building Blocks 133
• Component Configuration 139
• Points to Remember 141

CHAPTER 9

OTHER RTOS SERVICES

9.1 Introduction

A good real-time embedded operating system avoids implementing the kernel as a large, monolithic program. The kernel is developed instead as a micro-kernel. The goal of the micro-kernel design approach is to reduce essential kernel services into a small set and to provide a framework in which other optional kernel services can be implemented as independent modules. These modules can be placed outside the kernel. Some of these modules are part of special server tasks. This structured approach makes it possible to extend the kernel by adding additional services or to modify existing services without affecting users. This level of implementation flexibility is highly desirable. The resulting benefit is increased system configurability because each embedded application requires a specific set of system services with respect to its characteristics. This combination can be quite different from application to application.

The micro-kernel provides core services, including task-related services, the scheduler service, and synchronization primitives. This chapter discusses other common building blocks, as shown in Figure 9.1.

9.2 Other Building Blocks

These other common building blocks make up the additional kernel services that are part of various embedded applications. The other building blocks include the following:

• TCP/IP protocol stack,
• file system component,
• remote procedure call component,

133

Figure 9.1   Overview.

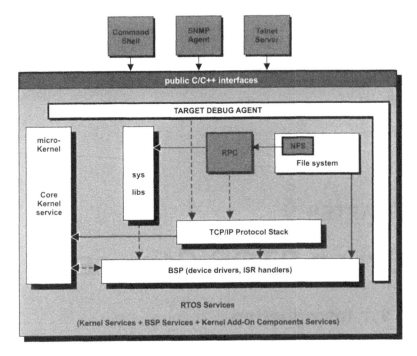

- command shell,
- target debut agent, and
- other components.

9.2.1   TCP/IP Protocol Stack

The network protocol stacks and components, as illustrated in Figure 9.2, provide useful system services to an embedded application in a networked environment. The TCP/IP protocol stack provides transport services to both higher layer, well-known protocols, including Simple Network Management Protocol (SNMP), Network File System (NFS), and Telnet, and to user-defined protocols. The transport service can be either reliable connection-oriented service over the TCP protocol or unreliable connectionless service over the UDP protocol. The TCP/IP protocol stack can operate over various types of physical connections and networks, including Ethernet, Frame Relay, ATM, and ISDN networks using different frame encapsulation protocols, including the point-to-point protocol. It is common to find the transport services offered through standard Berkeley socket interfaces.

9.2.2   File System Component

The file system component, as illustrated in Figure 9.3, provides efficient access to both local and network mass storage devices. These storage devices include but are not limited to CD-ROM, tape, floppy disk, hard disk, and flash memory devices. The file system

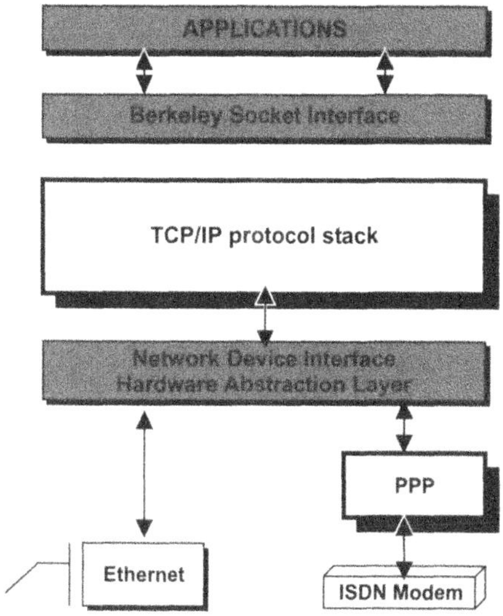

Figure 9.2   TCP/IP protocol stack
component.

component structures the storage device into supported formats for writing information to and for accessing information from the storage device. For example, CD-ROMs are formatted and managed according to ISO 9660 standard file system specifications; floppy disks and hard disks are formatted and managed according to MS-DOS FAT file system conventions and specifications; NFS allows local applications to access files on remote systems as an NFS client. Files located on an NFS server are treated exactly as though they were on a local disk. Because NFS is a protocol, not a file system format, local applications can access any format files supported by the NFS server. File system components found in some real-time RTOS provide high-speed proprietary file systems in place of common storage devices.

9.2.3   Remote Procedure Call Component

The remote procedure call (RPC) component allows for distributed computing. The RPC server offers services to external systems as remotely callable procedures. A remote RPC client can invoke these procedures over the network using the RPC protocol. To use a service provided by an RPC server, a client application calls routines, known as *stubs*, provided by the RPC client residing on the local machine.

The RPC client in turn invokes remote procedure calls residing in the RPC server on behalf of the calling application. The primary goal of RPC is to make remote procedure calls transparent to applications invoking the local call stubs. To the client application, calling a stub appears no different from calling a local procedure. The RPC client and server can run on top of different operating systems, as well as different types of hardware. As an example of such transparency, note that NFS relies directly upon RPC calls to support the illusion that all files are local to the client machine.

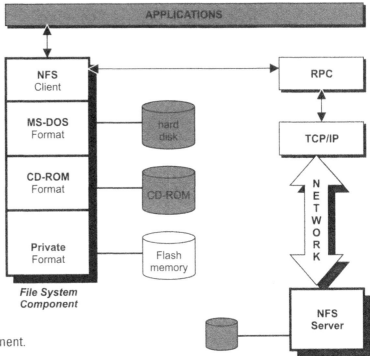

Figure 9.3   File system component.

To hide both the server remoteness, as well as platform differences from the client application, data that flows between the two computing systems in the RPC call must be translated to and from a common format. External data representation (XDR) is a method that represents data in an OS- and machine-independent manner. The RPC client translates data passed in as procedure parameters into XDR format before making the remote procedure call. The RPC server translates the XDR data into machine-specific data format upon receipt of the procedure call request. The decoded data is then passed to the actual procedure to be invoked on the server machine. This procedure's output data is formatted into XDR when returning it to the RPC client. The RPC concept is illustrated in Figure 9.4.

9.2.4   Command Shell

The *command shell*, also called the *command interpreter*, is an interactive component that provides an interface between the user and the real-time operating system. The user can invoke commands, such as ping, ls, loader, and route through the shell. The shell interprets these commands and makes corresponding calls into RTOS routines. These routines can be in the form of loadable program images, dynamically created programs

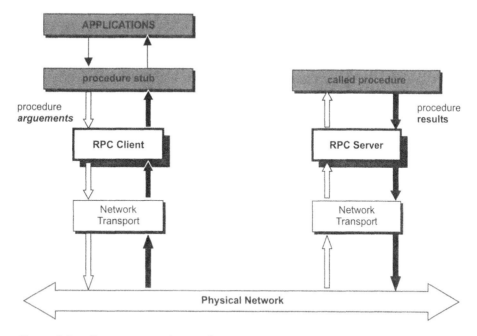

Figure 9.4   Remote procedure calls.

(dynamic tasks), or direct system function calls if supported by the RTOS. The programmer can experiment with different global system calls if the command shell supports this feature. With this feature, the shell can become a great learning tool for the RTOS in which it executes, as illustrated in Figure 9.5.

Some command shell implementations provide a programming interface. A programmer can extend the shell's functionality by writing additional commands or functions using the shell's application program interface (API). The shell is usually accessed from the host system using a terminal emulation program over a serial interface. It is possible to access the shell over the network, but this feature is highly implementation-dependent. The shell becomes a good debugging tool when it supports available debug agent commands. A host debugger is not always available and can be tedious to set up. On the other hand, the programmer can immediately begin debugging when a debug agent is present on the target system, as well as a command shell.

9.2.5   Target Debug Agent

Every good RTOS provides a target debug agent. Through either the target shell component or a simple serial connection, the debug agent offers the programmer a rich set of debug commands or capabilities. The debug agent allows the programmer to set up both execution and data access break points. In addition, the programmer can use the debug

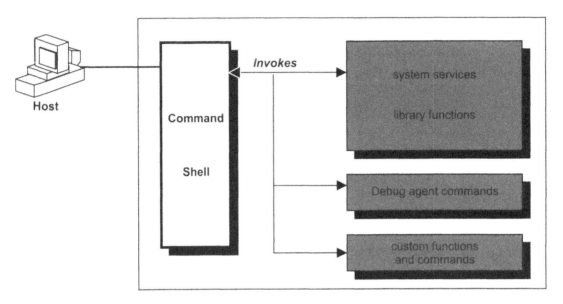

Figure 9.5   RTOS command shell.

agent to examine and modify system memory, system registers, and system objects, such as tasks, semaphores, and message queues. The host debugger can provide source-level debug capability by interacting with the target debug agent. With a host debugger, the user can debug the target system without having to understand the native debug agent commands. The target debug agent commands are mapped into host debugger commands that are more descriptive and easier to understand. Using an established debug protocol, the host debugger sends the user-issued debug commands to the target debug agent over the serial cable or the Ethernet network. The target debug agent acts on the commands and sends the results back to the host debugger. The host debugger displays the results in its user-friendly debug interface. The debug protocol is specific to the host debugger and its supported debug agent. Be sure to check the host debugging tools against the supported RTOS debug agents before making a purchase.

9.2.6   Other Components

What has been presented so far is a very small set of components commonly found in available RTOS. Other service components include the SNMP component. The target system can be remotely managed over the network by using SNMP. The standard I/O library provides a common interface to write to and read from system I/O devices. The standard system library provides common interfaces to applications for memory functions and string manipulation functions. These library components make it straightforward to port applications written for other operating systems as long as they use standard interfaces. The possible services components that an RTOS can provide are limited only by imagination. The more an embedded RTOS matures the more components and options it provides to the developer. These components enable powerful embedded applications programming, while at the same time save overall development costs. Therefore, choose the RTOS wisely.

9.3 Component Configuration

The available system memory in many embedded systems is limited. Therefore, only the necessary service components are selected into the final application image. Frequently programmers ask how to configure a service component into an embedded application. In a simplified view, the selection and consequently the configuration of service components are accomplished through a set of system configuration files. Look for these files in the RTOS development environment to gain a better understanding of available components and applicable configuration parameters.

The first level of configuration is done in a component inclusion header file. For example, call it sys_comp.h, as shown in Listing 9.1.

Listing 9.1   The sys_comp.h **inclusion header file.**

```
#define INCLUDE_TCPIP        1
#define INCLUDE_FILE_SYS     0
#define INCLUDE_SHELL        1
#define INCLUDE_DBG_AGENT    1
```

In this example, the target image includes the TCP/IP protocol stack, the command shell, and the debug agent. The file system is excluded because the sample target system does not have a mass storage device. The programmer selects the desired components through sys_comp.h.

The second level of configuration is done in a component-specific configuration file, sometimes called the component description file. For example, the TCP/IP component configuration file could be called net_conf.h, and the debug agent configuration file might be called the dbg_conf.h. The component-specific configuration file contains the user-configurable, component-specific operating parameters. These parameters contain default values. Listing 9.2 uses net_conf.h.

Listing 9.2   The net_conf.h **configuration file.**

```
#define NUM_PKT_BUFS        100
#define NUM_SOCKETS         20
#define NUM_ROUTES          35
#define NUM_NICS            40
```

In this example, four user-configurable parameters are present: the number of packet buffers to be allocated for transmitting and receiving network packets; the number of sockets to be allocated for the applications; the number of routing entries to be created in the routing table used for forwarding packets; and the number of network interface data structures to be allocated for installing network devices. Each parameter contains a default value, and the programmer is allowed to change the value of any parameter present in the configuration file. These parameters are applicable only to the TCP/IP protocol stack component.

Component-specific parameters must be passed to the component during the initialization phase. The component parameters are set into a data structure called the component configuration table. The configuration table is passed into the component initialization routine. This level is the third configuration level. Listing 9.3 shows the configuration file named net_conf.c, which continues to use the network component as the example.

Listing 9.3   The net_conf.c **configuration file.**

```
#include "sys_comp.h"
#include "net_conf.h"


#if (INCLUDE_TCPIP)
struct net_conf_parms  params;
params.num_pkt_bufs = NUM_PKT_BUFS;
params.num_sockets  = NUM_SOCKETS;
params.num_routes   = NUM_ROUTES;
params.num_NICS     = NUM_NICS;


tcpip_init(&params);


#endif
```

The components are pre-built and archived. The function tcpip_init is part of the component. If INCLUDE_TCPIP is defined as 1 at the time the application is built, the call to this function triggers the linker to link the component into the final executable image. At this point, the TCP/IP protocol stack is included and fully configured.

Obviously, the examples presented here are simple, but the concepts vary little in real systems. Manual configuration, however, can be tedious when it is required to wading through directories and files to get to the configuration files. When the configuration file does not offer enough or clear documentation on the configuration parameters, the process is even harder. Some host development tools offer an interactive and visual alternative to manual component configuration. The visual component configuration tool allows the programmer to select the offered components visually. The configurable parameters are also laid out visually and are easily editable. The outputs of the configuration tool are automatically generated files similar to sys_comp.h and net_conf.h. Any modification completed through the configuration tool regenerates these files.

9.4 Points to Remember

Some points to remember include the following:

- Micro-kernel design promotes a framework in which additional service components can be developed to extend the kernel's functionalities easily.
- Debug agents allow programmers to debug every piece of code running on target systems.
- Developers should choose a host debugger that understands many different RTOS debug agents.
- Components can be included and configured through a set of system configuration files.
- Developers should only include the necessary components to safeguard memory efficiency.

In this chapter...

- What are Exceptions and Interrupts? 144
- Applications of Exceptions and Interrupts 145
- A Closer Look at Exceptions and Interrupts 146
- Processing General Exceptions 150
- The Nature of Spurious Interrupts 163
- Points to Remember. 165

CHAPTER 10

EXCEPTIONS AND INTERRUPTS

10.1 Introduction

Exceptions and interrupts are part of a mechanism provided by the majority of embedded processor architectures to allow for the disruption of the processor's normal execution path. This disruption can be triggered either intentionally by application software or by an error, unusual condition, or some unplanned external event.

Many real-time operating systems provide wrapper functions to handle exceptions and interrupts in order to shield the embedded systems programmer from the low-level details. This application-programming layer allows the programmer to focus on high-level exception processing rather than on the necessary, but tedious, prologue and epilogue system-level processing for that exception. This isolation, however, can create misunderstanding and become an obstacle when the programmer is transformed from an embedded *applications* programmer into an embedded *systems* programmer.

Understanding the inner workings of the processor exception facility aids the programmer in making better decisions about when to best use this powerful mechanism, as well as in designing software that handles exceptions correctly. The aim of this chapter is to arm the programmer with this knowledge.

This chapter focuses on:

- the definitions of exception and interrupt,
- the applications of exceptions and interrupts,
- a closer look at exceptions and interrupts in terms of hardware support, classifications, priorities, and causes of spurious interrupts, and
- a detailed discussion on how to handle exceptions and interrupts.

10.2 What are Exceptions and Interrupts?

An *exception* is any event that disrupts the normal execution of the processor and forces the processor into execution of special instructions in a privileged state. Exceptions can be classified into two categories: synchronous exceptions and asynchronous exceptions.

Exceptions raised by internal events, such as events generated by the execution of processor instructions, are called *synchronous exceptions*. Examples of synchronous exceptions include the following:

- On some processor architectures, the read and the write operations must start at an even memory address for certain data sizes. Read or write operations that begin at an odd memory address cause a memory access error event and raise an exception (called an *alignment exception*).
- An arithmetic operation that results in a division by zero raises an exception.

Exceptions raised by external events, which are events that do not relate to the execution of processor instructions, are called *asynchronous exceptions*. In general, these external events are associated with hardware signals. The sources of these hardware signals are typically external hardware devices. Examples of asynchronous exceptions include the following:

- Pushing the reset button on the embedded board triggers an asynchronous exception (called the *system reset exception*).
- The communications processor module that has become an integral part of many embedded designs is another example of an external device that can raise asynchronous exceptions when it receives data packets.

An *interrupt*, sometimes called an *external interrupt*, is an asynchronous exception triggered by an event that an external hardware device generates. Interrupts are one class of exception. What differentiates interrupts from other types of exceptions, or more precisely what differentiates synchronous exceptions from asynchronous exceptions, is the source of the event. The event source for a synchronous exception is internally generated from the processor due to the execution of some instruction. On the other hand, the event source for an asynchronous exception is an external hardware device.

Because the term *interrupt* has been used extensively in other texts, therefore, the text that follows uses *exceptions* to mean *synchronous exceptions* and *interrupts* to mean *asynchronous exceptions*. The book uses *general exceptions* to mean both. The term *interrupts* and *external interrupts* are used interchangeably throughout the text.

Exceptions and interrupts are the necessary evils that exist in the majority of embedded systems. This facility, specific to the processor architecture, if misused, can become the source of troubled designs. While exceptions and interrupts introduce challenging design complications and impose strict coding requirements, they are nearly indispensable in embedded applications. The following sections describe the most common and important uses of these mechanisms.

10.3 Applications of Exceptions and Interrupts

From an application's perspective, exceptions and external interrupts provide a facility for embedded hardware (either internal or external to the processor) to gain the attention of application code. Interrupts are a means of communicating between the hardware and an application currently running on an embedded processor.

In general, exceptions and interrupts help the embedded engineer in three areas:

- internal errors and special conditions management,
- hardware concurrency, and
- service requests management.

10.3.1 Internal Errors and Special Conditions Management

Handling and appropriately recovering from a wide range of errors without coming to a halt is often necessary in the application areas in which embedded systems are typically employed.

Exceptions are either error conditions or special conditions that the processor detects while executing instructions. Error conditions can occur for a variety of reasons. The embedded system might be implementing an algorithm, for example, to calculate heat exchange or velocity for a cruise control. If some unanticipated condition occurs that causes a division by zero, overflow, or other math error, the application must be warned. In this case, the execution of the task performing the calculation halts, and a special exception service routine begins. This process gives the application an opportunity to evaluate and appropriately handle the error. Other types of errors include memory read or write failures (a common symptom of a stray pointer), or attempts to access floating-point hardware when not installed.

Many processor architectures have two modes of execution: normal and privileged. Some instructions, called *privileged instructions*, are allowed to execute only when the processor is in the privileged execution mode. An exception is raised when a privileged instruction is issued while the processor is in normal execution mode.

Special conditions are exceptions that are generated by special instructions, such as the TRAP instruction on the Motorola 68K processor family. These instructions allow a program to force the processor to move into privileged execution mode, consequently gaining access to a privileged instruction set. For example, the instruction used to disable external interrupts must be issued in privileged mode.

Another example of a special condition is the trace exception generated by the break point feature available on many processor architectures. The debugger agent, a special software program running on the embedded device, handles this exception, which makes using a host debugger to perform software break point and code stepping possible.

Although not all microcontrollers or embedded processors define the same types of exceptions or handle them in the same way, an exception facility is available and can assist the embedded systems engineer design a controlled response to these internal errors and special conditions.

10.3.2 Hardware Concurrency and Service Request Management

The ability to perform different types of work simultaneously is important in embedded systems. Many external hardware devices can perform device-specific operations in parallel to the core processor. These devices require minimum intervention from the core processor. The key to concurrency is knowing when the device has completed the work previously issued so that additional jobs can be given. External interrupts are used to achieve this goal.

For example, an embedded application running on a core processor issues work commands to a device. The embedded application continues execution, performing other functions while the device tries to complete the work issued. After the work is complete, the device triggers an external interrupt to the core processor, which indicates that the device is now ready to accept more commands. This method of hardware concurrency and use of external interrupts is common in embedded design.

Another use of external interrupts is to provide a communication mechanism to signal or alert an embedded processor that an external hardware device is requesting service. For example, an initialized programmable interval timer chip communicates with the embedded processor through an interrupt when a preprogrammed time interval has expired. (Chapter 11 discusses programmable interval timers in detail.) Similarly, the network interface device uses an interrupt to indicate the arrival of packets after the received packets have been stored into memory.

The capabilities of exceptions and their close cousins, external interrupts, empower embedded designs. Applying the general exception facility to an embedded design, however, requires properly handling general exceptions according to the source and associated cause of each particular general exception in question. The following section provides the needed background knowledge.

10.4 A Closer Look at Exceptions and Interrupts

General exceptions have classifications and are prioritized based on the classifications. It is possible there exists another level of priorities, imposed and enforced by the interrupt hardware, among the external interrupts. Understanding the hardware sources that can trigger general exceptions, the hardware that implements the transfer of control, and the mechanisms for determining where control vectors reside are all critical to properly installing general exception handlers and to writing correct general exception handlers.

10.4.1 Programmable Interrupt Controllers and External Interrupts

Most embedded designs have more than one source of external interrupts, and these multiple external interrupt sources are prioritized. To understand how this process is handled, a clear understanding of the concept of a *programmable interrupt controller* (PIC) is required.

The PIC is implementation-dependent. It can appear in a variety of forms and is sometimes given different names, however, all serve the same purpose and provide two main functionalities:

- Prioritizing multiple interrupt sources so that at any time the highest priority interrupt is presented to the core CPU for processing.
- Offloading the core CPU with the processing required to determine an interrupt's exact source.

The PIC has a set of interrupt request lines. An external source generates interrupts by asserting a physical signal on the interrupt request line. Each interrupt request line has a priority assigned to it. Figure 10.1 illustrates a PIC used in conjunction with four interrupt sources. Each interrupt source connects to one distinct interrupt request line: the airbag deployment sensor, the break deployment sensor, the fuel-level sensor detecting the amount of gasoline in the system, and a real-time clock.

Figure 10.1 translates into an interrupt table that captures this information more concisely. The *interrupt table* lists all available interrupts in the embedded system. In addition, several other properties help define the dynamic characteristics of the interrupt source. Table 10.1 is an example of an interrupt table for the hypothetical example shown in Figure 10.1. The information in the table illustrates all of the sources of external interrupts that the embedded system must handle.

Why is it important to know this information? Understanding the priorities of the interrupt sources enables the embedded systems programmer to better understand the concept of *nested interrupts*. The term refers to the ability of a higher priority interrupt source to preempt the processing of a lower priority interrupt. It is easy to see how low-priority interrupt sources are affected by higher priority interrupts and their execution times and frequency if this interrupt table is ordered by overall system priority. This information aids the embedded systems programmer in designing and implementing better ISRs that allow for nested interrupts.

The maximum frequency column of the interrupt table specifies the process time constraint placed on all ISRs that have the smallest impact on the overall system.

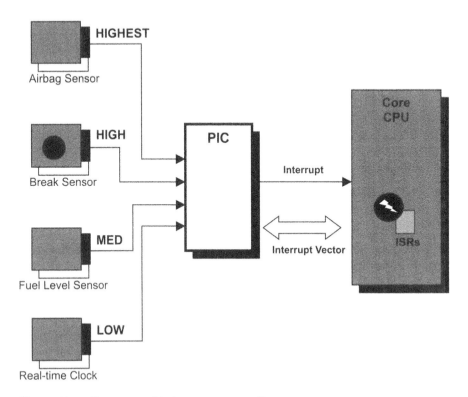

Figure 10.1 Programmable interrupt controller.

Table 10.1   Interrupt table.

Source	Priority	Vector Address	IRQ	Max Freq.	Description
Airbag Sensor	Highest	14h	8	N/A	Deploys airbag
Break Sensor	High	18h	7	N/A	Deploys the breaking system
Fuel Level Sensor	Med	1Bh	6	20Hz	Detects the level of gasoline
Real-Time Clock	Low	1Dh	5	100Hz	Clock runs at 10ms ticks

The vector address column specifies where in memory the ISR must be installed. The processor automatically fetches the instruction from one of these known addresses based on the interrupt number, which is specified in the IRQ column. This instruction begins the interrupt-specific service routine. In this example, the interrupt table contains a vector address column, but these values are dependent on processor and hardware design. In some designs, a column of indexes is applied to a formula used to calculate an actual vector address. In other designs, the processor uses a more complex formulation to obtain a vector address before fetching the instructions. Consult the hardware manual for specific details. Later sections of this chapter discuss the interrupt service routine in detail. In general, the vector table also covers the service routines for synchronous exceptions. The service routines are also called *vectors* in short.

10.4.2 Classification of General Exceptions

Although not all embedded processors implement exceptions in the same manner, most of the more recent processors have these types of exceptions:

- asynchronous—non-maskable,
- asynchronous—maskable,
- synchronous—precise, and
- synchronous—imprecise.

Asynchronous exceptions are classified into maskable and non-maskable exceptions. External interrupts are asynchronous exceptions. Asynchronous exceptions that can be blocked or enabled by software are called *maskable exceptions*. Similarly, asynchronous exceptions that cannot be blocked by software are called *non-maskable exceptions*. Non-maskable exceptions are always acknowledged by the processor and processed immediately. Hardware-reset exceptions are always non-maskable exceptions. Many embedded processors have a dedicated non-maskable interrupt (NMI) request line. Any device connected to the NMI request line is allowed to generate an NMI.

External interrupts, with the exception of NMIs, are the only asynchronous exceptions that can be disabled by software.

Synchronous exceptions can be classified into precise and imprecise exceptions. With *precise exceptions*, the processor's program counter points to the exact instruction that caused the exception, which is the *offending instruction*, and the processor knows where to resume execution upon return from the exception. With modern architectures that incorporate instruction and data pipelining, exceptions are raised to the processor in the order of written instruction, not in the order of execution. In particular, the architecture ensures that the instructions that follow the offending instruction and that were started in the instruction pipeline during the exception do not affect the CPU state. This chapter is concerned with precise exceptions.

Silicon vendors employ a number of advanced techniques (such as predictive instruction and data loading, instruction and data pipelining, and caching mechanisms) to streamline overall execution in order to increase chip performance. For example, the processor can do floating point and integer memory operations out of order with the non-sequential memory access mode. If an embedded processor implements heavy pipelining or pre-fetch algorithms, it can often be impossible to determine the exact instruction and associated data that caused an exception. This issue indicates an *imprecise exception*. Consequently, when some exceptions do occur, the reported program counter does not point to the offending instruction, which makes the program counter meaningless to the exception handler.

Why is it important to know this information? Knowing the type of exception for which an exception handler is written helps the programmer determine how the system is to recover from the exception, if the exception is at all recoverable.

10.4.3 General Exception Priorities

All processors handle exceptions in a defined order. Although not every silicon vendor uses the exact same order of exception processing, generally exceptions are handled according to these priorities, as shown in Table 10.2.

Table 10.2   Exception priorities.

Highest	Asynchronous	Non-maskable
↓	Synchronous	Precise
	Synchronous	Imprecise
Lowest	Asynchronous	Maskable

The highest priority level of exceptions is usually reserved for system resets, other significant events, or errors that warrant the overall system to reset. In many cases, hardware implementations for this exception also cause much, if not all, of the surrounding hardware to reset to a known state and condition. For this reason, this exception is treated as the highest level.

The next two priority levels reflect a set of errors and special execution conditions internal to the processor. A synchronous exception is generated and acknowledged only at certain states of the internal processor cycle. The sources of these errors are rooted in either the instructions or data that is passed along to be processed.

Typically, the lowest priority is an asynchronous exception external to the core processor. External interrupts (except NMIs) are the only exceptions that can be disabled by software.

From an application point of view, all exceptions have processing priority over operating system objects, including tasks, queues, and semaphores. Figure 10.2 illustrates a general priority framework observed in most embedded computing architectures.

10.5 Processing General Exceptions

Having introduced the fundamentals of exceptions and external interrupts, it is time to discuss processing exceptions and external interrupts. The overall exception handling

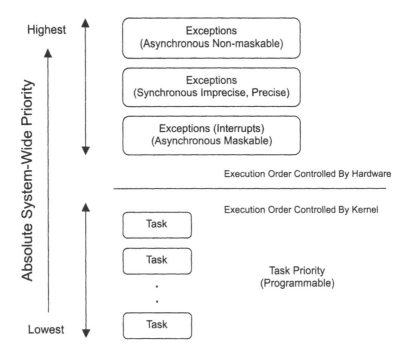

Figure 10.2   System-wide priority scheme.

mechanism is similar to the mechanism for interrupt handling. In a simplified view, the processor takes the following steps when an exception or an external interrupt is raised:

- Save the current processor state information.
- Load the exception or interrupt handling function into the program counter.
- Transfer control to the handler function and begin execution.
- Restore the processor state information after the handler function completes.
- Return from the exception or interrupt and resume previous execution.

A typical handler function does the following:

- Switch to an exception frame or an interrupt stack.
- Save additional processor state information.
- Mask the current interrupt level but allow higher priority interrupts to occur.
- Perform a minimum amount of work so that a dedicated task can complete the main processing.

10.5.1 Installing Exception Handlers

Exception service routines (ESRs) and interrupt service routines (ISRs) must be installed into the system before exceptions and interrupts can be handled. The installation of an ESR or ISR requires knowledge of the exception and interrupt table (called the *general exception table*).

The general exception table, as exemplified in Table 10.1, has a vector address column, which is sometimes also called the *vector table*. Each vector address points to the beginning of an ESR or ISR. Installing an ESR or ISR requires replacing the appropriate vector table entry with the address of the desired ESR or ISR.

The embedded system startup code typically installs the ESRs at the time of system initialization. Hardware device drivers typically install the appropriate ISRs at the time of driver initialization.

If either an exception or an interrupt occurs when no associated handler function is installed, the system suffers a system fault and may halt. To prevent this problem, it is common for an embedded RTOS to install default handler functions (i.e., functions that perform small amounts of work to ensure the proper reception of and the proper return from exceptions) into the vector table for every possible exception and interrupt in the system. Many RTOSes provide a mechanism that the embedded systems programmer can use to overwrite the default handler function with his or her own or to allow the programmer to insert further processing in addition to the default actions. If allowed, the embedded systems programmer can code specific actions before and after the default action is completed.

In this book, the general term *service routine* means either an ESR or an ISR when the distinction is not important.

10.5.2 Saving Processor States

When an exception or interrupt comes into context and before invoking the service routine, the processor must perform a set of operations to ensure a proper return of program execution after the service routine is complete. Just as tasks save information in task control blocks, exception and interrupt service routines also need to store blocks of information, called *processor state information*, somewhere in memory. The processor typically saves a minimum amount of its state information, including the status register (SR) that contains the current processor execution status bits and the program counter (PC) that contains the returning address, which is the instruction to resume execution after the exception. The ESR or the ISR, however, must do more to preserve more complete state information in order to properly resume the program execution that the exception preempted. A later section discusses this issue in more detail.

So, whose stack is used during the exception and interrupt processing?

As Chapter 5 discusses, in an embedded operating system environment, all task objects have a task control block (TCB). During task creation, a block of memory is reserved as

Stacks are used for the storage requirement of saving processor state information. In an embedded operating system environment, a *stack* is a statically reserved block of memory and an active dynamic pointer called a *stack pointer*, as shown in Figure 10.3. In some embedded architectures, such as Motorola's 68000 microprocessors, two separate stacks—the *user stack* (USP) and the *supervisor stack* (SSP)—are used. The USP is used when the processor executes in non-privileged mode. The SSP is used when the processor executes in privileged mode.

Section 10.3.1, "Internal Errors and Special Conditions Management" on page 145, discusses processor execution modes. On this type of architecture, the processor consciously selects SSP to store its state information during general exception handling. While some architectures offer special support for stack switching, the balance of this chapter assumes a simple environment with just one run-time stack.

As data is saved on the stack, the stack pointer is incremented to reflect the number of bytes copied onto the stack. This process is often called *pushing values on the stack*. When values are copied off the stack, the stack pointer is decremented by the equivalent number of bytes copied from the stack. This process is called *popping values off the stack*. The stack pointer always points to the first valid location in order to store data onto the stack. For purposes of this book, the stack grows up; however, a stack can grow in the opposite direction. Note that a typical stack does not store identifiers for the contents. Stack users are required to push and pop items onto and off the stack in a symmetric order. If this rule is not followed during exception or interrupt processing, unintended results are likely to occur.

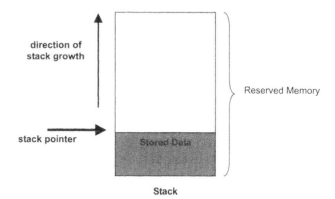

Figure 10.3   Store processor state information onto stack.

a stack for task use, as shown in Figure 10.4. High-level programming languages, such as C and C++, typically use the stack space as the primary vehicle to pass variables between functions and objects of the language.

The active stack pointer (SP) is reinitialized to that of the active task each time a task context switch occurs. The underlying real-time kernel performs this work. As mentioned earlier, the processor uses whichever stack the SP points to for storing its minimum state information before invoking the exception handler.

Figure 10.4 Task TCB and stack.

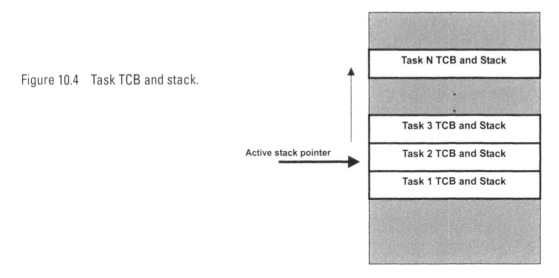

Although not all embedded architectures implement exception or interrupt processing in the same way, the general idea of sizing and reserving exception stack space is the same. In many cases, when general exceptions occur and a task is running, the task's stack is used to handle the exception or interrupt. If a lower priority ESR or ISR is running at the time of exception or interrupt, whichever stack the ESR or ISR is using is also the stack used to handle the new exception or interrupt. This default approach on stack usage can be problematic with nested exceptions or interrupts, which are discussed in detail shortly.

10.5.3 Loading and Invoking Exception Handlers

As discussed earlier, some differences exist between an ESR and an ISR in the precursory work the processor performs. This issue is caused by the fact that an external interrupt is the only exception type that can be disabled by software. In many embedded processor architectures, external interrupts can be disabled or enabled through a processor control register. This control register directly controls the operation of the PIC and determines which interrupts the PIC raises to the processor. In these architectures, all external interrupts are raised to the PIC. The PIC filters interrupts according to the setting of the control register and determines the necessary action. This book assumes this architecture model in the following discussions.

Formally speaking, an interrupt can be disabled, active, or pending. A *disabled interrupt* is also called a *masked interrupt*. The PIC ignores a disabled interrupt. A *pending interrupt* is an unacknowledged interrupt, which occurs when the processor is currently processing a higher priority interrupt. The pending interrupt is acknowledged and processed after all higher priority interrupts that were pending have been processed. An *active interrupt* is the one that the processor is acknowledging and processing. Being aware of

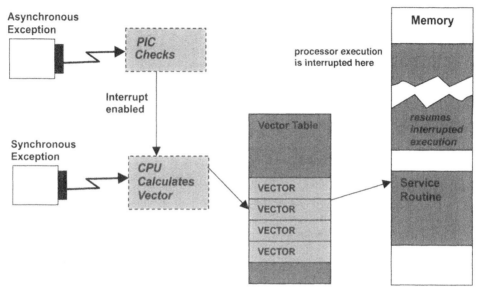

Figure 10.5   Loading exception vector.

the existence of a pending interrupt and raising this interrupt to the processor at the appropriate time is accomplished through hardware and is outside the concern of an embedded systems developer.

For synchronous exceptions, the processor first determines which exception has occurred and then calculates the correct index into the vector table to retrieve the ESR. This calculation is dependent on implementation. When an asynchronous exception occurs, an extra step is involved. The PIC must determine if the interrupt has been disabled (or masked). If so, the PIC ignores the interrupt and the processor execution state is not affected. If the interrupt is not masked, the PIC raises the interrupt to the processor and the processor calculates the interrupt vector address and then loads the exception vector for execution, as shown in Figure 10.5.

Some silicon vendors implement the table lookup in hardware, while others rely on software approaches. Regardless, the mechanisms are the same. When an exception occurs, a value or index is calculated for the table. The content of the table at this index or offset reflects the address of a service routine. The program counter is initialized with this vector address, and execution begins at this location. Before examining the general approach to an exception handler, let's first examine nested interrupts and their effect on the stack.

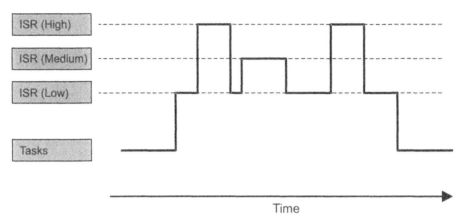

Figure 10.6   Interrupt nesting.

10.5.4 Nested Exceptions and Stack Overflow

Nested exceptions refer to the ability for higher priority exceptions to preempt the processing of lower priority exceptions. Much like a context switch for tasks when a higher priority one becomes ready, the lower priority exception is preempted, which allows the higher priority ESR to execute. When the higher priority service routine is complete, the earlier running service routine returns to execution. Figure 10.6 illustrates this process.

The task block in the diagram in this example shows a group of tasks executing. A low-priority interrupt then becomes active, and the associated service routine comes into context. While this service routine is running, a high-priority interrupt becomes active, and the lower priority service routine is preempted. The high-priority service routine runs to completion, and control returns to the low-priority service routine. Before the low-priority service routine completes, another interrupt becomes active. As before, the low-priority service routine is preempted to allow the medium-priority service routine to complete. Again, before the low-priority routine can finish, another high-priority interrupt becomes active and runs to completion. The low-priority service routine is finally able to run to completion. At that point, the previously running task can resume execution.

When interrupts can nest, the application stack must be large enough to accommodate the maximum requirements for the application's own nested function invocation, as well as the maximum exception or interrupt nesting possible, if the application executes with interrupts enabled. This issue is exactly where the effects of interrupt nesting on the application stack are most commonly observed.

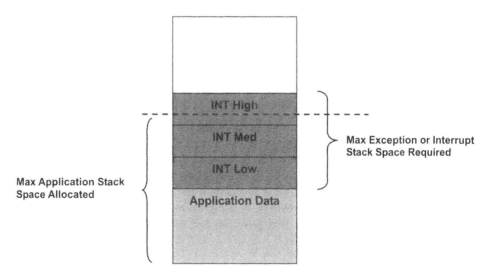

Figure 10.7   Nested interrupts and stack overflow.

As exemplified in Figure 10.4, N tasks have been created, each with its own TCB and statically allocated stack. Assuming the stack of the executing task is used for exceptions, a sample scenario, as shown in Figure 10.7, might look as follows:

1. Task 2 is currently running.
2. A low-priority interrupt is received.
3. Task 2 is preempted while exception processing starts for a low-priority interrupt.
4. The stack grows to handle exception processing storage needs.
5. A medium-priority interrupt is received before exception processing is complete.
6. The stack grows again to handle medium-priority interrupt processing storage requirements.
7. A high-priority interrupt is received before execution processing of the medium interrupt is complete.
8. The stack grows to handle high-priority interrupt processing storage needs.

In each case of exception processing, the size of the stack grows as has been discussed. Note that without a MMU, no bounds checking is performed when using a stack as a storage medium. As depicted in this example, the sum of the application stack space requirement and the exception stack space requirement is less than the actual stack space allocated by Task 2. Consequently, when data is copied onto the stack past the statically defined limits in this example, Task 3's TCB is corrupted, which is a *stack overflow*. Unfortunately, the corrupted TCB is not likely to be noticed until Task 3 is scheduled to run. These types of errors can be very hard to detect. They are a function of the combination of the running task and the exact frequency, timing, and sequence of interrupts or exceptions presented to the operating environment. This situation often gives a user or testing team the sense of a sporadic or flaky system. Sometimes, dependably recreating errors is almost impossible.

Two solutions to the problem are available: increasing the application's stack size to accommodate all possibilities and the deepest levels of exception and interrupt nesting, or having the ESR or ISR switch to its own exception stack, called an *exception frame*.

The maximum exception stack size is a direct function of the number of exceptions, the number of external devices connected to each distinct IRQ line, and the priority levels supported by the PIC. The simple solution is having the application allocate a large enough stack space to accommodate the worst case, which is if the lowest priority exception handler executes and is preempted by all higher priority exceptions or interrupts. A better approach, however, is using an independent exception frame inside the ESR or the ISR. This approach requires far less total memory than increasing every task stack by the necessary amount.

10.5.5 Exception Handlers

After control is transferred to the exception handler, the ESR or the ISR performs the actual work of exception processing. Usually the exception handler has two parts. The first part executes in the exception or interrupt context. The second half executes in a task context.

Exception Frames

The *exception frame* is also called the *interrupt stack* in the context of asynchronous exceptions.

Two main reasons exist for needing an exception frame. One reason is to handle nested exceptions. The other reason is that, as embedded architecture becomes more complex, the ESR or ISR consequently increases in complexity. Commonly, exception handlers are written in both machine assembly language and in a high-level programming language, such as C or C++. As mentioned earlier, the portion of the ESR or ISR written in C or C++ requires a stack to which to pass function parameters during invocation. This fact is also true if the ESR or ISR were to invoke a library function written in a high-level language.

The common approach to the exception frame is for the ESR or the ISR to allocate a block of memory, either statically or dynamically, before installing itself into the system. The exception handler then saves the current stack pointer into temporary memory storage, reinitializes the stack pointer to this private stack, and begins processing. This is depicted in Figure 10.8.

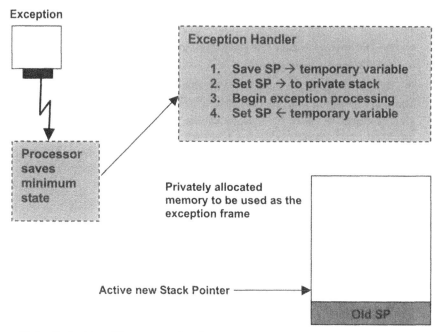

Figure 10.8   Switching SP to exception frame.

The exception handler can perform more housekeeping work, such as storing additional processor state information, onto this stack.

Differences between ESR and ISR

One difference between an ESR and an ISR is in the additional processor state information saved.

The three ways of masking interrupts are:

- Disable the device so that it cannot assert additional interrupts. Interrupts at all levels can still occur.
- Mask the interrupts of equal or lower priority levels, while allowing higher priority interrupts to occur. The device can continue to generate interrupts, but the processor ignores them.
- Disable the global system-wide interrupt request line to the processor (the line between the PIC and the core processor), as exemplified in Figure 10.1. Interrupts of any priority level do not reach the processor. This step is equivalent to masking interrupts of the highest priority level.

An ISR would typically deploy one of these three methods to disable interrupts for one or all of these reasons:

- the ISR tries to reduce the total number of interrupts raised by the device,
- the ISR is non-reentrant, and
- the ISR needs to perform some atomic operations.

Some processor architectures keep the information on which interrupts or interrupt levels are disabled inside the system status register. Other processor architectures use an interrupt mask register (IMR). Therefore, an ISR needs to save the current IMR onto the stack and disable interrupts according to its own requirements by setting new mask values into the IMR. The IMR only applies to maskable asynchronous exceptions and, therefore, is not saved by synchronous exception routines.

One other related difference between an ESR and an ISR is that an exception handler in many cases cannot prevent other exceptions from occurring, while an ISR can prevent interrupts of the same or lower priority from occurring.

Exception Timing

Discussions about the ESR or ISR, however, often mention keeping the ESR or ISR short. How so and how short should it be? To answer this question, let's focus the discussion on the external interrupts and the ISR.

It is the hardware designer's job to use the proper interrupt priority at the PIC level, but it is the ISR programmer's responsibility to know the timing requirements of each device when an ISR runs with either the same level or all interrupts disabled.

The embedded systems programmer, when designing and implementing an ISR, should be aware of the interrupt frequency of each device that can assert an interrupt. Table 10.1 contains a column called Maximum Frequency, which indicates how often a device can assert an interrupt when the device operates at maximum capacity. The allowed duration for an ISR to execute with interrupts disabled without affecting the system can be inferred from Table 10.1.

Without going into detail, an ISR, when executing with interrupts disabled, can cause the system to miss interrupts if the ISR takes too long. *Interrupt miss* is the situation in which an interrupt is asserted but the processor could not record the occurrence due to some busy condition. The interrupt service routine, therefore, is not invoked for that particular interrupt occurrence. This issue is typically true for a device that uses the edge-triggering mechanism to assert interrupts. The edge-triggering mechanism is discussed in "The Nature of Spurious Interrupts" on page 163, section 10.6.

The RTOS kernel scheduler cannot run when an ISR disables all system interrupts while it runs. As indicated earlier, interrupt processing has higher priority than task processing. Therefore, real-time tasks that have stringent deadlines can also be affected by a poorly designed ISR.

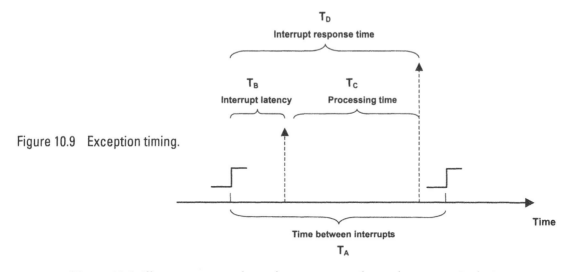

Figure 10.9   Exception timing.

Figure 10.9 illustrates a number of concepts as they relate to a single interrupt. In Figure 10.9, the value of T_A is based on the device interrupt frequency.

The interrupt latency, T_B, refers to the interval between the time when the interrupt is raised and the time when the ISR begins to execute. Interrupt latency is attributed to:

- The amount of time it takes the processor to acknowledge the interrupt and perform the initial housekeeping work.
- A higher priority interrupt is active at the time.
- The interrupt is disabled and then later re-enabled by software.

The first case is always a contributing factor to interrupt latency. As can be seen, interrupt latency can be unbounded. Therefore, the response time can also be unbounded. The interrupt latency is outside the control of the ISR. The processing time T_C, however, is determined by how the ISR is implemented.

The interrupt response time is $T_D = T_B + T_C$.

It is possible for the entire processing to be done within the context of the interrupt, that is, with interrupts disabled. Notice, however, that the processing time for a higher priority interrupt is a source of interrupt latency for the lower priority interrupt. Another approach is to have one section of ISR running in the context of the interrupt and another section running in the context of a task. The first section of the ISR code services the device so that the service request is acknowledged and the device is put into a known operational state so it can resume operation. This portion of the ISR packages the device service request and sends it to the remaining section of the ISR that executes within the context of a task. This latter part of the ISR is typically implemented as a dedicated daemon task.

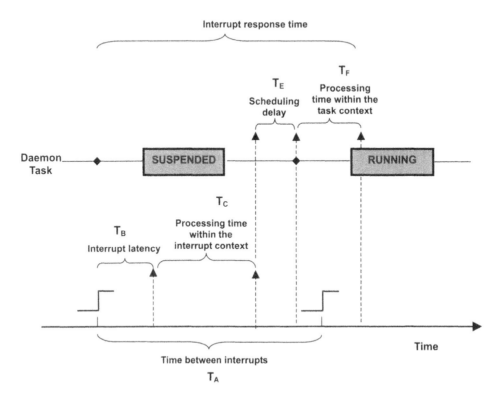

Figure 10.10 Interrupt processing in two contexts.

There are two main reasons to partition the ISR into two pieces. One is to reduce the processing time within the interrupt context. The other is a bit more complex in that the architecture treats the interrupt as having higher priority than a running task, but in practice that might not be the case. For example, if the device that controls the blinking of an LED reports a failure, it is definitely lower in priority than a task that must send a communication reply to maintain its connection with the peer. If the ISR for this particular interrupt were partitioned into two sections, the daemon task that continues the LED interrupt processing can have a lower task priority than the other task. This factor allows the other higher priority task to complete with limited impact. Figure 10.10 illustrates this concept.

The benefits to this concept are the following:

- Lower priority interrupts can be handled with less priority than more critical tasks running in the system.
- This approach reduces the chance of missing interrupts.

- This approach affords more concurrency because devices are being serviced minimally so that they can continue operations while their previous requests are accumulated without loss to the extent allowed by the system.

On the other hand, the interrupt response time increases, because now the interrupt response time is $T_D = T_B + T_C + T_E + T_F$. The increase in response time is attributed to the scheduling delay, and the daemon task might have to yield to higher priority tasks.

The scheduling delay happens when other higher priority tasks are either running or are scheduled to run. The scheduling delay also includes the amount of time needed to perform a context switch after the daemon task is moved from the ready queue to the run queue.

In conclusion, the duration of the ISR running in the context of the interrupt depends on the number of interrupts and the frequency of each interrupt source existing in the system. Although general approaches to designing an ISR exist, no one solution exists to implement an ISR so that it works in all embedded designs. Rather the embedded systems developer must design an ISR according to the considerations discussed in this section.

General Guides

On architectures where interrupt nesting is allowed:

- An ISR should disable interrupts of the same level if the ISR is non-reentrant.
- An ISR should mask all interrupts if it needs to execute a sequence of code as one atomic operation.
- An ISR should avoid calling non-reentrant functions. Some standard library functions are non-reentrant, such as many implementations of `malloc` and `printf`. Because interrupts can occur in the middle of task execution and because tasks might be in the midst of the "`malloc`" function call, the resulting behavior can be catastrophic if the ISR calls this same non-reentrant function.
- An ISR must never make any blocking or suspend calls. Making such a call might halt the entire system.

If an ISR is partitioned into two sections with one section being a daemon task, the daemon task does not have a high priority by default. The priority should be set with respect to the rest of the system.

10.6 The Nature of Spurious Interrupts

A *spurious interrupt* is a signal of very short duration on one of the interrupt input lines, and it is likely caused by a signal glitch.

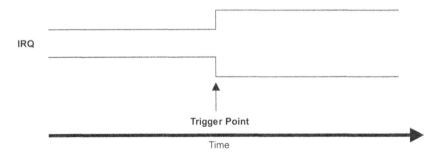

Figure 10.11 Edge triggering on either rising or falling edge.

An external device uses a triggering mechanism to raise interrupts to the core processor. Two types of triggering mechanisms are *level triggering* and *edge triggering*. Figure 10.11 illustrates the variants of edge triggers (rising edge or falling edge). This kind of triggering is typically used with a digital signal.

In contrast, level triggering is commonly used in conjunction with an analog signal. Figure 10.12 illustrates how level triggering might be implemented in a design. It is important to note that when using level triggering, the PIC or microcontroller silicon typically defines the trigger threshold value.

How do spurious interrupts occur? In real-world situations, digital and analog signals are not as clean as portrayed here. The environment, types of sensors or transducers, and the method in which wiring is laid out in an embedded design all have a considerable effect on how clean the signal might appear. For example, a digital signal from a switch might require debouncing, or an analog signal might need filtering. Figure 10.13 provides a good illustration of how both digital and analog signals can really look. While electronic methods for debouncing and filtering fall beyond the realm of this book, it is important nonetheless to understand that input signals, whether for interrupts or other inputs, might not be as clean as a developer might envision them. These signals, therefore, can represent a potential source for sporadic behavior.

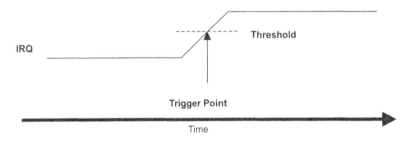

Figure 10.12 Level triggering.

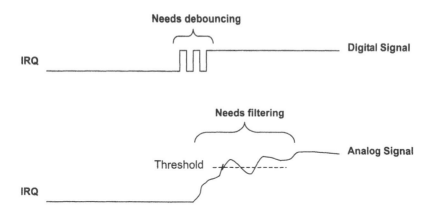

Figure 10.13 Real signals.

As can be seen, one reason for the occurrence of spurious interrupts is unstableness of the interrupt signal. Spurious interrupts can be caused when the processor detects errors while processing an interrupt request. The embedded systems programmer must be aware of spurious interrupts and know that spurious interrupts can occur and that this type of interrupt must be handled as any other type of interrupts. The default action from the kernel is usually sufficient.

10.7 Points to Remember

Some points to remember include the following:

- Exceptions are classified into synchronous and asynchronous exceptions.
- Exceptions are prioritized.
- External interrupts belong to the category of asynchronous exceptions.
- External interrupts are the only exceptions that can be disabled by software.
- Exceptions can be nested.
- Using a dedicated exception frame is one solution to solving the stack overflow problem that nested exceptions cause.
- Exception processing should consider the overall timing requirements of the system devices and tasks.
- Spurious interrupts can occur and should be handled as any other interrupts.

In this chapter...

- Real-Time Clocks and System Clocks 168
- Programmable Interval Timers. 169
- Timer Interrupt Service Routines. 171
- A Model for Implementing the Soft-Timer
  Handling Facility. 171
- Timing Wheels. 176
- Soft Timers and Timer Related Operations 182
- Points to Remember 185

CHAPTER 11

TIMER AND TIMER SERVICES

11.1 Introduction

In embedded systems, system tasks and user tasks often schedule and perform activities after some time has elapsed. For example, a RTOS scheduler must perform a context switch of a preset time interval periodically—among tasks of equal priorities—to ensure execution fairness when conducting a round-robin scheduling algorithm. A software-based memory refresh mechanism must refresh the dynamic memory every so often or data loss will occur. In embedded networking devices, various communication protocols schedule activities for data retransmission and protocol recovery. The target monitor software sends system information to the host-based analysis tool periodically to provide system-timing diagrams for visualization and debugging.

In any case, embedded applications need to schedule future events. Scheduling future activities is accomplished through timers using timer services.

Timers are an integral part of many real-time embedded systems. A *timer* is the scheduling of an event according to a predefined time value in the future, similar to setting an alarm clock.

A complex embedded system is comprised of many different software modules and components, each requiring timers of varying timeout values. Most embedded systems use two different forms of timers to drive time-sensitive activities: hard timers and soft timers. Hard timers are derived from physical timer chips that directly interrupt the processor when they expire. Operations with demanding requirements for precision or latency need the predictable performance of a hard timer. Soft timers are software events that are scheduled through a software facility.

167

A soft-timer facility allows for efficiently scheduling of non-high-precision software events. A practical design for the soft-timer handling facility should have the following properties:

- efficient timer maintenance, i.e., counting down a timer,
- efficient timer installation, i.e., starting a timer, and
- efficient timer removal, i.e., stopping a timer.

While an application might require several high-precision timers with resolutions on the order of microseconds or even nanoseconds, not all of the time requirements have to be high precision. Even demanding applications also have some timing functions for which resolutions on the order of milliseconds, or even of hundreds of milliseconds, are sufficient. Aspects of applications requiring timeouts with course granularity (for example, with tolerance for bounded inaccuracy) should use soft timers. Examples include the Transmission Control Protocol module, the Real-time Transport Protocol module, and the Address Resolution Protocol module.

Another reason for using soft timers is to reduce system-interrupt overhead. The physical timer chip rate is usually set so that the interval between consecutive timer interrupts is within tens of milliseconds or even within tens of microseconds. The interrupt latency and overhead can be substantial and can grow with the increasing number of outstanding timers. This issue particularly occurs when each timer is implemented by being directly interfaced with the physical timer hardware.

This chapter focuses on:

- real-time clocks versus system clocks,
- programmable interval timers,
- timer interrupt service routines,
- timer-related operations,
- soft timers, and
- implementing soft-timer handling facilities.

11.2 Real-Time Clocks and System Clocks

In some references, the term *real-time clock* is interchangeable with the term *system clock*. Within the context of this book, however, these terminologies are separate, as they are different on various architectures.

Real-time clocks exist in many embedded systems and track time, date, month, and year. Commonly, they are integrated with battery-powered DRAM as shown in Figure 11.1. This integrated real-time clock becomes independent of the CPU and the programmable interval timer, making the maintenance of real time between system power cycles possible.

The job of the system clock is identical to that of the real-time clock: to track either real-time or elapsed time following system power up (depending on implementation). The initial value of the system clock is typically retrieved from the real-time clock at power up or is set by the user. The programmable interval timer drives the system clock, i.e. the system clock increments in value per timer interrupt. Therefore, an important function performed at the timer interrupt is maintaining the system clock, as shown in Figure 11.2.

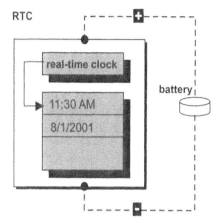

Figure 11.1   A real-time clock.

11.3 Programmable Interval Timers

The *programmable interval timer* (PIT), also known as the *timer chip*, is a device designed mainly to function as an event counter, elapsed time indicator, rate-controllable periodic event generator, as well as other applications for solving system-timing control problems.

The functionality of the PIT is commonly incorporated into the embedded processor, where it is called an *on-chip timer*. Dedicated stand-alone timer chips are available to reduce processor overhead. As different as the various timer chips can be, some general

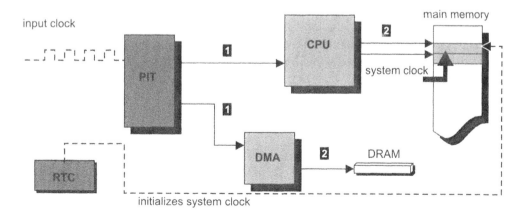

Figure 11.2   System clock initialization.

characteristics exist among them. For example, timer chips feature an input clock source with a fixed frequency, as well as a set of programmable timer control registers. The *timer interrupt rate* is the number of timer interrupts generated per second. The timer interrupt rate is calculated as a function of the input clock frequency and is set into a timer control register.

A related value is the *timer countdown value*, which determines when the next timer interrupt occurs. It is loaded in one of the timer control registers and decremented by one every input clock cycle. The remaining timer control registers determine the other modes of timer operation, such as whether periodic timer interrupts are generated and whether the countdown value should be automatically reloaded for the next timer interrupt.

Customized embedded systems come with schematics detailing the interconnection of the system components. From these schematics, a developer can determine which external components are dependent on the timer chip as the input clock source. For example, if a timer chip output pin interconnects with the control input pin of the DMA chip, the timer chip controls the DRAM refresh rate.

Timer-chip initialization is performed as part of the system startup. Generally, initialization of the timer chip involves the following steps:

- Resetting and bringing the timer chip into a known hardware state.
- Calculating the proper value to obtain the desired timer interrupt frequency and programming this value into the appropriate timer control register.
- Programming other timer control registers that are related to the earlier interrupt frequency with correct values. This step is dependent on the timer chip and is specified in detail by the timer chip hardware reference manual.
- Programming the timer chip with the proper mode of operation.
- Installing the timer interrupt service routine into the system.
- Enabling the timer interrupt.

The behavior of the timer chip output is programmable through the control registers, the most important of which is the *timer interrupt-rate register* (TINTR), which is as follows:

$$TINTR = F(x)$$

where x = frequency of the input crystal

Manufacturers of timer chips provide this function and the information is readily available in the programmer's reference manual.

The timer interrupt rate equals the number of timer interrupt occurrences per second. Each interrupt is called a *tick*, which represents a unit of time. For example, if the timer rate is 100 ticks, each tick represents an elapsed time of 10 milliseconds.

The periodic event generation capability of the PIT is important to many real-time kernels. At the heart of many real-time kernels is the announcement of the timer interrupt occurrence, or the *tick announcement*, from the ISR to the kernel, as well as to the kernel scheduler, if one exists. Many of these kernel schedulers run through their algorithms and conduct task scheduling at each tick.

11.4 Timer Interrupt Service Routines

Part of the timer chip initialization involves installing an interrupt service routine (ISR) that is called when the timer interrupt occurs. Typically, the ISR performs these duties:

- **Updating the system clock**—Both the absolute time and elapsed time is updated. *Absolute time* is time kept in calendar date, hours, minutes, and seconds. *Elapsed time* is usually kept in ticks and indicates how long the system has been running since power up.
- **Calling a registered kernel function to notify the passage of a preprogrammed period**—For the following discussion, the registered kernel function is called `announce_time_tick`.
- **Acknowledging the interrupt, reinitializing the necessary timer control register(s), and returning from interrupt.**

The `announce_time_tick` function is invoked in the context of the ISR; therefore, all of the restrictions placed on an ISR are applicable to `announce_time_tick`. In reality, `announce_time_tick` is part of the timer ISR. The `announce_time_tick` function is called to notify the kernel scheduler about the occurrence of a timer tick. Equally important is the announcement of the timer tick to the soft-timer handling facility. These concepts are illustrated in Figure 11.3.

The soft-timer handling facility is responsible for maintaining the soft timers at each timer tick.

11.5 A Model for Implementing the Soft-Timer Handling Facility

The functions performed by the soft-timer facility, called the *timer facility* from now on, include:

- allowing applications to start a timer,
- allowing applications to stop or cancel a previously installed timer, and
- internally maintaining the application timers.

The soft-timer facility is comprised of two components: one component lives within the timer tick ISR and the other component lives in the context of a task.

This approach is used for several reasons. If all of the soft-timer processing is done with the ISR and if the work spans multiple ticks (i.e., if the timer tick handler does not

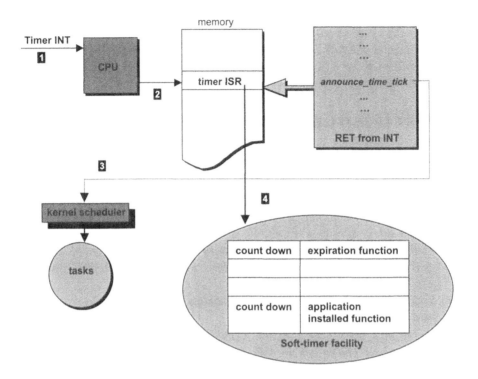

Figure 11.3   Steps in servicing the timer interrupt.

complete work before the next clock tick arrives), the system clock might appear to drift as seen by the software that tracks time. Worse, the timer tick events might be lost. Therefore, the timer tick handler must be short and must be conducting the least amount of work possible. Processing of expired soft timers is delayed into a dedicated processing task because applications using soft timers can tolerate a bounded timer inaccuracy. The *bounded timer inaccuracy* refers to the imprecision the timer may take on any value. This value is guaranteed to be within a specific range.

Therefore, a workable model for implementing a soft-timer handling facility is to create a dedicated processing task and call it a worker task, in conjunction with its counter part that is part of the system timer ISR. The ISR counterpart is given a fictitious name of ISR_timeout_fn for this discussion.

The system timer chip is programmed with a particular interrupt rate, which must accommodate various aspects of the system operation. The associated timer tick granularity is typically much smaller than the granularity required by the application-level soft timers. The ISR_timeout_fn function must work with this value and notify the worker task appropriately.

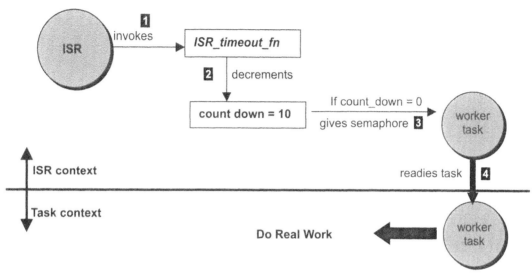

Figure 11.4   A model for soft-timer handling facility.

In the following example, assume that an application requires three soft timers. The timeout values equal 200ms, 300ms, and 500ms. The least common denominator is 100ms. If each hardware timer tick represents 10ms, then 100ms translates into a countdown value of 10. The ISR_timeout_fn keeps track of this countdown value and decrements it by one during each invocation. The ISR_timeout_fn notifies the worker task by a "give" operation on the worker task's semaphore after the countdown value reaches zero, effectively allowing the task to be scheduled for execution. The ISR_timeout_fn then reinitializes the countdown value back to 10. This concept is illustrated in Figure 11.4.

In the ISR-to-processing-task model, the worker task must maintain an application-level, timer-countdown table based on 100ms granularity. In this example, the timer table has three countdown values: 2, 3, and 5 representing the 200ms, 300ms, and the 500ms application-requested timers. An application-installed, timer-expiration function is associated with each timer. This concept is illustrated in Figure 11.5.

The three soft timers, which are simply called timers unless specified otherwise, are decremented by the worker task each time it runs. When the counter reaches zero, the application timer has expired. In this example, the 200ms timer and the associated function App_timeout_fn_1, which the application installs, is invoked. As shown in Figures 11.4 and 11.5, a single ISR-level timer drives three application timers at the task-level, providing a good reason why these timers are called soft timers. The decrease in the number of ISR timers installed improves the overall system performance.

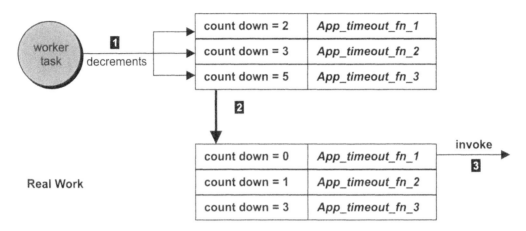

Figure 11.5   Servicing the timer interrupt in the task context.

These application-installed timers are called *soft timers* because processing is not syn-chronized with the hardware timer tick. It is a good idea to explore this concept further by examining possible delays that can occur along the delivery path of the timer tick.

11.5.1 Possible Processing Delays

The first delay is the event-driven, task-scheduling delay. As shown in the previous example, the maintenance of soft timers is part of ISR_timeout_fn and involves decre-menting the expiration time value by one. When the expiration time reaches zero, the timer expires and the associated function is invoked. Because ISR_timeout_fn is part of the ISR, it must perform the smallest amount of work possible and postpone major work to a later stage outside the context of the ISR. Typical implementations perform real work either inside a worker task that is a dedicated daemon task or within the application that originally installed the timer. The minimum amount of work completed within the ISR by the installed function involves triggering an asynchronous event to the worker task, which typically translates into the kernel call event_send, should one exist. Alternatively, the triggering can also translate into the release of a semaphore on which the worker task is currently blocked. The notification delay caused by event generation from the ISR to the daemon task is the first level of delay, as shown in Figure 11.7. Note that the hypothetical kernel function event_send and the semaphore release function must be callable from within an ISR.

The second delay is the priority-based, task-scheduling delay. In a typical RTOS, tasks can execute at different levels of execution priorities. For example, a worker task that performs timer expiration-related functions might not have the highest execution prior-ity. In a priority-based, kernel-scheduling scheme, a worker task must wait until all other higher priority tasks complete execution before being allowed to continue. With a

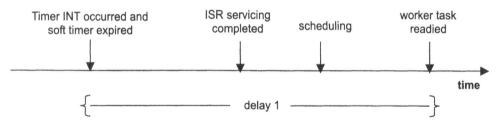

Figure 11.6   Level 1 delays—timer event notification delay.

round-robin scheduler, the worker task must wait for its scheduling cycle in order to execute. This process represents the second level of delay as shown in Figure 11.7.

Another delay is introduced when an application installs many soft timers. This issue is explored further in the next section when discussing the concept of timing wheels.

11.5.2 Implementation Considerations

A soft-timer facility should allow for efficient timer insertion, timer deletion and cancellation, and timer update. These requirements, however, can conflict with each other in practice. For example, imagine the linked list-timer implementation shown in Figure 11.8. The fastest way to start a timer is to insert it either at the head of the timer list or at the tail of the timer list if the timer entry data structure contains a double-linked list.

Because the timer list is not sorted in any particular order, maintaining timer ticks can prove costly. Updating the timer list at each tick requires the worker task to traverse the entire linked list and update each timer entry. When the counter reaches zero, the callout function is invoked. A timer handle is returned to the application in a successful timer installation. The cancellation of a timer also requires the worker task to traverse the entire list. Each timer entry is compared to the timer handle, and, when a match is found, that particular timer entry is removed from the timer list.

As shown in Figure 11.9, while timer installation can be performed in constant time, timer cancellation and timer update might require $O(N)$ in the worst case.

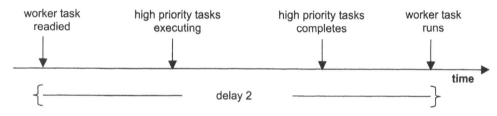

Figure 11.7   Level 2 delays—priority-based, task-scheduling delays.

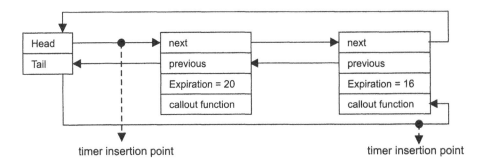

Figure 11.8   Maintaining soft timers.

Sorting expiration times in ascending order results in efficient timer bookkeeping. In the example, only the first timer-entry update is necessary, because all the other timers are decremented implicitly. In other words, when inserting new timers, the timeout value is modified according to the first entry before inserting the timer into the list.

As shown in Figure 11.10, while timer bookkeeping is performed in constant time, timer installation requires search and insertion. The cost is $O(\log(N))$, where N is the number of entries in the timer list. The cost of timer cancellation is also $O(\log(N))$.

11.6 Timing Wheels

As shown in Figure 11.11, the *timing wheel* is a construct with a fixed-size array in which each slot represents a unit of time with respect to the precision of the soft-timer

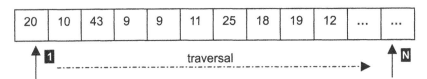

Figure 11.9   Unsorted soft timers.

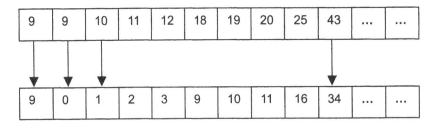

Figure 11.10 Sorted soft timers.

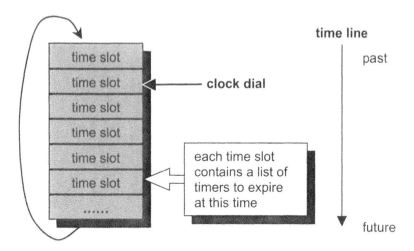

Figure 11.11 Timing wheel.

facility. The timing wheel approach has the advantage of the sorted timer list for updating the timers efficiently, and it also provides efficient operations for timer installation and cancellation.

The soft-timer facility installs a periodic timeout (a clock tick) using the underlying timer hardware. This hardware-based periodic timer, drives all of the soft timers installed within the facility. The frequency of the timeout determines the precision of the soft-timer facility. For example, if the precision defines a tick occurrence every 50ms, each slot represents the passing of 50ms, which is the smallest timeout that can be installed into the timer facility. In addition, a doubly linked list of timeout event handlers (also named *callback functions* or *callbacks* for short) is stored within each slot, which is invoked upon timer expiration. This list of timers represents events with the same expiration time.

Each timer slot is represented in Figure 11.12.

The clock dial increments to the next time slot on each tick and wraps to the beginning of the time-slot array when it increments past the final array entry. The idea of the timing wheel is derived from this property. Therefore, when installing a new timer event, the current location of the clock dial is used as the reference point to determine the time slot

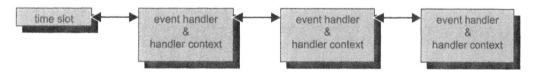

Figure 11.12 Timeout event handlers.

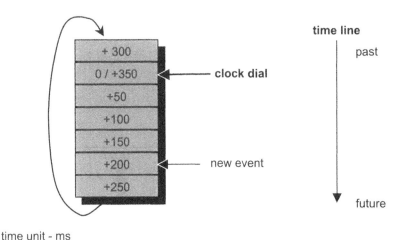

time unit - ms

Figure 11.13 Installing a timeout event.

in which the new event handler will be stored. Consider the following example as depicted in Figure 11.13. Assume each time slot represents the passing of 50ms, which means that 50ms has elapsed between ticks.

The time slot marked *+200* is the slot in which to store an event handler if the developer wants to schedule a 200ms timeout in the future. The location of the clock dial is the "beginning of time" on the time line, in other words, the reference point. At a minimum, the timer handle returned to the calling application is the array index.

11.6.1 Issues

A number of issues are associated with the timing wheel approach. The number of slots in the timing wheel has a limit, whatever that might be for the system. The example in Figure 11.13 makes this problem obvious. The maximum schedulable event is 350ms. How can a 400ms timer be scheduled? This issue causes an overflow condition in the timing wheel. One approach is to deny installation of timers outside the fixed range. A better solution is to accumulate the events causing the overflow condition in a temporary event buffer until the clock dial has turned enough so that these events become schedulable. This solution is illustrated in Figure 11.14.

For example, in order to schedule a 400ms timeout when the clock dial is at location 1, this event must be saved in the event overflow buffer until the clock dial reaches location 2. To schedule a 500ms timer when clock dial is at location 1, this event must be saved in the event overflow buffer until the clock dial reaches location 3. The expired events at location 2 and location 3 must be serviced first, and then the new events installed. The event overflow buffer must be examined to see if new events need to be scheduled when the clock dial moves at each clock tick to the next slot. This process

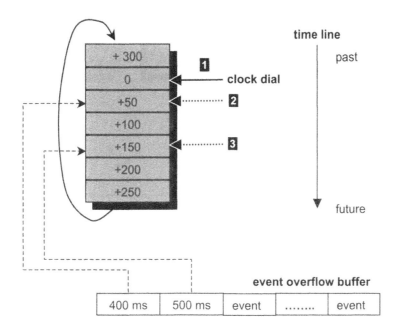

Figure 11.14 Timing wheel overflow event buffer.

implies that the events in the overflow buffer must be sorted in increasing order. New events are inserted in order and can be expensive if the overflow buffer contains a large number of entries.

Another issue associated with the timing wheel approach is the precision of the installed timeouts. Consider the situation in which a 150ms timer event is being scheduled while the clock is ticking but before the tick announcement reaches the timing wheel. Should the timer event be added to the +150ms slot or placed in the +200ms slot? On average, the error is approximately half the size of the tick. In this example, the error is about 25ms.

One other important issue relates to the invocation time of the callbacks installed at each time slot. In theory, the callbacks should all be invoked at the same time at expiration, but in reality, this is impossible. The work performed by each callback is unknown; therefore, the execution length of each callback is unknown. Consequently, no guarantee or predictable measures exist concerning when a callback in a later position of the list can be called, even in a worst-case scenario. This issue introduces non-determinism into the system and is undesirable. Figure 11.15 illustrates the problem.

Event handler 1 is invoked at $t1$ when the timeout has just expired. Similarly, event handler n is invoked at tn when the previous $(n–1)$ event handlers have finished execution. The interval x and y is non-deterministic because the length of execution of each handler is unknown. These intervals are also unbounded.

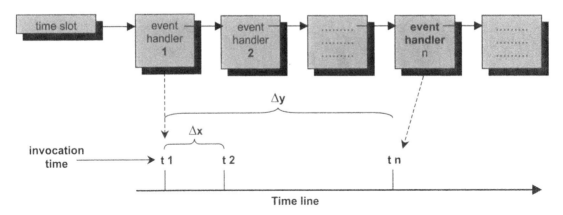

Figure 11.15 Unbounded soft-timer handler invocation.

Ideally, the timer facility could guarantee an upper bound; for example, regardless of the number of timers already installed in the system, event handler *n* is invoked no later than 200ms from the actual expiration time.

This problem is difficult, and the solution is application specific.

11.6.2 Hierarchical Timing Wheels

The timer overflow problem presented in the last section can be solved using the *hierarchical timing wheel* approach.

The soft-timer facility needs to accommodate timer events spanning a range of values. This range can be very large. For example accommodating timers ranging from 100ms to 5 minutes requires a timing wheel with 3,000 ($5 \times 60 \times 10$) entries. Because the timer facility needs to have a granularity of at least 100ms and there is a single array representing the timing wheel,

$10 \times 100\text{ms} = 1 \text{ sec}$
10 entries/sec

$60 \text{ sec} = 1 \text{ minute}$
60×10 entries / min

therefore:

$5 \times 60 \times 10$ = total number of entries needed for the timing wheel with a granularity of 100ms.

A hierarchical timing wheel is similar to a digital clock. Instead of having a single timing wheel, multiple timing wheels are organized in a hierarchical order. Each timing wheel in the hierarchy set has a different granularity. A clock dial is associated with each timing wheel. The clock dial turns by one unit when the clock dial at the lower

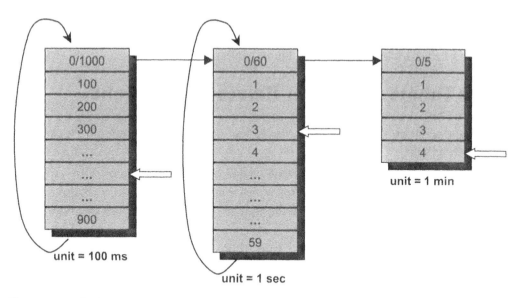

Figure 11.16 A hierarchical timing wheel.

level of the hierarchy wraps around. Using a hierarchical timing wheel requires only 75 (10 + 60 +5) entries to allow for timeouts with 100ms resolution and duration of up to 5 minutes.

With a hierarchical timing wheels, there are multiple arrays, therefore

$10 \times 100ms = 1$ sec
10 entries/sec
the 1st array (leftmost array as shown in Figure 11.16)

60 sec = 1 minute
60 entries / min
the 2nd array (middle array shown in Figure 11.16)

5 entries for 5 minutes
3rd array

therefore:

5 + 60 + 10 = total number of entries needed for the hierarchal timing wheels.

The reduction in space allows for the construction of higher precision timer facilities with a large range of timeout values. Figure 11.16 depicts this concept.

For example, it is possible to install timeouts of 2 minutes, 4 seconds, and 300 milliseconds. The timeout handler is installed at the 2-minute slot first. The timeout handler determines that there are still 4.3 seconds to go when the 2 minutes is up. The handler installs itself at the 4-second timeout slot. Again, when 4 seconds have elapsed, the same handler determines that 300 milliseconds are left before expiring the timer. Finally, the handler is reinstalled at the 300-millisecond timeout slot. The real required work is performed by the handler when the last 300ms expire.

11.7 Soft Timers and Timer Related Operations

Many RTOSs provide a set of timer-related operations for external software components and applications through API sets. These common operations can be cataloged into these groups:

- **group 1**—provides low-level hardware related operations,
- **group 2**—provides soft-timer-related services, and
- **group 3**—provides access either to the storage of the real-time clock or to the system clock.

Not all of the operations in each of these three groups, however, are offered by all RTOSs, and some RTOSs provides additional operations not mentioned here.

The first group of operations is developed and provided by the BSP developers. The group is considered low-level system operations. Each operation in the group is given a fictitious function name for this discussion. Actual function names are implementation dependent.

Table 11.1   Group 1 Operations.

Typical Operations	Description
sys_timer_enable	Enables the system timer chip interrupts. As soon as this operation is invoked, the timer interrupts occur at the preprogrammed frequency, assuming that the timer chip has been properly initialized with the desired values. Only after this operation is complete can kernel task scheduling take place.
sys_timer_disable	Disables the system timer chip interrupts. After this operation is complete, the kernel scheduler is no longer in effect. Other system-offered services based on time ticks are disabled by this operation as well.
sys_timer_connect	Installs the system timer interrupt service routine into the system exception vector table. The new timer ISR is invoked automatically on the next timer interrupt. The installed function is either part of the BSP or the kernel code and represents the "timer ISR" depicted in Figure 11.3, page 172. Input Parameters: 1. New timer interrupt service routine
sys_timer_getrate	Returns the system clock rate as the number of ticks per second that the timer chip is programmed to generate.

Table 11.1   Group 1 Operations. (Continued)

Typical Operations	Description
	Output Parameter: 1. Ticks per second
sys_timer_setrate	Sets the system clock rate as the number of ticks per second the timer chip generates. Internally, this operation reprograms the PIT to obtain the desired frequency.
	Input Parameters: 1. Ticks per second
sys_timer_getticks	Returns the elapsed timer ticks since system power up. This figure is the total number of elapsed timer ticks since the system was first powered on.
	Output Parameters: 1. Total number of elapsed timer ticks

The second group of timer-related operations includes the core timer operations that are heavily used by both the system modules and applications. Either an independent timer-handling facility or a built-in one that is part of the kernel offers these operations. Each operation in the group is given a fictitious function name for this discussion. Actual function names are implementation dependent.

The timer_create and timer_start operations allow the caller to start a timer that expires some time in the future. The caller-supplied function is invoked at the time of expiration, which is specified as a time relative with respect to when the timer_start operation is invoked. Through these timer operations, applications can install soft timers for various purposes. For example, the TCP protocol layer can install retransmission timers, the IP protocol layer can install packet-reassembly discard timers, and a device driver can poll an I/O device for input at predefined intervals.

Table 11.2   Group 2 Operations.

Typical Operations	Description
timer_create	Creates a timer. This operation allocates a soft-timer structure. Any software module intending to install a soft timer must first create a timer structure. The timer structure contains control information that allows the timer-handling facility to update and expire soft timers. A timer created by this operation refers to an entry in the soft-timers array depicted in Figure 11.3.
	Input Parameter: Expiration time User function to be called at the timer expiration

Table 11.2   Group 2 Operations. (Continued)

Typical Operations	Description
	Output Parameter: An ID identifying the newly created timer structure
	Note: This timer structure is implementation dependent. The returned timer ID is also implementation dependent.
timer_delete	Deletes a timer. This operation deletes a previously created soft timer, freeing the memory occupied by the timer structure.
	Input Parameter: 1. An ID identifying a previously created timer structure
	Note: This timer ID is implementation dependent.
timer_start	Starts a timer. This operation installs a previously created soft timer into the timer-handling facility. The timer begins running at the completion of this operation.
	Input Parameter: 1. An ID identifying a previously created timer structure
timer_cancel	Cancels a currently running timer. This operation cancels a timer by removing the currently running timer from the timer-handling facility.
	Input Parameter: 1. An ID identifying a previously created timer structure

The third group is mainly used by user-level applications. The operations in this group interact either with the system clock or with the real-time clock. A system utility library offers these operations. Each operation in the group is given a fictitious function name for this discussion. Actual function names are implementation dependent.

Table 11.3   Group 3 Operations.

Typical Operations	Description
clock_get_time	Gets the current clock time, which is the current running value either from the system clock or from the real-time clock.
	Output Parameter: A time structure containing seconds, minutes, or hours[1]
clock_set_time	Sets the clock to a specified time. The new time is set either into the system clock or into the real-time clock.
	Input Parameter: A time structure containing seconds, minutes, or hours[1]

1.   The time structure is implementation dependent.

11.8 Points to Remember

Some points to remember include the following:

- Hardware timers (hard timers) are handled within the context of the ISR. The timer handler must conform to general restrictions placed on the ISR.
- The kernel scheduler depends on the announcement of time passing per tick.
- Soft timers are built on hard timers and are less accurate because of various delays.
- A soft-timer handling facility should allow for efficient timer installation, cancellation, and timer bookkeeping.
- A soft-timer facility built using the timing-wheel approach provides efficient operations for installation, cancellation, and timer bookkeeping.

In this chapter...

- The I/O Subsystem 192
- Basic I/O Concepts 188
- Points to Remember 197

CHAPTER 12

I/O SUBSYSTEM

12.1 Introduction

All embedded systems include some form of input and output (I/O) operations. These I/O operations are performed over different types of I/O devices. A vehicle dashboard display, a touch screen on a PDA, the hard disk of a file server, and a network interface card are all examples of I/O devices found in embedded systems. Often, an embedded system is designed specifically to handle the special requirements associated with a device. A cell phone, pager, and a handheld MP3 player are a few examples of embedded systems built explicitly to deal with I/O devices.

I/O operations are interpreted differently depending on the viewpoint taken and place different requirements on the level of understanding of the hardware details.

From the perspective of a system software developer, I/O operations imply communicating with the device, programming the device to initiate an I/O request, performing actual data transfer between the device and the system, and notifying the requestor when the operation completes. The system software engineer must understand the physical properties, such as the register definitions, and access methods of the device. Locating the correct instance of the device is part of the device communications when multiple instances of the same device are present. The system engineer is also concerned with how the device is integrated with rest of the system. The system engineer is likely a device driver developer because the system engineer must know to handle any errors that can occur during the I/O operations.

From the perspective of the RTOS, I/O operations imply locating the right device for the I/O request, locating the right device driver for the device, and issuing the request to the device driver. Sometimes the RTOS is required to ensure synchronized access to the

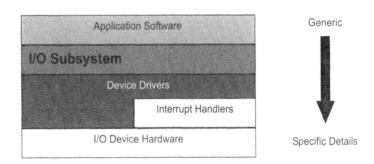

Figure 12.1   I/O subsystem and the layered model.

device. The RTOS must facilitate an abstraction that hides both the device characteristics and specifics from the application developers.

From the perspective of an application developer, the goal is to find a simple, uniform, and elegant way to communicate with all types of devices present in the system. The application developer is most concerned with presenting the data to the end user in a useful way.

Each perspective is equally important and is examined in this chapter. This chapter focuses on:

- basic hardware I/O concepts,
- the structure of the I/O subsystem, and
- a specific implementation of an I/O subsystem.

12.2 Basic I/O Concepts

The combination of I/O devices, associated device drivers, and the I/O subsystem comprises the overall I/O system in an embedded environment. The purpose of the I/O subsystem is to hide the device-specific information from the kernel as well as from the application developer and to provide a uniform access method to the peripheral I/O devices of the system. This section discusses some fundamental concepts from the perspective of the device driver developer.

Figure 12.1 illustrates the I/O subsystem in relation to the rest of the system in a layered software model. As shown, each descending layer adds additional detailed information to the architecture needed to manage a given device.

12.2.1 Port-Mapped vs. Memory-Mapped I/O and DMA

The bottom layer contains the I/O device hardware. The I/O device hardware can range from low-bit rate serial lines to hard drives and gigabit network interface adaptors. All I/O devices must be initialized through device control registers, which are usually external to the CPU. They are located on the CPU board or in the devices themselves. During operation, the device registers are accessed again and are programmed to process data

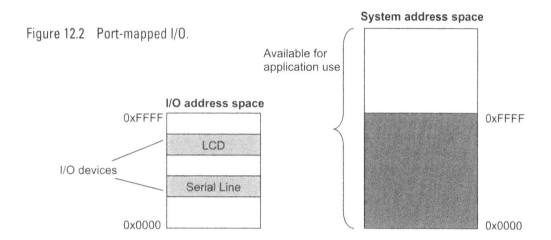

Figure 12.2   Port-mapped I/O.

transfer requests, which is called *device control*. To access these devices, it is necessary for the developer to determine if the device is port mapped or memory mapped. This information determines which of two methods, port-mapped I/O or memory-mapped I/O, is deployed to access an I/O device.

When the I/O device address space is separate from the system memory address space, special processor instructions, such as the IN and OUT instructions offered by the Intel processor, are used to transfer data between the I/O device and a microprocessor register or memory.

The I/O device address is referred to as the *port number* when specified for these special instructions. This form of I/O is called *port-mapped I/O*, as shown in Figure 12.2.

The devices are programmed to occupy a range in the I/O address space. Each device is on a different I/O port. The I/O ports are accessed through special processor instructions, and actual physical access is accomplished through special hardware circuitry. This I/O method is also called *isolated I/O* because the memory space is isolated from the I/O space, thus the entire memory address space is available for application use.

The other form of device access is memory-mapped I/O, as shown in Figure 12.3. In *memory-mapped I/O*, the device address is part of the system memory address space. Any machine instruction that is encoded to transfer data between a memory location and the processor or between two memory locations can potentially be used to access the I/O device. The I/O device is treated as if it were another memory location. Because the I/O address space occupies a range in the system memory address space, this region of the memory address space is not available for an application to use.

The memory-mapped I/O space does not necessarily begin at offset 0 in the system address space, as illustrated in Figure 12.3. It can be mapped anywhere inside the address space. This issue is dependent on the system implementation.

Commonly, tables describing the mapping of a device's internal registers are available in the device hardware data book. The device registers appear at different offsets in this map. Sometimes the information is presented in the "base + offset" format. This format indicates that the addresses in the map are relative, i.e., the offset must be added to the start address of the I/O space for port-mapped I/O or the offset must be added to the base address of the system memory space for mem-ory-mapped I/O in order to access a particular register on the device.

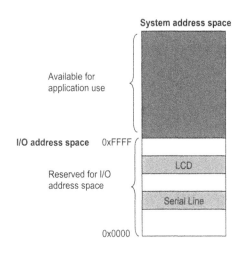

Figure 12.3 Memory-mapped I/O.

The processor has to do some work in both of these I/O methods. Data transfer between the device and the system involves transferring data between the device and the proces-sor register and then from the processor register to memory. The transfer speed might not meet the needs of high-speed I/O devices because of the additional data copy involved. Direct memory access (DMA) chips or controllers solve this problem by allow-ing the device to access the memory directly without involving the processor, as shown in Figure 12.4. The processor is used to set up the DMA controller before a data transfer operation begins, but the processor is bypassed during data transfer, regardless of whether it is a read or write operation. The transfer speed depends on the transfer speed of the I/O device, the speed of the memory device, and the speed of the DMA controller.

In essence, the DMA controller provides an alternative data path between the I/O device and the main memory. The processor sets up the transfer operation by specifying the source address, the destination memory address, and the length of the transfer to the DMA controller.

12.2.2 Character-Mode vs. Block-Mode Devices

I/O devices are classified as either character-mode devices or block-mode devices. The classification refers to how the device handles data transfer with the system.

Character-mode devices allow for unstructured data transfers. The data transfers typically take place in serial fashion, one byte at a time. Character-mode devices are usually simple devices, such as the serial interface or the keypad. The driver buffers the data in cases where the transfer rate from system to the device is faster than what the device can handle.

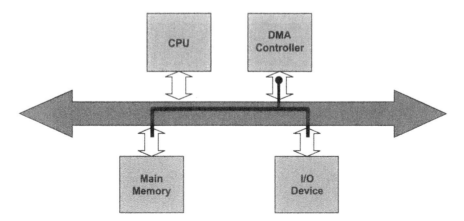

Figure 12.4   DMA I/O.

Block-mode devices transfer data one block at time, for example, 1,024 bytes per data transfer. The underlying hardware imposes the block size. Some structure must be imposed on the data or some transfer protocol enforced. Otherwise an error is likely to occur. Therefore, sometimes it is necessary for the block-mode device driver to perform additional work for each read or write operation, as shown in Figure 12.5.

As illustrated in Figure 12.5, when servicing a write operation with large amounts of data, the device driver must first divide the input data into multiple blocks, each with a device-specific block size. In this example, the input data is divided into four blocks, of which all but the last block is of the required block size. In practice, the last partition often is smaller than the normal device block size.

Each block is transferred to the device in separate write requests. The first three are straightforward write operations. The device driver must handle the last block differently from the first three because the last block has a different size. The method used to process this last block is device specific. In some cases, the driver pads the block to the required size. The example in Figure 12.5 is based on a hard-disk drive. In this case, the device driver first performs a read operation of the affected block and replaces the affected region of the block with the new data. The modified block is then written back.

Another strategy used by block-mode device drivers for small write operations is to accumulate the data in the driver cache and to perform the actual write after enough data has accumulated for a required block size. This technique also minimizes the number of device accesses. Some disadvantages occur with this approach. First, the device driver is more complex. For example, the block-mode device driver for a hard disk must know if the cached data can satisfy a read operation. The delayed write associated with caching can also cause data loss if a failure occurs and if the driver is shut down and

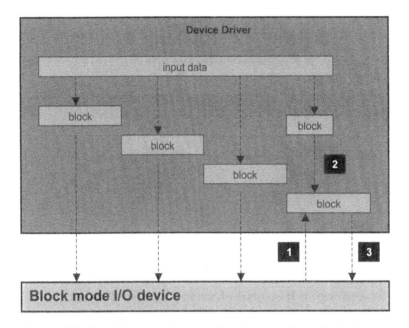

Figure 12.5   Servicing a write operation for a block-mode device.

unloaded ungracefully. Data caching in this case implies data copying that can result in lower I/O performance.

12.3 The I/O Subsystem

Each I/O device driver can provide a driver-specific set of I/O application programming interfaces to the applications. This arrangement requires each application to be aware of the nature of the underlying I/O device, including the restrictions imposed by the device. The API set is driver and implementation specific, which makes the applications using this API set difficult to port. To reduce this implementation--dependence, embedded systems often include an *I/O subsystem*.

> The I/O subsystem defines a standard set of functions for I/O operations in order to hide device peculiarities from applications. All I/O device drivers conform to and support this function set because the goal is to provide uniform I/O to applications across a wide spectrum of I/O devices of varying types.

The following steps must take place to accomplish uniform I/O operations at the application-level.

1. The I/O subsystem defines the API set.
2. The device driver implements each function in the set.
3. The device driver exports the set of functions to the I/O subsystem.
4. The device driver does the work necessary to prepare the device for use. In addition, the driver sets up an association between the I/O subsystem API set and the corresponding device-specific I/O calls.
5. The device driver loads the device and makes this driver and device association known to the I/O subsystem. This action enables the I/O subsystem to present the illusion of an abstract or virtual instance of the device to applications.

This section discusses one approach to uniform I/O. This approach is general, and the goal is to offer insight into the I/O subsystem layer and its interaction with the application layer above and the device driver layer below. Another goal is to give the reader an opportunity to observe how the pieces are put together to provide uniform I/O capability in an embedded environment.

12.3.1 Standard I/O Functions

The I/O subsystem presented in the example in this section defines a set of functions as the standard I/O function set. Table 12.1 lists those functions that are considered part of the set in the general approach to uniform I/O. Again, remember that the example approach is used for illustration purposes in describing and discussing the I/O subsystem in general. The number of functions in the standard I/O API set, function names, and functionality of each is dependent on the embedded system and implementation. The next few sections put these functions into perspective.

Note that all these functions operate on a so-called "virtual instance" of the I/O device. In other words, these functions do not act directly on the I/O device, but rather on the driver, which passes the operations to the I/O device. When the open, read, write, and close operations are described, these operations should be understood as acting indirectly on an I/O device through the agency of a virtual instance.

The create function creates a virtual instance of an I/O device in the I/O subsystem, making the device available for subsequent operations, such as open, read, write, and ioctl. This function gives the driver an opportunity to prepare the device for use. Preparations might include mapping the device into the system memory space, allocating an available interrupt request line (IRQ) for the device, installing an ISR for the IRQ, and initializing the device into a known state. The driver allocates memory to store instance-specific information for subsequent operations. A reference to the newly created device instance is returned to the caller.

The destroy function deletes a virtual instance of an I/O device from the I/O subsystem. No more operations are allowed on the device after this function completes. This function gives the driver an opportunity to perform cleanup operations, such as un-mapping the device from the system memory space, de-allocating the IRQ, and removing the ISR

Table 12.1   I/O functions.

Function	Description
Create	Creates a virtual instance of an I/O device
Destroy	Deletes a virtual instance of an I/O device
Open	Prepares an I/O device for use.
Close	Communicates to the device that its services are no longer required, which typically initiates device-specific cleanup operations.
Read	Reads data from an I/O device
Write	Writes data into an I/O device
Ioctl	Issues control commands to the I/O device (I/O control)

from the system. The driver frees the memory that was used to store instance-specific information.

The open function prepares an I/O device for subsequent operations, such as read and write. The device might have been in a disabled state when the create function was called. Therefore, one of the operations that the open function might perform is enabling the device. Typically, the open operation can also specify modes of use; for example, a device might be opened for read-only operations or write-only operations or for receiving control commands. The reference to the newly opened I/O device is returned to the caller. In some implementations, the I/O subsystem might supply only one of the two functions, create and open, which implements most of the functionalities of both create and open due to functional overlaps between the two operations.

The close function informs a previously opened I/O device that its services are no longer required. This process typically initiates device-specific cleanup operations. For example, closing a device might cause it to go to a standby state in which it consumes little power. Commonly, the I/O subsystem supplies-only one of the two functions, destroy and close, which implements most of the functionalities of both destroy and close, in the case where one function implements both the create and open operations.

The read function retrieves data from a previously opened I/O device. The caller specifies the amount of data to retrieve from the device and the location in memory where the data is to be stored. The caller is completely isolated from the device details and is not concerned with the I/O restrictions imposed by the device.

The write function transfers data from the application to a previously opened I/O device. The caller specifies the amount of data to transfer and the location in memory holding the data to be transferred. Again, the caller is isolated from the device I/O details.

The Ioctl function is used to manipulate the device and driver operating parameters at runtime.

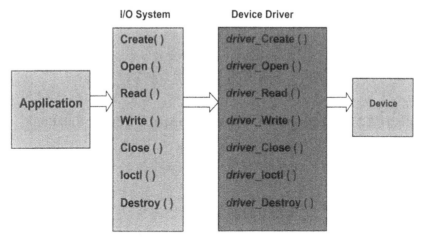

Figure 12.6   I/O function mapping.

An application is concerned with only two things in the context of uniform I/O: the device on which it wishes to perform I/O operations and the functions presented in this section. The I/O subsystem exports this API set for application use.

12.3.2 Mapping Generic Functions to Driver Functions

The individual device drivers provide the actual implementation of each function in the uniform I/O API set. Figure 12.6 gives an overview of the relationship between the I/O API set and driver internal function set.

As illustrated in Figure 12.6, the I/O subsystem-defined API set needs to be mapped into a function set that is specific to the device driver for any driver that supports uniform I/O. The functions that begin with the *driver_* prefix in Figure 12.6 refer to implementations that are specific to a device driver. The uniform I/O API set can be represented in the C programming language syntax as a structure of function pointers, as shown in the left-hand side of Listing 12.1.

Listing 12.1   C structure defining the uniform I/O API set.

```
typedef struct
{
        int (*Create)( );
        int (*Open) ( );
        int (*Read)( );
        int (*Write) ( );
```

Listing 12.1 C structure defining the uniform I/O API set. (Continued)

```
        int (*Close) ( );
        int (*Ioctl) ( );
        int (*Destroy) ( );
} UNIFORM_IO_DRV;
```

Listing 12.2 Mapping uniform I/O API to specific driver functions.

```
UNIFORM_IO_DRV ttyIOdrv;
ttyIOdrv.Create = tty_Create;
ttyIOdrv.Open = tty_Open;
ttyIOdrv.Read = tty_Read;
ttyIOdrv.Write = tty_Write;
ttyIOdrv.Close = tty_Close;
ttyIOdrv.Ioctl = tty_Ioctl;
ttyIOdrv.Destroy = tty_Destroy;
```

The mapping process involves initializing each function pointer with the address of an associated internal driver function, as shown in Listing 12.2. These internal driver functions can have any name as long as they are correctly mapped.

An I/O subsystem usually maintains a *uniform I/O driver table*. Any driver can be installed into or removed from this driver table by using the utility functions that the I/O subsystem provides. Figure 12.7 illustrates this concept.

Each row in the table represents a unique I/O driver that supports the defined API set. The first column of the table is a generic name used to associate the uniform I/O driver with a particular type of device. In Figure 12.7, a uniform I/O driver is provided for a serial line terminal device, tty. The table element at the second row and column contains a pointer to the internal driver function, tty_Create(). This pointer, in effect, constitutes an association between the generic create function and the driver-specific create function. The association is used later when creating virtual instances of a device.

These pointers are written to the table when a driver is installed in the I/O subsystem, typically by calling a utility function for driver installation. When this utility function is called, a reference to the newly created driver table entry is returned to the caller.

12.3.3 Associating Devices with Device Drivers

As discussed in the section on standard I/O functions, the create function is used to create a virtual instance of a device. The I/O subsystem tracks these virtual instances using the *device table*. A newly created virtual instance is given a unique name and is inserted into the device table, as shown in Figure 12.8. Figure 12.8 also illustrates the device table's relationship to the driver table.

Driver Table

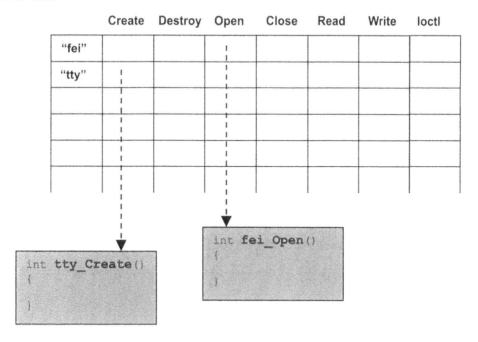

Figure 12.7   Uniform I/O driver table.

Each entry in the device table holds generic information, as well as instance-specific information. The generic part of the device entry can include the unique name of the device instance and a reference to the device driver. In Figure 12.8, a device instance name is constructed using the generic device name and the instance number. The device named tty0 implies that this I/O device is a serial terminal device and is the first instance created in the system. The driver-dependent part of the device entry is a block of memory allocated by the driver for each instance to hold instance-specific data. The driver initializes and maintains it. The content of this information is dependent on the driver implementation. The driver is the only entity that accesses and interprets this data.

A reference to the newly created device entry is returned to the caller of the create function. Subsequent calls to the open and destroy functions use this reference.

12.4 Points to Remember

Some points to remember include the following:

- Interfaces between a device and the main processor occur in two ways: port mapped and memory mapped.
- DMA controllers allows data transfer bypassing the main processor.
- I/O subsystems must be flexible enough to handle a wide range of I/O devices.

- Uniform I/O hides device peculiarities from applications.
- The I/O subsystem maintains a driver table that associates uniform I/O calls with driver-specific I/O routines.
- The I/O subsystem maintains a device table and forms an association between this table and the driver table.

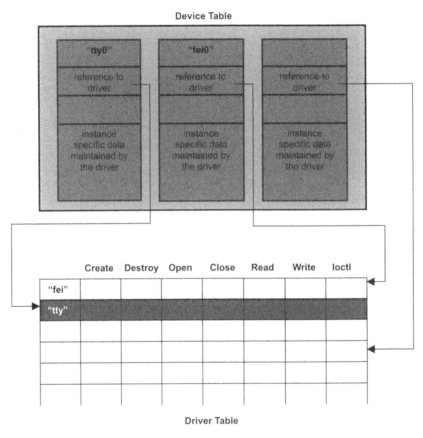

Figure 12.8   Associating devices with drivers.

In this chapter...

- Dynamic Memory Allocation in Embedded
  Systems 200
- Fixed-Size Memory Management in
  Embedded Systems 208
- Blocking vs. Non-Blocking Memory
  Functions 209
- Hardware Memory Management Units . 211
- Points to Remember 212

CHAPTER 13

MEMORY MANAGEMENT

13.1 Introduction

Embedded systems developers commonly implement custom memory-management facilities on top of what the underlying RTOS provides. Understanding memory management is therefore an important aspect of developing for embedded systems.

Knowing the capability of the memory management system can aid application design and help avoid pitfalls. For example, in many existing embedded applications, the dynamic memory allocation routine, `malloc`, is called often. It can create an undesirable side effect called memory fragmentation. This generic memory allocation routine, depending on its implementation, might impact an application's performance. In addition, it might not support the allocation behavior required by the application.

Many embedded devices (such as PDAs, cell phones, and digital cameras) have a limited number of applications (tasks) that can run in parallel at any given time, but these devices have small amounts of physical memory onboard. Larger embedded devices (such as network routers and web servers) have more physical memory installed, but these embedded systems also tend to operate in a more dynamic environment, therefore making more demands on memory. Regardless of the type of embedded system, the common requirements placed on a memory management system are minimal fragmentation, minimal management overhead, and deterministic allocation time.

This chapter focuses on:

- memory fragmentation and memory compaction,
- an example implementation of the `malloc` and `free` functions,
- fixed-size, pool-based memory management,

199

- blocking vs. non-blocking memory functions, and
- the hardware memory management unit (MMU).

13.2 Dynamic Memory Allocation in Embedded Systems

Chapter 3 shows that the program code, program data, and system stack occupy the physical memory after program initialization completes. Either the RTOS or the kernel typically uses the remaining physical memory for dynamic memory allocation. This memory area is called the *heap*. Memory management in the context of this chapter refers to the management of a contiguous block of physical memory, although the concepts introduced in this chapter apply to the management of non-contiguous memory blocks as well. These concepts also apply to the management of various types of physical memory. In general, a memory management facility maintains internal information for a heap in a reserved memory area called the *control block*. Typical internal information includes:

- the starting address of the physical memory block used for dynamic memory allocation,
- the overall size of this physical memory block, and
- the allocation table that indicates which memory areas are in use, which memory areas are free, and the size of each free region.

This chapter examines aspects of memory management through an example implementation of the `malloc` and `free` functions for an embedded system.

13.2.1 Memory Fragmentation and Compaction

In the example implementation, the heap is broken into small, fixed-size blocks. Each block has a unit size that is power of two to ease translating a requested size into the corresponding required number of units. In this example, the unit size is 32 bytes. The dynamic memory allocation function, `malloc`, has an input parameter that specifies the size of the allocation request in bytes. `malloc` allocates a larger block, which is made up of one or more of the smaller, fixed-size blocks. The size of this larger memory block is at least as large as the requested size; it is the closest to the multiple of the unit size. For example, if the allocation requests 100 bytes, the returned block has a size of 128 bytes (4 units x 32 bytes/unit). As a result, the requestor does not use 28 bytes of the allocated memory, which is called memory fragmentation. This specific form of fragmentation is called internal fragmentation because it is internal to the allocated block.

The allocation table can be represented as a bitmap, in which each bit represents a 32-byte unit. Figure 13.1 shows the states of the allocation table after a series of invocations of the `malloc` and `free` functions. In this example, the heap is 256 bytes.

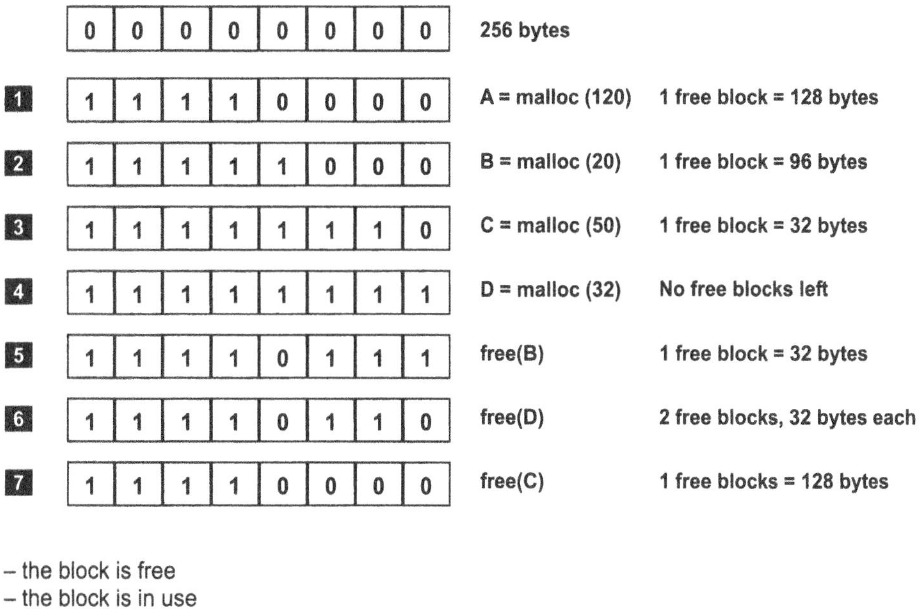

	0	0	0	0	0	0	0	0	256 bytes	
1	1	1	1	1	0	0	0	0	A = malloc (120)	1 free block = 128 bytes
2	1	1	1	1	1	0	0	0	B = malloc (20)	1 free block = 96 bytes
3	1	1	1	1	1	1	1	0	C = malloc (50)	1 free block = 32 bytes
4	1	1	1	1	1	1	1	1	D = malloc (32)	No free blocks left
5	1	1	1	1	0	1	1	1	free(B)	1 free block = 32 bytes
6	1	1	1	1	0	1	1	0	free(D)	2 free blocks, 32 bytes each
7	1	1	1	1	0	0	0	0	free(C)	1 free blocks = 128 bytes

0 – the block is free
1 – the block is in use

Figure 13.1   States of a memory allocation map.

Step 6 shows two free blocks of 32 bytes each. Step 7, instead of maintaining three separate free blocks, shows that all three blocks are combined to form a 128-byte block. Because these blocks have been combined, a future allocation request for 96 bytes should succeed.

Figure 13.2 shows another example of the state of an allocation table. Note that two free 32-byte blocks are shown. One block is at address 0x10080, and the other at address 0x101C0, which cannot be used for any memory allocation requests larger than 32 bytes. Because these isolated blocks do not contribute to the contiguous free space needed for a large allocation request, their existence makes it more likely that a large request will fail or take too long. The existence of these two trapped blocks is considered external fragmentation because the fragmentation exists in the table, not within the blocks themselves. One way to eliminate this type of fragmentation is to compact the area adjacent to these two blocks. The range of memory content from address 0x100A0 (immediately following the first free block) to address 0x101BF (immediately preceding the second free block is shifted 32 bytes lower in memory, to the new range of 0x10080 to 0x1019F, which effectively combines the two free blocks into one 64-byte block. This new free block is still considered memory fragmentation if future allocations are potentially larger than 64 bytes. Therefore, memory compaction continues until all of the free blocks are combined into one large chunk.

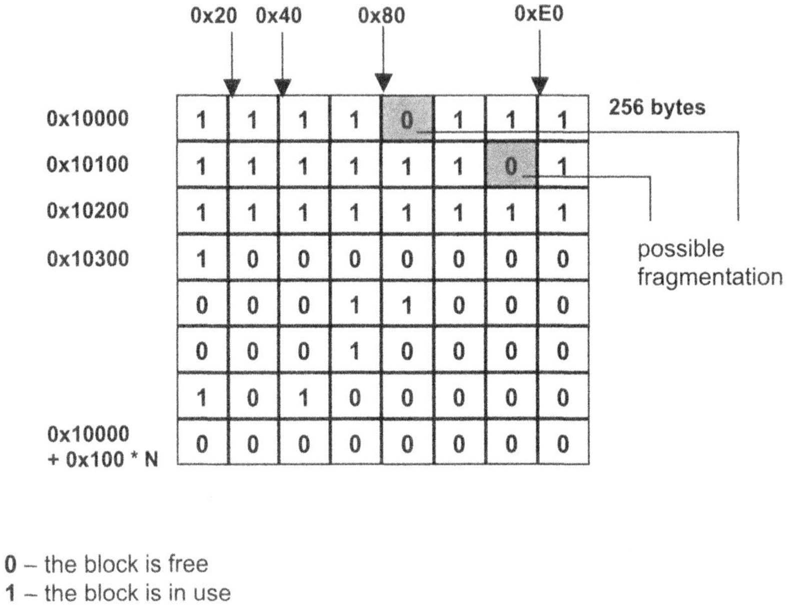

0 – the block is free
1 – the block is in use

Figure 13.2   Memory allocation map with possible fragmentation.

Several problems occur with memory compaction. It is time-consuming to transfer memory content from one location to another. The cost of the copy operation depends on the length of the contiguous blocks in use. The tasks that currently hold ownership of those memory blocks are prevented from accessing the contents of those memory locations until the transfer operation completes. Memory compaction is almost never done in practice in embedded designs. The free memory blocks are combined only if they are immediate neighbors, as illustrated in Figure 13.1.

Memory compaction is allowed if the tasks that own those memory blocks reference the blocks using virtual addresses. Memory compaction is not permitted if tasks hold physical addresses to the allocated memory blocks.

In many cases, memory management systems should also be concerned with architecture-specific memory alignment requirements. *Memory alignment* refers to architecture-specific constraints imposed on the address of a data item in memory. Many embedded processor architectures cannot access multi-byte data items at any address. For example, some architecture requires multi-byte data items, such as integers and long integers, to be allocated at addresses that are a power of two. Unaligned memory addresses result in bus errors and are the source of memory access exceptions.

Some conclusions can be drawn from this example. An efficient memory manager needs to perform the following chores quickly:

- Determine if a free block that is large enough exists to satisfy the allocation request. This work is part of the `malloc` operation.
- Update the internal management information. This work is part of both the `malloc` and `free` operations.
- Determine if the just-freed block can be combined with its neighboring free blocks to form a larger piece. This work is part of the `free` operation.

The structure of the allocation table is the key to efficient memory management because the structure determines how the operations listed earlier must be implemented. The allocation table is part of the overhead because it occupies memory space that is excluded from application use. Consequently, one other requirement is to minimize the management overhead.

13.2.2 An Example of `malloc` and `free`

The following is an example implementation of `malloc`'s allocation algorithm for an embedded system. A static array of integers, called the *allocation array*, is used to implement the allocation map. The main purpose of the allocation array is to decide if neighboring free blocks can be merged to form a larger free block. Each entry in this array represents a corresponding fixed-size block of memory. In this sense, this array is similar to the map shown in Figure 13.2, but this one uses a different encoding scheme. The number of entries contained in the array is the number of fixed-size blocks available in the managed memory area. For example, 1MB of memory can be divided into 32,768 32-byte blocks. Therefore, in this case, the array has 32,768 entries.

To simplify the example for better understanding of the algorithms involved, just 12 units of memory are used. Figure 13.3 shows the example allocation array.

In Figure 13.3, let the allocation-array index start at 0. Before any memory has been allocated, one large free block is present, which consists of all 12 units of available memory. The allocation array uses a simple encoding scheme to keep track of allocated and free blocks of memory. To indicate a range of contiguous free blocks, a positive number is placed in the first and last entry representing the range. This number is equal to the number of free blocks in the range. For example, in the first array shown on the left, the number of free units (12 in this case) is placed in the entries at index 0 and index 11.

Placing a negative number in the first entry and a zero in the last entry indicates a range of allocated blocks. The number placed in the first entry is equal to –1 times the number of allocated blocks.

In this example, the first allocation request is for three units. The array labeled 1 in Figure 13.3 represents the state of the allocation array after this first allocation request is made. The value of –3 at index 9 and the value of 0 at index 11 marks the range of the allocated block. The size of the free block is now reduced to nine. Step 3 in Figure 13.3

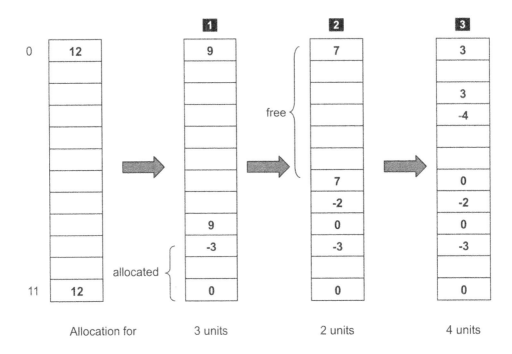

Figure 13.3   Static array implementation of the allocation map.

shows the state of the allocation array at the completion of three allocation requests. This array arrangement and the marking of allocated blocks simplify the merging operation that takes place during the `free` operation, as explained later in this chapter.

Not only does this allocation array indicate which blocks are free, but it also implicitly indicates the starting address of each block, because a simple relationship exists between array indices and starting addresses, as shown

```
starting address = offset + unit_size*index
```

When allocating a block of memory, `malloc` uses this formula to calculate the starting address of the block. For example, in Figure 13.3, the first allocation for three units begins at index 9. If the offset in the formula is 0x10000 and the unit size is 0x20 (32 decimal), the address returned for index 9 is

```
0x10000 + 0x20*9 = 0x10120
```

13.2.3 Finding Free Blocks Quickly

In this memory management scheme, `malloc` always allocates from the largest available range of free blocks. The allocation array described is not arranged to help `malloc` perform this task quickly. The entries representing free ranges are not sorted by size. Find-

Figure 13.4 Free blocks in a heap
arrangement.

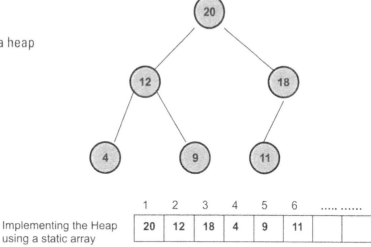

Implementing the Heap
using a static array

1	2	3	4	5	6		
20	12	18	4	9	11		

The left child of a node k is at position 2k.
The right child of a node k is at position 2k+1.

ing the largest range always entails an end-to-end search. For this reason, a second data structure is used to speed up the search for the free block that can satisfy the allocation request. The sizes of free blocks within the allocation array are maintained using the heap data structure, as shown in Figure 13.4. The heap data structure is a complete binary tree with one property: the value contained at a node is no smaller than the value in any of its child nodes.

The size of each free block is the key used for arranging the heap. Therefore, the largest free block is always at the top of the heap. The `malloc` algorithm carves the allocation out of the largest available free block. The remaining portion is reinserted into the heap. The heap is rearranged as the last step of the memory allocation process.

Although the size of each free range is the key that organizes the heap, each node in the heap is actually a data structure containing at least two pieces of information: the size of a free range and its starting index in the allocation array. The `malloc` operation involves the following steps:

1. Examine the heap to determine if a free block that is large enough for the allocation request exists.
2. If no such block exists, return an error to the caller.
3. Retrieve the starting allocation-array index of the free range from the top of the heap.
4. Update the allocation array by marking the newly allocated block, as illustrated in Figure 13.3.

5. If the entire block is used to satisfy the allocation, update the heap by deleting the largest node. Otherwise update the size.

6. Rearrange the heap array.

Before any memory has been allocated, the heap has just one node, signifying that the entire memory region is available as one, large, free block. The heap continues to have a single node either if memory is allocated consecutively without any free operations or if each memory free operation results in the deallocated block merging with its immediate neighbors. The heap structure in Figure 13.4 represents free blocks interleaved with blocks in use and is similar to the memory map in Figure 13.2.

The heap can be implemented using another static array, called the *heap array*, as shown in Figure 13.4. The array index begins at 1 instead of 0 to simplify coding in C. In this example, six free blocks of 20, 18, 12, 11, 9, and 4 blocks are available. The next memory allocation uses the 20-block range regardless of the size of the allocation request. Note that the heap array is a compact way to implement a binary tree. The heap array stores no pointers to child nodes; instead, child-parent relationships are indicated by the positions of the nodes within the array.

13.2.4 The free Operation

Note that the bottom layer of the malloc and free implementation is shown in Figure 13.3 and Figure 13.4. In other words, another layer of software tracks, for example, the address of an allocated block and its size. Let's assume that this software layer exists and that the example is not concerned with it other than that this layer feeds the necessary information into the free function.

The main operation of the free function is to determine if the block being freed can be merged with its neighbors. The merging rules are

1. If the starting index of the block is not 0, check for the value of the array at (index −1). If the value is positive (not a negative value or 0), this neighbor can be merged.

2. If (index + number of blocks) does not exceed the maximum array index value, check for the value of the array at (index + number of blocks). If the value is positive, this neighbor can be merged.

These rules are illustrated best through an example, as shown in Figure 13.5.

Figure 13.5 shows two scenarios worth discussion. In the first scenario, the block starting at index 3 is being freed. Following rule #1, look at the value at index 2. The value is 3; therefore, the neighboring block can be merged. The value of 3 indicates that the neighboring block is 3 units large. The block being freed is 4 units large, so following rule #2, look at the value at index 7. The value is −2; therefore, the neighboring block is still in use and cannot be merged. The result of the free operation in the first scenario is shown as the second table in Figure 13.5.

In the second scenario, the block at index 7 is being freed. Following rule #1, look at the value at index 6, which is 0. This value indicates the neighboring block is still in

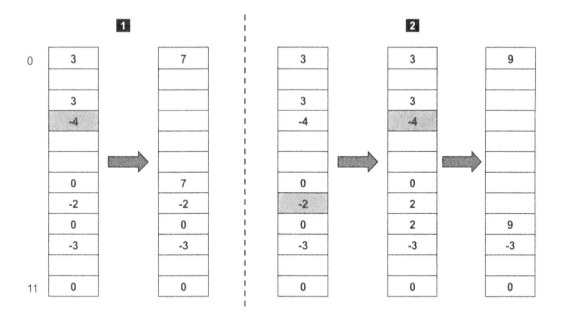

Figure 13.5   The free operation.

use. Following rule #2, look at the value at index 9, which is −3. Again, this value indicates that this block is also in use. The newly freed block remains as independent piece. After applying the two merge rules, the next free operation of the block starting at index 3 results in the allocation table shown as the last table in Figure 13.5.

When a block is freed, the heap must be updated accordingly. Therefore, the free operation involves the following steps:

1. Update the allocation array and merge neighboring blocks if possible.
2. If the newly freed block cannot be merged with any of its neighbors, insert a new entry into the heap array.
3. If the newly freed block can be merged with one of its neighbors, the heap entry representing the neighboring block must be updated, and the updated entry rearranged according to its new size.
4. If the newly freed block can be merged with both of its neighbors, the heap entry representing one of the neighboring blocks must be deleted from the heap, and the heap entry representing the other neighboring block must be updated and rearranged according to its new size.

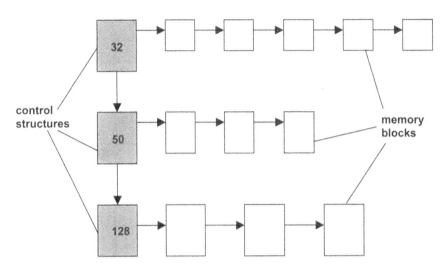

Figure 13.6   Management based on memory pools.

13.3 Fixed-Size Memory Management in Embedded Systems

Another approach to memory management uses the method of fixed-size memory pools. This approach is commonly found in embedded networking code, such as in embedded protocol stacks implementation.

As shown in Figure 13.6, the available memory space is divided into variously sized memory pools. All blocks of the same memory pool have the same size. In this example, the memory space is divided into three pools of block sizes 32, 50, and 128 respectively. Each memory-pool control structure maintains information such as the block size, total number of blocks, and number of free blocks. In this example, the memory pools are linked together and sorted by size. Finding the smallest size adequate for an allocation requires searching through this link and examining each control structure for the first adequate block size.

A successful allocation results in an entry being removed from the memory pool. A successful deallocation results in an entry being inserted back into the memory pool. The memory pool structure shown in Figure 13.6 is a singly linked list. Therefore, memory allocation and deallocation takes place at the beginning of this list.

This method is not as flexible as the algorithm introduced earlier in "Dynamic Memory Allocation in Embedded Systems" on page 200 and also has some drawbacks. In real-time embedded systems, a task's memory requirement often depends on its operating environment. This environment can be quite dynamic. This method does not work well for embedded applications that constantly operate in dynamic environments because it is nearly impossible to anticipate the memory block sizes that the task might commonly use. This issue results in increased internal memory fragmentation per allocation. In addition, the number of blocks to allocate for each size is also impossible to predict. In many cases, the memory pools are constructed based on a number of assumptions. The result is that some memory pools are under used or not used at all, while others are overused.

On the other hand, this memory allocation method can actually reduce internal fragmentation and provide high utilization for static embedded applications. These applications are those with predictable environments, a known number of running tasks at the start of application execution, and initially known required memory block sizes.

One advantage of this memory management method is that it is more deterministic than the heap method algorithm. In the heap method, each `malloc` or `free` operation can potentially trigger a rearrangement of the heap. In the memory-pool method, memory blocks are taken or are returned from the beginning of the list so the operation takes constant time. The memory pool does not require restructuring.

13.4 Blocking vs. Non-Blocking Memory Functions

The `malloc` and `free` functions do not allow the calling task to block and wait for memory to become available. In many real-time embedded systems, tasks compete for the limited system memory available. Oftentimes, the memory exhaustion condition is only temporary. For some tasks when a memory allocation request fails, the task must backtrack to an execution checkpoint and perhaps restart an operation. This issue is undesirable as the operation can be expensive. If tasks have built-in knowledge that the memory congestion condition can occur but only momentarily, the tasks can be designed to be more flexible. If such tasks can tolerate the allocation delay, the tasks can choose to wait for memory to become available instead of either failing entirely or backtracking.

For example, the network traffic pattern on an Ethernet network is bursty. An embedded networking node might receive few packets for a period and then suddenly be flooded with packets at the highest allowable bandwidth of the physical network. During this traffic burst, tasks in the embedded node that are in the process of sending data can experience temporary memory exhaustion problems because much of the available memory is used for packet reception. These sending tasks can wait for the condition to subside and then resume their operations.

In practice, a well-designed memory allocation function should allow for allocation that permits blocking forever, blocking for a timeout period, or no blocking at all. This chapter uses the memory-pool approach to demonstrate how to implement a blocking memory allocation function.

As shown in Figure 13.7, a blocking memory allocation function can be implemented using both a counting semaphore and a mutex lock. These synchronization primitives are

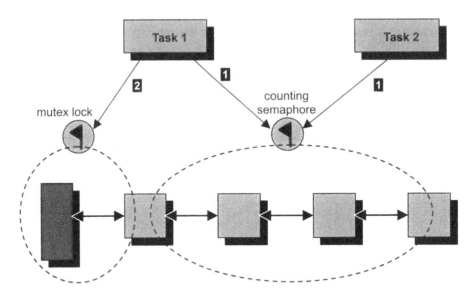

Figure 13.7   Implementing a blocking allocation function using a mutex and a counting semaphore.

created for each memory pool and are kept in the control structure. The counting semaphore is initialized with the total number of available memory blocks at the creation of the memory pool. Memory blocks are allocated and freed from the beginning of the list.

Multiple tasks can access the free-blocks list of the memory pool. The control structure is updated each time an allocation or a deallocation occurs. Therefore, a mutex lock is used to guarantee a task exclusive access to both the free-blocks list and the control structure. A task might wait for a block to become available, acquire the block, and then continue its execution. In this case, a counting semaphore is used.

For an allocation request to succeed, the task must first successfully acquire the counting semaphore, followed by a successful acquisition of the mutex lock.

The successful acquisition of the counting semaphore reserves a piece of the available blocks from the pool. A task first tries to acquire the counting semaphore. If no blocks are available, the task blocks on the counting semaphore, assuming the task is prepared to wait for it. If a resource is available, the task acquires the counting semaphore successfully. The counting semaphore token count is now one less than it was. At this point, the task has reserved a piece of the available blocks but has yet to obtain the block.

Next, the task tries to lock the mutex. If another task is currently getting a block out of the memory pool or if another task is currently freeing a block back into the memory pool, the mutex is in the locked state. The task blocks waiting for the mutex to unlock. After the task locks the mutex, the task retrieves the resource from the list.

The counting semaphore is released when the task finishes using the memory block.

The pseudo code for memory allocation using a counting semaphore and mutex lock is provided in Listing 13.1.

Listing 13.1   Pseudo code for memory allocation.

```
Acquire(Counting_Semaphore)
Lock(mutex)
Retrieve the memory block from the pool
Unlock(mutex)
```

The pseudo code for memory deallocation using a mutex lock and counting semaphore is provided in Listing 13.2.

Listing 13.2   Pseudo code for memory deallocation.

```
Lock(mutex)
Release the memory block back to into the pool
Unlock(mutex)
Release(Counting_Semaphore)
```

This implementation shown in Listing 13.1 and 13.2 enables the memory allocation and deallocation functions to be safe for multitasking. The deployment of the counting semaphore and the mutex lock eliminates the priority inversion problem when blocking memory allocation is enabled with these synchronization primitives. Chapter 6 discusses semaphores and mutexes. Chapter 16 discusses priority inversions.

13.5 Hardware Memory Management Units

Thus far, the discussion on memory management focuses on the management of physical memory. Another topic is the management of virtual memory. Virtual memory is a technique in which mass storage (for example, a hard disk) is made to appear to an application as if the mass storage were RAM. Virtual memory address space (also called *logical address space*) is larger than the actual physical memory space. This feature allows a program larger than the physical memory to execute. The *memory management unit* (MMU) provides several functions. First, the MMU translates the virtual address to a physical address for each memory access. Second, the MMU provides memory protection.

The address translation function differs from one MMU design to another. Many commercial RTOSes do not support implementation of virtual addresses, so this chapter does not discuss address translation. Instead, the chapter discusses the MMU's memory protection feature, as many RTOSes do support it.

If an MMU is enabled on an embedded system, the physical memory is typically divided into *pages*. A set of attributes is associated with each memory page. Information on attributes can include the following:

- whether the page contains code (i.e., executable instructions) or data,
- whether the page is readable, writable, executable, or a combination of these, and
- whether the page can be accessed when the CPU is not in privileged execution mode, accessed only when the CPU is in privileged mode, or both.

All memory access is done through MMU when it is enabled. Therefore, the hardware enforces memory access according to page attributes. For example, if a task tries to write to a memory region that only allows for read access, the operation is considered illegal, and the MMU does not allow it. The result is that the operation triggers a memory access exception.

13.6 Points to Remember

Some points to remember include the following:

- Dynamic memory allocation in embedded systems can be built using a fixed-size blocks approach.
- Memory fragmentation can be classified into either external memory fragmentation or internal memory fragmentation.
- Memory compaction is generally not performed in real-time embedded systems.
- Management based on memory pools is commonly found in networking-related code.
- A well-designed memory allocation function should allow for blocking allocation.
- Blocking memory allocation function can be designed using both a counting semaphore and a mutex.
- Many real-time embedded RTOSes do not implement virtual addressing when the MMU is present.
- Many of these RTOSes do take advantage of the memory protection feature of the MMU.

In this chapter...

- An Outside-In Approach to Decomposing
  Applications .214
- Guidelines and Recommendations for
  Identifying Concurrency 217
- Schedulability Analysis—Rate Monotonic
  Analysis 225
- Points to Remember 229

CHAPTER 14

MODULARIZING AN APPLICATION FOR CONCURRENCY

14.1 Introduction

Many activities need to be completed when designing applications for real-time systems. One group of activities requires identifying certain elements. Some of the more important elements to identify include:

1. system requirements,
2. inputs and outputs,
3. real-time deadlines,
4. events and event response times,
5. event arrival patterns and frequencies,
6. required objects and other components,
7. tasks that need to be concurrent,
8. system schedulability, and
9. useful or needed synchronization protocols for inter-task communications.

Depending on the design methodologies and modeling tools that a design team is using, the list of steps to be taken can vary, as well as the execution order. Regardless of the methodology, eventually a design team must consider how to decompose the application into concurrent tasks (Step 7).

This chapter provides guidelines and discussions on how real-time embedded applications can be decomposed. Many design teams use formalized object-oriented development techniques and modeling languages, such as UML, to model their real-time systems initially. The concepts discussed in this section are complementary to object-oriented design approaches; much emphasis is placed on decomposing the application into separate tasks to achieve concurrency. Through examples, approaches to decomposing applications into concurrent tasks are discussed. In addition, general guidelines for designing concurrency in a real-time application are provided.

These guidelines and recommendations are based on a combination of things—lessons learned from current engineering design practices, work done by H. Gomaa, current UML modeling approaches, and work done by other researchers in the real-time field. Our guidelines provide high-level strategies on proceeding with decomposing real-time applications for concurrency. Our recommendations, on the other hand, are specific strategies focusing on the implementation of concurrency. Both the guidelines and recommendations might not necessarily cover every exception that can arise when designing a real-time embedded application. If two guidelines or recommendations appear to contain opposing thoughts, they should be treated as constituting a tradeoff that the designer needs to consider.

At the completion of the application decomposition process, robust systems must validate the schedulability of the newly formed tasks. Quantitative schedulability analysis on a real-time system determines whether the system as designed is schedulable. A real-time system is considered schedulable if every task in the system can meet its deadline.

This chapter also focuses on the schedulability analysis (Step 8). In particular, the chapter introduces a formal method known as Rate Monotonic Analysis (RMA).

14.2 An Outside-In Approach to Decomposing Applications

In most cases, designers insist on a set of requirements before beginning work on a real-time embedded system. If the requirements are not fully defined, one of the first activities is to ensure that many of these requirements are solidified. Ambiguous areas also need to be fleshed out. The detailed requirements should be captured in a document, such as a Software Requirements Specification (SRS). Only then can an engineering team make a reasonable attempt at designing a system. A high-level example of a mobile phone design is provided to show how to decompose an application into concurrent units of execution.

Commonly, decomposing an application is performed using an *outside-in approach*. This approach follows a process of identifying the inputs and outputs of a system and expressing them in a simple high-level context diagram. A context diagram for the mobile application is illustrated in Figure 14.1. The circle in the center of the diagram represents the software application. Rectangular boxes represent the input and output devices for this application. In addition, arrows, labeled with meaningful names,

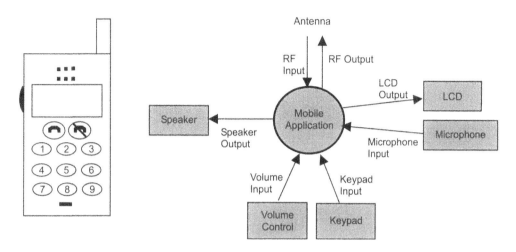

Figure 14.1 High-level context diagram of a mobile handheld unit.

represent the flow of the input and output communications. For the sake of simplicity, not all components (i.e., battery, input for hands-free ear plug, input for external power, and power on/off button) are illustrated.

The diagram shows that mobile handset application provides interfaces for the following I/O devices:

- antenna,
- speaker,
- volume control,
- keypad,
- microphone, and
- LCD.

The following inputs are identified:

- RF input,
- volume input,
- keypad input, and
- microphone input.

The following outputs are identified:

- RF output,
- speaker output, and
- LCD output.

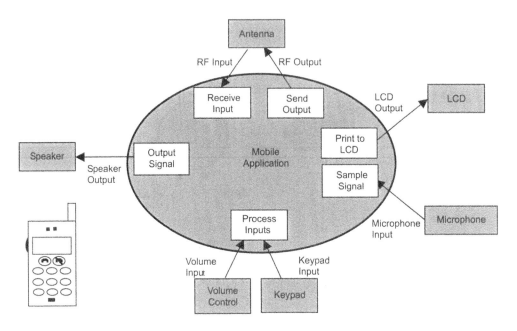

Figure 14.2   Using the outside-in approach to decompose an application into tasks.

After the inputs and outputs are identified, a first cut at decomposing the application can be made. Figure 14.2 shows an expanded diagram of the circle identifying some of the potential tasks into which the application can decompose. These tasks are along the edges of the newly drawn application, which means they probably must interact with the outside world. Note that these tasks are not the only ones required, but the process provides a good starting point. Upon further analysis, additional tasks may be identified, or existing tasks may be combined as more details are considered.

Some inputs and outputs in a handheld mobile device can require more than one dedicated task to handle processing. Conversely, in some cases, a single task can handle multiple devices. Looking at the example, the antenna can have two tasks assigned to it—one for handling the incoming voice channel and one for handling the outgoing voice channel. Printing to the LCD can be a relatively simple activity and can be handled with one task. Similarly, sampling the input voice from the microphone can also be handled with one task for now but might require another task if heavy computation is required for sampling accuracy. Note that one task can handle the input keys and the volume control. Finally, a task is designated for sending the output to the speaker.

This example illustrates why the decomposition method is called outside-in: an engineering team can continue this way to decompose the overall application into tasks from the outside in.

14.3 Guidelines and Recommendations for Identifying Concurrency

The outside-in approach to decomposing an application is an example of one practical way to identify types of concurrent tasks that are dependent on or interact with I/O devices. The mobile handset example expands a high-level context diagram to determine some of the obvious tasks required to handle certain events or actions. Further refinement of this diagram would yield additional tasks. More formalized ways of identifying concurrency exist, however. Many guidelines are provided in this section to help the reader identify concurrency in an application. First, let's introduce a couple of concepts that are important to understanding concurrency.

14.3.1 Units of Concurrency

It is important to encapsulate concurrency within an application into manageable units. A *unit of concurrency* can be a task or a process; it can be any schedulable thread of execution that can compete for the CPU's processing time. Although ISRs are not scheduled to run concurrently with other routines, they should also be considered in designing for concurrency because they follow a preemptive policy and are units of execution competing for CPU processing time. The primary objective of this decomposition process is to optimize parallel execution to maximize a real-time application's performance and responsiveness. If done correctly, the result can be a system that meets all of its deadlines robustly and responsively. If done incorrectly, real-time deadlines can be compromised, and the system's design may not be acceptable.

14.3.2 Pseudo versus True Concurrent Execution

Concurrent tasks in a real-time application can be scheduled to run on a single processor or multiple processors. Single-processor systems can achieve pseudo concurrent execution, in which an application is decomposed into multiple tasks maximizing the use of a single CPU. It is important to note that on a single-CPU system, only one *program counter* (also called an *instruction pointer*) is used, and, hence, only one instruction can be executed at any time. Most applications in this environment use an underlying scheduler's multitasking capabilities to interleave the execution of multiple tasks; therefore, the term *pseudo concurrent execution* is used.

In contrast, true concurrent execution can be achieved when multiple CPUs are used in the designs of real-time embedded systems. For example, if two CPUs are used in a system, two concurrent tasks can execute in parallel at one time, as shown in Figure 14.3. This parallelism is possible because two program counters (one for each CPU) are used, which allows for two different instructions to execute simultaneously.

In the case of multiple CPU systems, the underlying RTOS typically is *distributed,* which means that various components, or copies of RTOS components, can execute on different CPUs. On such systems, multiple tasks can be assigned to run on each CPU, just as

"Pseudo" Concurrent Execution   **"True" Concurrent Execution**

Figure 14.3   Pseudo and true concurrent (parallel) execution.

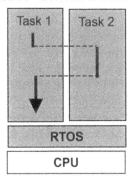
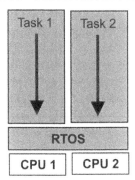

they do on single-CPU systems. In this case, even though two or more CPUs allow true concurrent execution, each CPU might actually be executing in a pseudo-concurrent fashion.

Unless explicitly stated, this book refers to both pseudo and true parallel execution as concurrent execution for the sake of simplicity.

Following the outside-in approach, certain types of tasks can be identified near the application edge (i.e., where an application needs to create an interface with an I/O device), whereas other tasks can be internal to the application. From the mobile handheld example, if a design team were to further decompose the application, these internal tasks would be identified. Applications, such as calculator or calendar programs, are some examples of internal tasks or groupings of tasks that can exist within the overall handheld mobile application. These internal tasks are decoupled from the I/O devices; they need no device-specific information in order to run

14.3.3 Some Guidelines

Guideline 1: Identify Device Dependencies

- Guideline 1a: Identify Active I/O Devices
- Guideline 1b: Identify Passive I/O Devices

Guideline 2: Identify Event Dependencies

Guideline 3: Identify Time Dependencies

- Guideline 3a: Identify Critical and Urgent Activities
- Guideline 3b: Identify Different Periodic Execution Rates
- Guideline 3c: Identify Temporal Cohesion

Guideline 4: Identify Computationally Bound Activities

Guideline 5: Identify Functional Cohesion

Figure 14.4   Some general properties of active and passive devices.

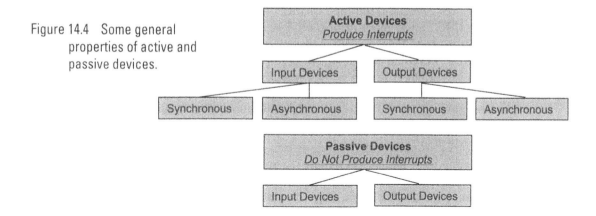

Guideline 6: Identify Tasks that Serve Specific Purposes

Guideline 7: Identify Sequential Cohesion

Guideline 1: Identify Device Dependencies

All real-time systems interface with the physical world through some devices, such as sensors, actuators, keyboards, or displays. An application can have a number of I/O devices interfacing to it. Not all devices, however, act as both input and output devices. Some devices can act just as inputs or just as outputs. Other devices can act as both. The discussions in this book refer to all of these devices as I/O devices.

The outside-in approach focuses on looking at the I/O devices in a system and assigning a task to each device. The basic concept is that unsynchronized devices need separate handling. For simple device interactions, processing within an ISR may suffice; however, for additional device processing, a separate task or set of tasks may be assigned. Both active and passive I/O devices should be considered for identifying potential areas of an application that can be decomposed into concurrent tasks.

As shown in Figure 14.4, hardware I/O devices can be categorized as two types:

- Active I/O devices
- Passive I/O devices

Active I/O devices generate interrupts to communicate with an application. These devices can generate interrupts in a periodic fashion or in synch with other active devices. These devices are referred to in this book as *synchronous*. Active devices can also generate interrupts aperiodically, or asynchronously, with respect to other devices. These devices are referred to in this book as *asynchronous*.

Passive I/O devices do not generate interrupts. Therefore, the application must initiate communications with a passive I/O device. Applications can communicate with passive devices in a periodic or aperiodic fashion.

Active devices generate interrupts whether they are sending input to or receiving output from the CPU. Active input devices send an interrupt to the CPU when the device has new input ready to be processed. The new input can be a large buffer of data, a small unit of data, or even no data at all. An example of the latter is a sensor that generates an interrupt every time it detects some event. On the other hand, an active output device sends an interrupt to the CPU when the device has finished delivering the previous output from the CPU to the physical world. This interrupt announces to the CPU and the application that the output device has completed the last request and is ready to handle the next request.

Passive input or output devices require the application to generate the necessary requests in order to interact with them. Passive input devices produce an input only when the application requests. The application can make these requests either periodically or aperiodically. In the case of the former, the application runs in a periodic loop and makes a request every time through the loop, called *polling a device*. For aperiodic requests, the application makes the request only when it needs the data, based on an event asynchronous to the application itself, such as an interrupt from another device or a message from another executing task.

Special care must be taken when polling a passive input device, especially when sampling a signal that has sharp valleys or peaks. If the polling frequency is too low, a chance exists that a valley or peak might be missed. If the polling frequency is too high, extra performance overhead might be incurred that uses unnecessary CPU cycles.

Guideline 1a: Identify Active Devices

Active input or output I/O devices use interrupts to communicate with real-time applications. Every time an active input device needs to send data or notification of an event to a real-time application, the device generates an interrupt. The interrupt triggers an ISR that executes the minimum code needed to handle the input. If a lot of processing is required, the ISR usually hands off the process to an associated task through an inter-task communication mechanism.

Similarly, active output devices also generate interrupts when they need to communicate with applications. However, interrupts from active output devices are generated when they are ready to receive the next piece of data or notification of some event from the application. The interrupts trigger the appropriate ISR that hands off the required processing to an associated task using an inter-task communication mechanism.

The diagram for both an active I/O device acting as an input or an output to an application and for a device generating interrupts in a synchronous or asynchronous manner is similar to the one illustrated in Figure 14.5.

Some typical tasks that can result from identifying an active I/O device in a real-time application are listed in Table 14.1.

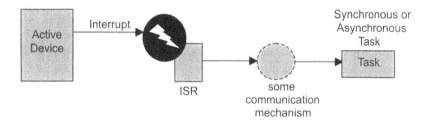

Figure 14.5   General communication mechanisms for active I/O devices.

Table 14.1   Common tasks that interface with active I/O devices.

Task Type	Description
Asynchronous Active Device I/O Task	Assigned to active I/O devices that generate aperiodic interrupts or whose operation is asynchronous with respect to other I/O devices.
Synchronous Active Device I/O Task	Assigned to active I/O devices that generate periodic interrupts or whose operation is synchronous with respect to other I/O devices.
Resource Control Device I/O Task	Assigned for controlling the access to a shared I/O device or a group of devices.
Event Dispatch Device I/O Task	Assigned for dispatching events to other tasks from one or more I/O devices.

Recommendation 1: Assign separate tasks for separate active asynchronous I/O devices.   Active I/O devices that interact with real-time applications do so at their own rate. Each hardware device that uses interrupts to communicate with an application and whose operation is asynchronous with respect to other I/O devices should be considered to have their own separate tasks.

Recommendation 2: Combine tasks for I/O devices that generate infrequent interrupts having long deadlines.   In the initial design, each active I/O device can have a separate task assigned to handle processing. Sometimes, however, combining the processing of two I/O devices into a single task makes sense. For example, if two I/O devices generate aperiodic or asynchronous interrupts infrequently and have relatively long deadlines, a single task might suffice.

Recommendation 3: Assign separate tasks to devices that have different input and output rates.   Generally speaking, a task that handles a device with a high I/O frequency should have a higher task priority than a task that handles a device with a lower frequency. Higher I/O frequency implies shorter, allowable processing time. However, the importance of the I/O operation, and the consequences of delayed I/O, should be taken into account when assigning task priorities with respect to I/O frequency.

Recommendation 4: Assign higher priorities to tasks associated with interrupt-generating devices. A task that needs to interface with a particular I/O device must be set to a high-enough priority level so that the task can keep up with the device. This requirement exists because the task's execution speed is usually constrained by the speed of the interrupts that an associated I/O device generates and not necessarily the processor on which the application is running.

For I/O devices that generate periodic interrupts, the interrupt period dictates how long a task must handle processing. If the period is very short, tasks associated with these devices need to be set at high priorities.

For I/O devices that generate aperiodic interrupts, it can be difficult to predict how long an associated task will have to process the request before the next interrupt comes in. In some cases, interrupts can occur rapidly. In other cases, however, the interrupts can occur with longer time intervals between them. A rule of thumb is that these types of tasks need their priorities set high to ensure that all interrupt requests can be handled, including ones that occur within short time intervals. If an associated task's priority is set too low, the task might not be able to execute fast enough to meet the hardware device's needs.

Recommendation 5: Assign a resource control task for controlling access to I/O devices. Sometimes multiple tasks need to access a single hardware I/O device. In this case, the device can only serve one task at a time; otherwise, data may be lost or corrupted. An efficient approach is to assign a *resource control task* to that device (also known as a *resource monitor task*). This task can be used to receive multiple I/O requests from different tasks, so that the resource control task can send the I/O requests in a controlled and sequential manner to the I/O device.

This resource control task is not limited to working with just one I/O device. In some cases, one resource task can handle multiple requests that might need to be dispatched to one or more I/O devices.

Recommendation 6: Assign an event dispatch task for I/O device requests that need to be handed off to multiple tasks. Events or requests that come from an I/O device can be propagated across multiple tasks. A single task assigned as an event dispatch task can receive all requests from I/O devices and can dispatch them to the appropriate tasks accordingly.

Guideline 1b: Identify Passive Devices

Passive devices are different from active devices because passive devices do not generate interrupts. They sit passively until an application's task requests them to do something meaningful. Whether the request is for an input or an output, an application's task needs to initiate the event or data transfer sequence. The ways that tasks communicate with these devices is either by polling them in a periodic manner or by making a request whenever the task needs to perform input or output.

The diagram either for a passive I/O device acting as an input or an output to an application or for communicating with the application periodically or aperiodically is similar to the one illustrated in Figure 14.6.

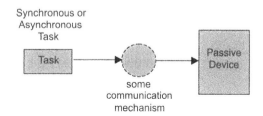

Some typical tasks that can result from identifying a passive I/O device in a real-time application are listed in Table 14.2.

Figure 14.6   General communication mechanisms for passive I/O devices.

Table 14.2   Common tasks that interface with passive I/O devices.

Task Type	Description
Aperiodic Passive Device I/O Task	Assigned to passive I/O devices and issues requests to those devices on an as-needed basis.
Periodic Passive Device I/O Task	Assigned to passive I/O devices and polls those devices in a periodic fashion.
Resource Control Device I/O Task	Assigned for controlling the access to a shared hardware I/O device or a group of devices.
Event Dispatch Device I/O Task	Assigned for dispatching events to other tasks from one or more I/O devices.

Recommendation 1: Assign a single task to interface with passive I/O devices when communication with such devices is aperiodic and when deadlines are not urgent.   Some applications need to communicate with a passive I/O device aperiodically. This device might be a sensor or display. If the deadlines are relatively long, these requests for one or more passive I/O devices can be handled with one task.

Recommendation 2: Assign separate polling tasks to send periodic requests to passive I/O devices.   Commonly, a real-time application might need to sample a signal or some data repeatedly from a passive I/O device. This process can be done effectively in a periodic polling loop. In order to avoid over-sampling or under-sampling the data, assign a separate task to each passive I/O device that needs to be polled at different rates.

Recommendation 3: Trigger polling requests via timer events. More than one way exists to perform timing-based polling loops. One common mistake is using a time delay within the loop that is equal to the period of the sampling rate. This method can be problematic because the loop won't take exactly the same amount of time to execute each time through—the loop is subject to interrupts and preemption from higher priority tasks. A better process is to use a timer to trigger an event after every cycle. A more accurate periodic rate can be maintained using this approach.

Recommendation 4: Assign a high relative priority to polling tasks with relatively short periods. Tasks that are set up to poll passive I/O devices for inputs may do so at different rates. If the period is very short, less time is available to process incoming data before the next cycle. In this case, these tasks with faster polling loops need to be set with higher priorities. Designers, however, need to remember that this process must be done carefully, as heavy polling can use extra CPU cycles and result in increased overhead.

Guideline 2: Identify Event Dependencies

Events in a real-time application can propagate across multiple tasks. Whether an event is generated externally from an I/O device or internally from within the application, a need exists for creating a task or a group of tasks that can properly handle the event as it is propagated through the application. Externally generated events are discussed in the pervious sections, so the focus here is on internally generated events. Examples of events that can be generated internally to an application include when error conditions arise or faults are detected. An event in this case is generated and propagated outward to an I/O device or an internal corrective action is taken.

Guideline 3: Identify Time Dependencies

Before designing a real-time application, take time to understand and itemize each of the timing deadlines required for the application. After the timing deadlines have been identified, separate tasks can be assigned to handle the separate deadlines. Task priorities can be assigned based on the criticality or urgency of each deadline.

Guideline 3a: Identify Critical and Urgent Activities

Note the difference between criticality and urgency. *Critical tasks* are tasks whose failure would be disastrous. The deadline might be long or short but must always be met, or else the system does not fulfill the specifications. An *urgent task* is a task whose timing deadline is relatively short. Meeting this deadline might or might not be critical. Both urgent and critical tasks are usually set to higher relative priorities.

Guideline 3b: Identify Different Periodic Execution Rates

Each rate-driven activity runs independently of any other rate. Periodic activities can be identified, and activities can be grouped into tasks with similar rates.

Guideline 3c: Identify Temporal Cohesion

Real-time systems may contain sequences of code that always execute at the same time, although they are functionally unrelated. Such sequences exhibit *temporal cohesion*. Examples are different activities driven by the same external stimulus (i.e., a timer). Grouping such sequences into one task reduces system overhead.

Guideline 4: Identify Computationally Bound Activities

Some activities in a real-time application require a lot of CPU time compared to the time required for other operations, such as performing I/O. These activities, known as *computationally bound activities*, can be number-crunching activities and typically have relatively long deadlines. These types of activities are usually set to lower relative priorities so that they do not monopolize the CPU. In some cases, these types of tasks can be time-sliced at a common priority level, where each gets time to execute when tasks that are more critical don't need to run.

Guideline 5: Identify Functional Cohesion

Functional cohesion requires collecting groups of functions or sequences of code that perform closely related activities into a single task. In addition, if two tasks are closely coupled (pass lots of data between each other), they should also be considered for combination into one task. Grouping these closely related or closely coupled activities into a singe task can help eliminate synchronization and communication overhead.

Guideline 6: Identify Tasks that Serve Specific Purposes

Tasks can also be grouped according to the specific purposes they serve. One example of a task serving a clear purpose is a safety task. Detection of possible problems, setting alarms, and sending notifications to the user, as well as setting up and executing corrective measures, are just some examples that can be coordinated in a safety task or group of tasks. Other tasks can also exist in a real-time system that can serve a specific purpose.

Guideline 7: Identify Sequential Cohesion

Sequential cohesion groups activities that must occur in a given sequence into one task to further emphasize the requirement for sequential operation. A typical example is a sequence of computations that must be carried out in a predefined order. For example, the result of the first computation provides input to the next computation and so on.

14.4 Schedulability Analysis—Rate Monotonic Analysis

After an embedded application has been decomposed into ISRs and tasks, the tasks must be scheduled to run in order to perform required system functionality. Schedulability analysis determines if all tasks can be scheduled to run and meet their deadlines based on the deployed scheduling algorithm while still achieving optimal processor utilization.

Note that schedulability analysis looks only at how systems meet temporal requirements, not functional requirements.

The commonly practiced analytical method for real-time systems is *Rate Monotonic Analysis* (RMA). Liu and Layland initially developed the mathematical model for RMA in 1973. (This book calls their RMA model the basic RMA because it has since been extended by later researchers.) The model is developed over a scheduling mechanism called *Rate Monotonic Scheduling* (RMS), which is the preemptive scheduling algorithm with rate monotonic priority assignment as the task priority assignment policy. *Rate monotonic priority assignment* is the method of assigning a task its priority as a monotonic function of the execution rate of that task. In other words, the shorter the period between each execution, the higher the priority assigned to a task.

A set of assumptions is associated with the basic RMA. These assumptions are that:

- all of the tasks are periodic,
- the tasks are independent of each other and that no interactions occur among tasks,
- a task's deadline is the beginning of its next period,
- each task has a constant execution time that does not vary over time,
- all of the tasks have the same level of criticality, and
- aperiodic tasks are limited to initialization and failure recovery work and that these aperiodic tasks do not have hard deadlines.

14.4.1 Basic RMA Schedulability Test

Equation 14.1 is used to perform the basic RMA schedulability test on a system.

$$\frac{C_1}{T_1} + \ldots + \frac{C_n}{T_n} \le U(n) = n(2^{1/n} - 1) \qquad \text{Eq. 14.1}$$

$$1 \le i \le n$$

where:

        C_i = worst-case execution time associated with periodic task i
        T_i = period associated with task i
        n = number of tasks

$U(n)$ is the utilization factor. The right side of the equation is the theoretical processor utilization bound. If the processor utilization for a given set of tasks is less than the theoretical utilization bound, this set of tasks is schedulable. The value of U decreases as n increases and eventually converges to 69% when n becomes infinite.

Let's look at a sample problem and see how the formula is implemented. Table 14.3 summarizes the properties of three tasks that are scheduled using the RMS.

Table 14.3   Properties of tasks.

Periodic Task	Execution Time	Period (milliseconds)
Task 1	20	100
Task 2	30	150
Task 3	50	300

Using Equation 14.1, the processor utilization for this sample problem is calculated as follows

$$\frac{20}{100} + \frac{30}{150} + \frac{50}{300} \leq U(3) = 3(2^{1/3} - 1)$$

$$56.67\% \leq U(3) = 77.98\%$$

Total utilization for the sample problem is at 57%, which is below the theoretical bound of 77%. This system of three tasks is schedulable, i.e., every task can meet its deadline.

14.4.2 Extended RAM Schedulability Test

The basic RMA is limiting. The second assumption associated with basic RMA is impractical because tasks in real-time systems have inter-dependencies, and task synchronization methods are part of many real-time designs. Task synchronization, however, lies outside the scope of basic RMA.

Deploying inter-task synchronization methods implies some tasks in the system will experience blocking, which is the suspension of task execution because of resource contention. Therefore, the basic RMA is extended to account for task synchronization. Equation 14.2 provides the equation for the extended RMA schedulability test.

$$\frac{C_1}{T_1} + \dots + \frac{C_i}{T_i} + \frac{B_i}{T_i} \leq U(i) = i(2^{1/i} - 1), (1 \leq i \leq n) \qquad \text{Eq. 14.2}$$

where:

> C_i = worst case execution time associated with periodic task i
> T_i = period associated with task i
> B_i = the longest duration of blocking that can be experienced by i
> n = number of tasks

This equation is best demonstrated with an example. This example uses the same three tasks provided in Table 14.3 and inserts two shared resources, as shown in Figure 14.7. In this case, the two resources represent a shared memory (resource #1) and an I/O bus (resource #2).

Task #1 makes use of resource #2 for 15ms at a rate of once every 100ms. Task #2 is a little more complex. It is the only task that uses both resources. Resource #1 is used for 5ms, and resource #2 is used for 10ms. Task #2 must run at a rate of once every 150ms.

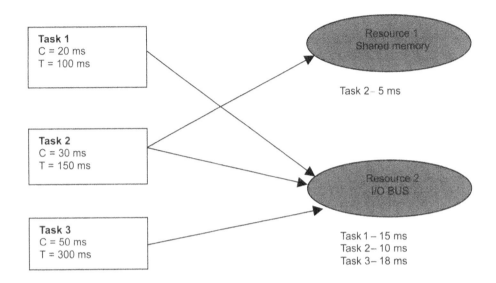

Figure 14.7   Example setup for extended RMA.

Task #3 has the lowest frequency of the tasks and runs once every 300ms. Task #3 also uses resource #2 for 18ms.

Now looking at schedulability, Equation 14.2 yields three separate equations that must be verified against a utility bound. Let's take a closer look at the first equation

$$\frac{20}{100} + \frac{18}{100} \le U(1) = 1(2 - 1)$$

$$38\% \le U(1) = 100\%$$

Either task #2 or task #3 can block task #1 by using resource #2. The blocking factor B_1 is the greater of the times task #2 or task #3 holds the resource, which is 18ms, from task #3. Applying the numbers to Equation 14.2, the result is below the utility bound of 100% for task #1. Hence, task #1 is schedulable.

Looking at the second equation, task #2 can be blocked by task #3. The blocking factor B_2 is 18ms, which is the time task #3 has control of resource #2, as shown

$$\frac{20}{100} + \frac{30}{150} + \frac{18}{150} \le U(2) = 2(2^{1/2} - 1)$$

$$52\% \le U(2) = 82.84\%$$

Task #2 is also schedulable as the result is below the utility bound for two tasks. Now looking at the last equation, note that B_n is always equal to 0. The blocking factor for the lowest level task is always 0, as no other tasks can block it (they all preempt it if they need to), as shown

$$\frac{20}{100} + \frac{30}{150} + \frac{50}{300} \leq U(3) = 3(2^{1/3} - 1)$$

$$56.67\% \leq U(3) = 77.98\%$$

Again, the result is below the utility bound for the three tasks, and, therefore, all tasks are schedulable.

Other extensions are made to basic RMA for dealing with the rest of the assumptions associated with basic RMA, such as accounting for aperiodic tasks in real-time systems. Consult the listed references for additional readings on RMA and related materials.

14.5 Points to Remember

Some points to remember include the following:

- An outside-in approach can be used to decompose applications at the top level.
- Device dependencies can be used to decompose applications.
- Event dependencies can be used to decompose applications.
- Timing dependencies can be used to decompose applications.
- Levels of criticality of workload involved can be used to decompose applications.
- Functional cohesion, temporal cohesion, or sequential cohesion can be used either to form a task or to combine tasks.
- Rate Monotonic Scheduling can be summarized by stating that a task's priority depends on its period—the shorter the period, the higher the priority. RMS, when implemented appropriately, produces stable and predictable performance.
- Schedulability analysis only looks at how systems meet temporal requirements, not functional requirements.
- Six assumptions are associated with the basic RMA:
    - all of the tasks are periodic,
    - the tasks are independent of each other and that no interactions occur among tasks,
    - a task's deadline is the beginning of its next period,
    - each task has a constant execution time that does not vary over time,
    - all of the tasks have the same level of criticality, and
    - aperiodic tasks are limited to initialization and failure recovery work and that these aperiodic tasks do not have hard deadlines.
- Basic RMA does not account for task synchronization and aperiodic tasks.

In this chapter...

- Synchronization 231
- Communication 236
- Resource Synchronization Methods. . 238
- Critical Section Revisited 240
- Common Practical Design Patterns . . 241
- Specific Solution Design Patterns . . . 247
- Points to Remember 258

CHAPTER 15

SYNCHRONIZATION AND COMMUNICATION

15.1 Introduction

Software applications for real-time embedded systems use concurrency to maximize efficiency. As a result, an application's design typically involves multiple concurrent threads, tasks, or processes. Coordinating these activities requires inter-task synchronization and communication.

This chapter focuses on:

- resource synchronization,
- activity synchronization,
- inter-task communication, and
- ready-to-use embedded design patterns.

15.2 Synchronization

Synchronization is classified into two categories: *resource synchronization* and *activity synchronization*. Resource synchronization determines whether access to a shared resource is safe, and, if not, when it will be safe. Activity synchronization determines whether the execution of a multithreaded program has reached a certain state and, if it hasn't, how to wait for and be notified when this state is reached.

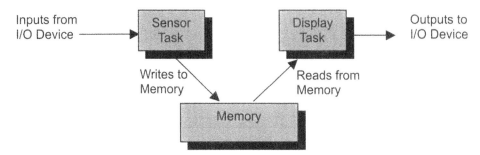

Figure 15.1   Multiple tasks accessing shared memory.

15.2.1 **Resource Synchronization**

Access by multiple tasks must be synchronized to maintain the integrity of a shared resource. This process is called *resource synchronization*, a term closely associated with critical sections and mutual exclusions.

Mutual exclusion is a provision by which only one task at a time can access a shared resource. A *critical section* is the section of code from which the shared resource is accessed.

As an example, consider two tasks trying to access shared memory. One task (the sensor task) periodically receives data from a sensor and writes the data to shared memory. Meanwhile, a second task (the display task) periodically reads from shared memory and sends the data to a display. The common design pattern of using shared memory is illustrated in Figure 15.1.

Problems arise if access to the shared memory is not exclusive, and multiple tasks can simultaneously access it. For example, if the sensor task has not completed writing data to the shared memory area before the display task tries to display the data, the display would contain a mixture of data extracted at different times, leading to erroneous data interpretation.

> A mutual exclusion algorithm ensures that one task's execution of a critical section is not interrupted by the competing critical sections of other concurrently executing tasks.

The section of code in the sensor task that writes input data to the shared memory is a critical section of the sensor task. The section of code in the display task that reads data from the shared memory is a critical section of the display task. These two critical sections are called *competing critical sections* because they access the same shared resource.

One way to synchronize access to shared resources is to use a client-server model, in which a central entity called a *resource server* is responsible for synchronization. Access requests are made to the resource server, which must grant permission to the requestor before the requestor can access the shared resource. The resource server determines the eligibility of the requestor based on pre-assigned rules or run-time heuristics.

While this model simplifies resource synchronization, the resource server is a bottleneck. Synchronization primitives, such as semaphores and mutexes, and other methods introduced in a later section of this chapter, allow developers to implement complex mutual exclusion algorithms. These algorithms in turn allow dynamic coordination among competing tasks without intervention from a third party.

15.2.2 Activity Synchronization

In general, a task must synchronize its activity with other tasks to execute a multi-threaded program properly. *Activity synchronization* is also called *condition synchronization* or *sequence control*. Activity synchronization ensures that the correct execution order among cooperating tasks is used. Activity synchronization can be either synchronous or asynchronous.

One representative of activity synchronization methods is *barrier synchronization*. For example, in embedded control systems, a complex computation can be divided and distributed among multiple tasks. Some parts of this complex computation are I/O bound, other parts are CPU intensive, and still others are mainly floating-point operations that rely heavily on specialized floating-point coprocessor hardware. These partial results must be collected from the various tasks for the final calculation. The result determines what other partial computations each task is to perform next.

The point at which the partial results are collected and the duration of the final computation is a *barrier*. One task can finish its partial computation before other tasks complete theirs, but this task must wait for all other tasks to complete their computations before the task can continue.

Barrier synchronization comprises three actions:

- a task posts its arrival at the barrier,
- the task waits for other participating tasks to reach the barrier, and
- the task receives notification to proceed beyond the barrier.

A later section of this chapter shows how to implement barrier synchronization using mutex locks and condition variables.

As shown in Figure 15.2, a group of five tasks participates in barrier synchronization. Tasks in the group complete their partial execution and reach the barrier at various times; however, each task in the group must wait at the barrier until all other tasks have reached the barrier. The last task to reach the barrier (in this example, task T5) broadcasts a notification to the other tasks. All tasks cross the barrier at the same time (conceptually in a uniprocessor environment due to task scheduling. We say "conceptually"

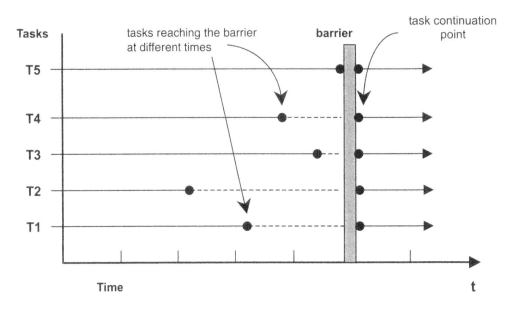

Figure 15.2   Visualization of barrier synchronization.

because in a uniprocessor environment, only one task can execute at any given time. Even though all five tasks have crossed the barrier and may continue execution, the task with the highest priority will execute next.

Another representative of activity synchronization mechanisms is *rendezvous synchronization*, which, as its name implies, is an execution point where two tasks meet. The main difference between the barrier and the rendezvous is that the barrier allows activity synchronization among two or more tasks, while rendezvous synchronization is between two tasks.

In rendezvous synchronization, a synchronization and communication point called an *entry* is constructed as a function call. One task defines its entry and makes it public. Any task with knowledge of this entry can call it as an ordinary function call. The task that defines the entry accepts the call, executes it, and returns the results to the caller. The issuer of the entry call establishes a rendezvous with the task that defined the entry.

Rendezvous synchronization is similar to synchronization using event-registers, which Chapter 8 introduces, in that both are synchronous. The issuer of the entry call is blocked if that call is not yet accepted; similarly, the task that accepts an entry call is blocked when no other task has issued the entry call. Rendezvous differs from event-register in that bidirectional data movement (input parameters and output results) is possible.

A derivative form of rendezvous synchronization, called *simple rendezvous* in this book, uses kernel primitives, such as semaphores or message queues, instead of the entry call to

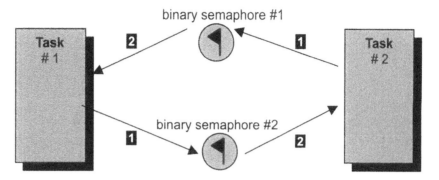

Figure 15.3   Simple rendezvous without data passing.

achieve synchronization. Two tasks can implement a simple rendezvous without data passing by using two binary semaphores, as shown in Figure 15.3.

Both binary semaphores are initialized to 0. When task #1 reaches the rendezvous, it gives semaphore #2, and then it gets on semaphore #1. When task #2 reaches the rendezvous, it gives semaphore #1, and then it gets on semaphore #2. Task #1 has to wait on semaphore #1 before task #2 arrives, and vice versa, thus achieving rendezvous synchronization.

15.2.3 Implementing Barriers

Barrier synchronization is used for activity synchronization. Listing 15.1 shows how to implement a barrier-synchronization mechanism using a mutex and a condition variable.

Listing 15.1   Pseudo code for barrier synchronization.

```
typedef struct {
    mutex_t    br_lock;      /* guarding mutex */
    cond_t     br_cond;      /* condition variable */
    int        br_count;     /* num of tasks at the barrier */
    int        br_n_threads; /* num of tasks participating in the barrier
                                synchronization */
} barrier_t;


barrier(barrier_t *br)                                               1
{
    mutex_lock(&br->br_lock);                                       2
    br->br_count++;                                                 3
```

Listing 15.1 Pseudo code for barrier synchronization. (Continued)

```
    if (br->br_count < br->br_n_threads)                          4
       cond_wait(&br->br_cond, &br->br_lock);                     5
    else
    {
       br->br_count = 0;                                          6
       cond_broadcast(&br->br_cond);                              7
    }
    mutex_unlock(&br->br_lock);                                   8
}
```

Each participating task invokes the function barrier for `barrier` synchronization. The guarding mutex for `br_count` and `br_n_threads` is acquired on line #2. The number of waiting tasks at the barrier is updated on line #3. Line #4 checks to see if all of the participating tasks have reached the barrier.

If more tasks are to arrive, the caller waits at the barrier (the blocking wait on the condition variable at line #5). If the caller is the last task of the group to enter the barrier, this task resets the barrier on line #6 and notifies all other tasks that the barrier synchronization is complete. Broadcasting on the condition variable on line #7 completes the barrier synchronization.

15.3 Communication

Tasks communicate with one another so that they can pass information to each other and coordinate their activities in a multithreaded embedded application. Communication can be signal-centric, data-centric, or both. In *signal-centric communication*, all necessary information is conveyed within the event signal itself. In *data-centric communication*, information is carried within the transferred data. When the two are combined, data transfer accompanies event notification.

When communication involves data flow and is unidirectional, this communication model is called *loosely coupled communication*. In this model, the data producer does not require a response from the consumer. Figure 15.4 illustrates an example of loosely coupled communication.

For example, an ISR for an I/O device retrieves data from a device and routes the data to a dedicated processing task. The ISR neither solicits nor requires feedback from the processing task. By contrast, in *tightly coupled communication*, the data movement is bidirectional. The data producer synchronously waits for a response to its data transfer before resuming execution, or the response is returned asynchronously while the data producer continues its function.

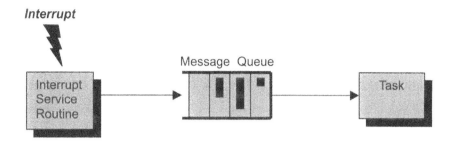

Figure 15.4 Loosely coupled ISR-to-task communication using message queues.

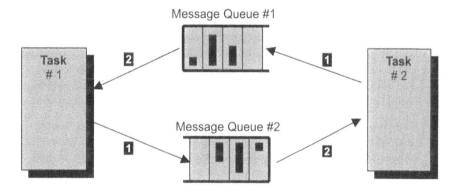

Figure 15.5 Tightly coupled task-to-task communication using message queues.

In tightly coupled communication, as shown in Figure 15.5, task #1 sends data to task #2 using message queue #2 and waits for confirmation to arrive at message queue #1. The data communication is bidirectional. It is necessary to use a message queue for confirmations because the confirmation should contain enough information in case task #1 needs to re-send the data. Task #1 can send multiple messages to task #2, i.e., task #1 can continue sending messages while waiting for confirmation to arrive on message queue #2.

Communication has several purposes, including the following:

- transferring data from one task to another,
- signaling the occurrences of events between tasks,
- allowing one task to control the execution of other tasks,
- synchronizing activities, and
- implementing custom synchronization protocols for resource sharing.

The first purpose of communication is for one task to transfer data to another task. Between the tasks, there can exist data dependency, in which one task is the data producer and another task is the data consumer. For example, consider a specialized processing task that is waiting for data to arrive from message queues or pipes or from shared memory. In this case, the data producer can be either an ISR or another task. The consumer is the processing task. The data source can be an I/O device or another task.

The second purpose of communication is for one task to signal the occurrences of events to another task. Either physical devices or other tasks can generate events. A task or an ISR that is responsible for an event, such as an I/O event, or a set of events can signal the occurrences of these events to other tasks. Data might or might not accompany event signals. Consider, for example, a timer chip ISR that notifies another task of the passing of a time tick.

The third purpose of communication is for one task to control the execution of other tasks. Tasks can have a master/slave relationship, known as *process control*. For example, in a control system, a master task that has the full knowledge of the entire running system controls individual subordinate tasks. Each subtask is responsible for a component, such as various sensors of the control system. The master task sends commands to the subordinate tasks to enable or disable sensors. In this scenario, data flow can be either unidirectional or bidirectional if feedback is returned from the subordinate tasks.

The fourth purpose of communication is to synchronize activities. The computation example given in "Activity Synchronization" on page 233, section 15.2.2, shows that when multiple tasks are waiting at the execution barrier, each task waits for a signal from the last task that enters the barrier, so that each task can continue its own execution. In this example, it is insufficient to notify the tasks that the final computation has completed; additional information, such as the actual computation results, must also be conveyed.

The fifth purpose of communication is to implement additional synchronization protocols for resource sharing. The tasks of a multithreaded program can implement custom, more-complex resource synchronization protocols on top of the system-supplied synchronization primitives.

15.4 Resource Synchronization Methods

Chapter 6 discusses semaphores and mutexes that can be used as resource synchronization primitives. Two other methods, interrupt locking and preemption locking, can also be deployed in accomplishing resource synchronization.

15.4.1 Interrupt Locks

Interrupt locking (disabling system interrupts) is the method used to synchronize exclusive access to shared resources between tasks and ISRs. Some processor architecture designs allow for a fine-grained, interrupt-level lock, i.e., an interrupt lock level is specified so that asynchronous events at or below the level of the disabled interrupt are blocked for the duration of the lock. Other processor architecture designs allow only coarse-grained locking, i.e., all system interrupts are disabled.

When interrupts are disabled at certain levels, even the kernel scheduler cannot run because the system becomes non-responsive to those external events that can trigger task re-scheduling. This process guarantees that the current task continues to execute until it voluntarily relinquishes control. As such, interrupt locking can also be used to synchronize access to shared resources between tasks.

Interrupt locking is simple to implement and involves only a few instructions. However, frequent use of interrupt locks can alter overall system timing, with side effects including missed external events (resulting in data overflow) and clock drift (resulting in missed deadlines). Interrupt locks, although the most powerful and the most effective synchronization method, can introduce indeterminism into the system when used indiscriminately. Therefore, the duration of interrupt locks should be short, and interrupt locks should be used only when necessary to guard a task-level critical region from interrupt activities.

A task that enabled interrupt locking must avoid blocking. The behavior of a task making a blocking call (such as acquiring a semaphore in blocking mode) while interrupts are disabled is dependent on the RTOS implementation. Some RTOSes block the calling task and then re-enable the system interrupts. The kernel disables interrupts again on behalf of the task after the task is ready to be unblocked. The system can hang forever in RTOSes that do not support this feature.

15.4.2 Preemption Locks

Preemption locking (disabling the kernel scheduler) is another method used in resource synchronization. Many RTOS kernels support priority-based, preemptive task scheduling. A task disables the kernel preemption when it enters its critical section and re-enables the preemption when finished. The executing task cannot be preempted while the preemption lock is in effect.

On the surface, preemption locking appears to be more acceptable than interrupt locking. Closer examination reveals that preemption locking introduces the possibility for priority inversion. Even though interrupts are enabled while preemption locking is in effect, actual servicing of the event is usually delayed to a dedicated task outside the context of the ISR. The ISR must notify that task that such an event has occurred.

This dedicated task usually executes at a high priority. This higher priority task, however, cannot run while another task is inside a critical region that a preemption lock is guarding. In this case, the result is not much different from using an interrupt lock. The priority inversion, however, is bounded. Chapter 16 discusses priority inversion in detail.

The problem with preemption locking is that higher priority tasks cannot execute, even when they are totally unrelated to the critical section that the preemption lock is guarding. This process can introduce indeterminism in a similar manner to that caused by the interrupt lock. This indeterminism is unacceptable to many systems requiring consistent real-time response.

For example, consider two medium-priority tasks that share a critical section and that use preemption locking as the synchronization primitive. An unrelated print server daemon task runs at a much higher priority; however, the printer daemon cannot send a command to the printer to eject one page and feed the next while either of the medium tasks is inside the critical section. This issue results in garbled output or output mixed from multiple print jobs.

The benefit of preemption locking is that it allows the accumulation of asynchronous events instead of deleting them. The I/O device is maintained in a consistent state because its ISR can execute. Unlike interrupt locking, preemption locking can be expensive, depending on its implementation.

In the majority of RTOSes when a task makes a blocking call while preemption is disabled, another task is scheduled to run, and the scheduler disables preemption after the original task is ready to resume execution.

15.5 Critical Section Revisited

Many sources give the impression that a mutual exclusion algorithm similar to either the interrupt lock or the preemption lock should be used to guard a critical section. One implication is that the critical section should be kept short. This idea bears further examination.

The critical section of a task is a section of code that accesses a shared resource. A competing critical section is a section of code in another task that accesses the same resource. If these tasks do not have real-time deadlines and guarding the critical section is used only to ensure exclusive access to the shared resource without side effects, then the duration of the critical section is not important.

Imagine that a system has two tasks: one that performs some calculations and stores the results in a shared variable and another that reads that shared variable and displays its value. Using a chosen mutual exclusion algorithm to guard the critical section ensures that each task has exclusive access to the shared variable. These tasks do not have real-time requirements, and the only constraint placed on these two tasks is that the write operation precedes the read operation on the shared variable.

If another task without a competing critical section exists in the system but does have real-time deadlines to meet, the task must be allowed to interrupt either of the other two tasks, regardless of whether the task to be interrupted is in its critical section, in order to guarantee overall system correctness. Therefore, in this particular example, the duration of the critical sections of the first two tasks can be long, and higher priority task should be allowed to interrupt.

If the first two tasks have real-time deadlines and the time needed to complete their associated critical sections impacts whether the tasks meet their deadlines, this critical section should run to completion without interruption. The preemption lock becomes useful in this situation.

Therefore, it is important to evaluate the criticality of the critical section and the overall system impact before deciding on which mutual exclusion algorithm to use for guarding a critical section. The solution to the mutual exclusion problem should satisfy the following conditions:

- only one task can enter its critical section at any given time,
- fair access to the shared resource by multiple competing tasks is provided, and
- one task executing its critical section must not prevent another task executing a non-competing critical section.

15.6 Common Practical Design Patterns

This section presents a set of common inter-tasks synchronization and communication patterns designed from real-life scenarios. These design patterns are ready to be used in real-world embedded designs.

In these design patterns, the operation of event register manipulation is considered an atomic operation. The numberings shown in these design patterns indicate the execution orders.

15.6.1 Synchronous Activity Synchronization

Multiple ways of implementing synchronous activity synchronization are available, including:

- task-to-task synchronization using binary semaphores,
- ISR-to-task synchronization using binary semaphores,
- task-to-task synchronization using event registers,
- ISR-to-task synchronization using event registers,
- ISR-to-task synchronization using counting semaphores, and
- simple rendezvous with data passing.

Task-to-Task Synchronization Using Binary Semaphores

In this design pattern, two tasks synchronize their activities using a binary semaphore, as shown in Figure 15.6. The initial value of the binary semaphore is 0. Task #2 has to wait for task #1 to reach an execution point, at which time, task #1 signals to task #2 its arrival at the execution point by giving the semaphore and changing the value of the binary semaphore to 1. At this point, depending on their execution priorities, task #2 can run if it has higher priority. The value of the binary semaphore is reset to 0 after the synchronization. In this design pattern, task #2 has execution dependency on task #1.

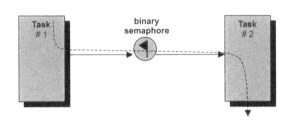

Figure 15.6   Task-to-task synchronization using binary semaphores.

ISR-to-Task Synchronization Using Binary Semaphores

In this design pattern, a task and an ISR synchronize their activities using a binary semaphore, as shown in Figure 15.7. The initial value of the binary semaphore is 0. The task has to wait for the ISR to signal the occurrence of an asynchronous event. When the event occurs and the associated ISR runs, it signals to the task by giving the semaphore and changing the value of the binary semaphore to 1. The ISR runs to completion before the task gets the chance to resume execution. The value of the binary semaphore is reset to 0 after the task resumes execution.

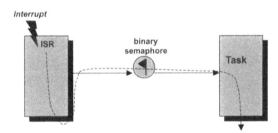

Figure 15.7   ISR-to-task synchronization using binary semaphores.

Task-to-Task Synchronization Using Event Registers

In this design pattern, two tasks synchronize their activities using an event register, as shown in Figure 15.8. The tasks agree on a bit location in the event register for signaling. In this example, the bit location is the first bit. The initial value of the event bit is 0. Task #2 has to wait for task #1 to reach an execution point. Task #1 signals to task #2 its arrival at that point by setting the event bit to 1. At this point, depending on execution priority, task #2 can run if it has higher priority. The value of the event bit is reset to 0 after synchronization.

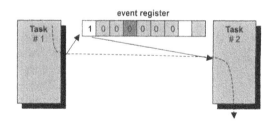

Figure 15.8   Task-to-task synchronization using event registers.

ISR-to-Task Synchronization Using Event Registers

In this design pattern, a task and an ISR synchronize their activities using an event register, as shown in Figure 15.9. The task and the ISR agree on an event bit location for signaling. In this example, the bit location is the first bit. The initial value of the event bit is 0. The task has to wait for the ISR to signal the occurrence of an asynchronous event. When the event occurs and the associated ISR runs, it signals to the task by changing the event bit to 1. The ISR runs to completion before the task gets the chance to resume execution. The value of the event bit is reset to 0 after the task resume execution.

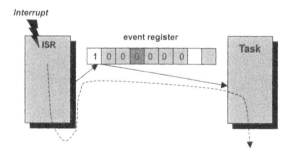

Figure 15.9   ISR-to-task synchronization using event registers.

ISR-to-Task Synchronization Using Counting Semaphores

In Figures 15.6, 15.7, 15.8, and 15.9, multiple occurrences of the same event cannot accumulate. A counting semaphore, however, is used in Figure 15.10 to accumulate event occurrences and for task signaling. The value of the counting semaphore increments by one each time the ISR gives the semaphore. Similarly, its value is decremented by one each time the task gets the semaphore. The task runs as long as the counting semaphore is non-zero.

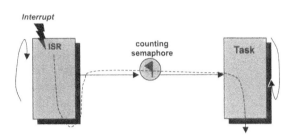

Figure 15.10 ISR-to-task synchronization using counting semaphores.

Simple Rendezvous with Data Passing

Two tasks can implement a simple rendezvous and can exchange data at the rendezvous point using two message queues, as shown in Figure 15.11. Each message queue can hold a maximum of one message. Both message queues are initially empty. When task #1 reaches the rendezvous, it puts data into message queue #2 and waits for a message to arrive on message queue #1. When task #2 reaches the rendezvous, it puts data into message queue #1 and waits for

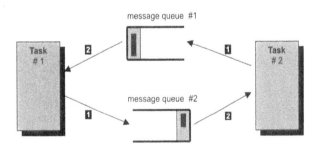

Figure 15.11 Task-to-task rendezvous using two message queues.

data to arrive on message queue #2. Task #1 has to wait on message queue #1 before task #2 arrives, and vice versa, thus achieving rendezvous synchronization with data passing.

15.6.2 Asynchronous Event Notification Using Signals

One task can synchronize with another task in urgent mode using the signal facility. The signaled task processes the event notification asynchronously. In Figure 15.12, a task generates a signal to another task. The receiving task diverts from its normal execution path and executes its asynchronous signal routine.

Figure 15.12 Using signals for urgent data communication.

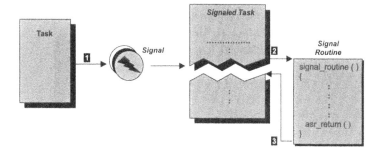

15.6.3 Resource Synchronization

Multiple ways of accomplishing resource synchronization are available. These methods include accessing shared memory with mutexes, interrupt locks, or preemption locks and sharing multiple instances of resources using counting semaphores and mutexes.

Shared Memory with Mutexes

In this design pattern, task #1 and task #2 access shared memory using a mutex for synchronization. Each task must first acquire the mutex before accessing the shared memory. The task blocks if the mutex is already locked, indicating that another task is accessing the shared memory. The task releases the mutex after it completes its operation on the shared memory. Figure 15.13 shows the order of execution with respect to each task.

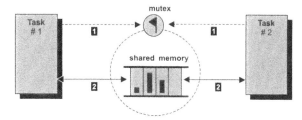

Figure 15.13 Task-to-task resource synchronization—shared memory guarded by mutex.

Shared Memory with Interrupt Locks

In this design pattern, the ISR transfers data to the task using shared memory, as shown in Figure 15.14. The ISR puts data into the shared memory, and the task removes data from the shared memory and subsequently processes it. The interrupt lock is used for synchronizing access to the shared memory. The task must acquire and release the interrupt lock to avoid the interrupt disrupting its execution. The ISR does not need to be aware of the existence of the interrupt lock unless nested interrupts are supported (i.e., interrupts are enabled while an ISR executes) and multiple ISRs can access the data.

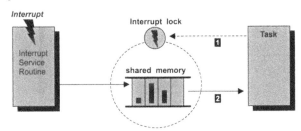

Figure 15.14 ISR-to-task resource synchronization—shared memory guarded by interrupt lock.

Shared Memory with Preemption Locks

In this design pattern, two tasks transfer data to each other using shared memory, as shown in Figure 15.15. Each task is responsible for disabling preemption before accessing the shared memory. Unlike using a binary semaphore or a mutex lock, no waiting is invovled when using a preemption lock for synchronization.

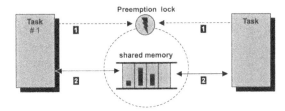

Figure 15.15 Task-to-task resource synchronization—shared memory guarded by preemption lock.

Sharing Multiple Instances of Resources Using Counting Semaphores and Mutexes

Figure 15.16 depicts a typical scenario where N tasks share M instances of a single resource type, for example, M printers. The counting semaphore tracks the number of available resource instances at any given time. The counting semaphore is initialized with the value M. Each task must acquire the counting semaphore before accessing the shared resource. By acquiring the counting semaphore, the task effectively reserves an instance of the resource. Having the counting semaphore alone is insufficient. Typically, a control structure associated with the resource instances is used. The control structure maintains information such as which resource instances are in use and which are available for allocation. The control information is updated each time a resource instance is either allocated to or released by a task. A mutex is deployed to guarantee that each task has exclusive access to the control structure. Therefore, after a task successfully acquires

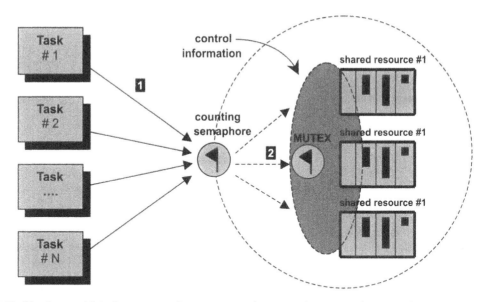

Figure 15.16 Sharing multiple instances of resources using counting semaphores and mutexes.

the counting semaphore, the task must acquire the mutex before the task can either allocate or free an instance.

15.7 **Specific Solution Design Patterns**

This section presents more complex design patterns for synchronization and communication. Multiple synchronization primitives can be found in a single design pattern.

15.7.1 **Data Transfer with Flow Control**

Task-to-task communication commonly involves data transfer. One task is a producer, and the other is a data consumer. Data processing takes time, and the consumer task might not be able to consume the data as fast as the producer can produce it. The producer can potentially overflow the communication channel if a higher priority task preempts the consumer task. Therefore, the consumer task might need to control the rate at which the producer task generates the data. This process is accomplished through a counting semaphore, as shown in Figure 15.17. In this case, the counting semaphore is a permission to produce data.

The data buffer in this design pattern is different from an RTOS-supplied message queue. Typically, a message queue has a built-in flow control mechanism. Assume that this message buffer is a custom data transfer mechanism that is not supplied by the RTOS.

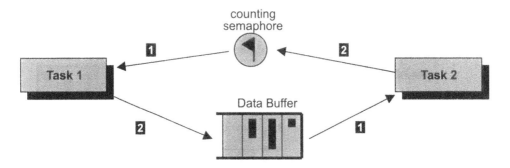

Figure 15.17 Using counting semaphores for flow control.

As shown in Figure 15.17, task #1 is the data producer, while task #2 is the consumer. Task #1 can introduce data into the buffer as long as the task can successfully acquire the counting semaphore. The counting semaphore may be initialized to a value less than the maximum allowable token value. Task #2 can increase the token value with the give operation and may decrease the token value by the take operation depending on how fast the task can consume data. Listing 15.2 shows the pseudo code for this design pattern.

Listing 15.2   Pseudo code for data transfer with flow control.

```
Acquire(Counting_Semaphore)        Consume data from MsgQueue
Produce data into msgQueue         Give(Counting_Semaphore)
```
data producing task   **data consuming task**

15.7.2 Asynchronous Data Reception from Multiple Data Communication Channels

Commonly, a daemon task receives data from multiple input sources, which implies that data arrives on multiple message queues. A task cannot block and wait for data on multiple message queues. Therefore, in such cases, multiple sources may use a single semaphore to signal the arrival of data. A task cannot block and wait on multiple semaphores either.

The task blocks and waits on the semaphore. Each ISR inserts data in the corresponding message queue followed by a give operation on the semaphore.

As shown in Figure 15.18, a single interrupt lock is sufficient to protect against multiple interrupt sources, as long as the masked interrupt level covers these sources. Both the interrupt service routines use a single semaphore as the signal channel.

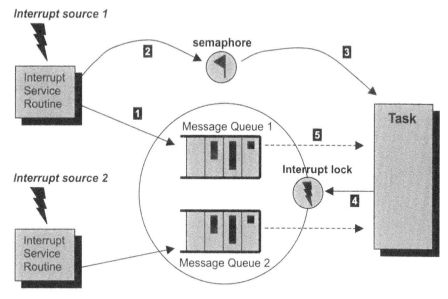

Figure 15.18 Task waiting on multiple input sources.

Listing 15.3 shows the code that the task runs when multiple input message queues are present. Note that the semaphore used in this case is a binary semaphore.

Listing 15.3   Pseudo code for task waiting on multiple input sources.

```
while (Get(Binary_Semaphore))
      disable(interrupts)
      for (each msgQueue)
            get msgQueueLength
            for (msgQueueLength)
                  remove a message
                  enable(interrupts)
                  process the message
                  disable(interrupts)
            endfor
      endfor
      enable(interrupts)
end while
```

Some RTOS kernels do not have the event-register object. Implementing the event register using the common basic primitives found in the majority of the RTOS kernels can be quite useful when porting applications from one RTOS to another.

The event-register object can be implemented using a shared variable, an interrupt lock, and a semaphore. The shared variable stores and retrieves the events. The interrupt lock guards the shared variable because ISRs can generate events through the event register. The semaphore blocks the task wanting to receive desired events.

```
Event_Receive(wanted_events)
{
        task_cb.wanted_events = wanted_events
        While (TRUE)
                Get(task_cb.event_semaphore)
                disable(interrupts)
                events = wanted_events XOR task_cb.recvd_events
                task_cb.wanted_events = task_cb.wanted_event AND (NOT
                events)
                enable(interrupts)
                If (events is not empty)
                        return (events)
                endIf
        endWhile
}
```

The variable `task_cb` refers to the task control block, in which the kernel keeps its private, task-specific information. Note that the unwanted events are not cleared because the task can call `event_receive` some time later.

```
Event_Send(events)
{
        disable(interrupts)
        task_cb.recvd_events = task_cb.recvd_events OR events
        enable(interrupts)
        Give(task_cb.event_semaphore)
}
```

15.7.3 Multiple Input Communication Channels

A daemon task usually has multiple data input sources and multiple event input sources, as shown in Figure 15.19. Consider a daemon task that processes data from an I/O device and has a periodic timer, which is used for recovery if the device is stuck in an inconsistent state. The system timer ISR signals the periodic timer event; this event does not carry data. In such situations, an event register combined with a counting semaphore is a much better alternative than using counting semaphores alone for signaling (see Figure 15.10).

With an event register, each event bit is pre-allocated to a source. In this design pattern, one event bit is assigned to the I/O task #1 and another bit is assigned to the timer ISR. The task blocks on an event register, and an event from either source activates the task. The I/O task first inserts the data associated with an I/O device into the message queue. Then the I/O task signals this event to the task by setting the event's assigned bit in the event register. The timer ISR sets the event bit; this event is no more than a tick announcement to the task. After the task resumes execution, it performs the appropriate action according to the event-register state.

Because the event register is only used as a signaling mechanism, a counting semaphore is used to keep track of the total number of tick occurrences. Listing 15.4 puts this discussion into perspective. The addition of the counting semaphore does not increase the code complexity.

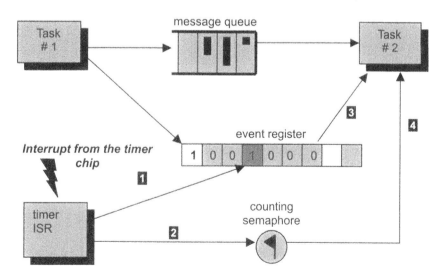

Figure 15.19 Task with multiple input communication channels.

Listing 15.4   Pseudo code for using a counting semaphore for event accumulation combined with an event-register used for event notification.

```
while (the_events = wait for events from Event-Register)
      if (the_events & EVENT_TYPE_DEVICE)
            while (Get message from msgQueue)
                  process the message
            endwhile
      endif

      if (the_events & EVENT_TYPE_TIMER)
            counter = 0
            disable(interrupts)
            while (Get(Counting_Semaphore))
                  counter = counter + 1
            endwhile
            enable(interrupts)
            if (counter > 1)
                  recovery time
            else
                  process the timer tick
            endif
      endif
endwhile
```

15.7.4 Using Condition Variables to Synchronize between Readers and Writers

The design pattern shown in Figure 15.20 demonstrates the use of condition variables. A condition variable can be associated with the state of a shared resource. In this example, multiple tasks are trying to insert messages into a shared message queue. The predicate of the condition variable is "the message queue is full." Each writer task tries first to insert the message into the message queue. The task waits (and is blocked) if the message queue is currently full. Otherwise, the message is inserted, and the task continues its execution path.

Note the message queue shown in Figure 15.20 is called a "simple message queue." For the sake of this example, the reader should assume this message queue is a simple buffer with structured content. This simple message queue is not the same type of message queue that is provided by the RTOS.

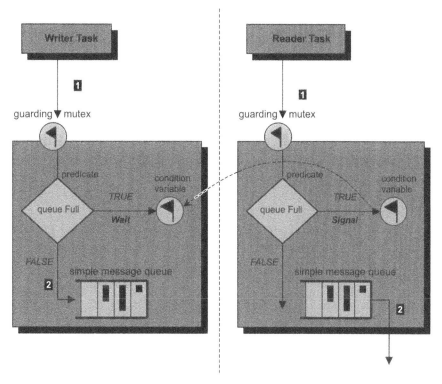

Figure 15.20 Using condition variables for task synchronization.

Dedicated reader (or consumer) tasks periodically remove messages from the message queue. The reader task signals on the condition variable if the message queue is full, in effect waking up the writer tasks that are blocked waiting on the condition variable. Listing 15.5 shows the pseudo code for reader tasks and Listing 15.6 shows the pseudo code for writer tasks.

Listing 15.5   Pseudo code for reader tasks.

```
Lock(guarding_mutex)
Remove message from message queue
If (msgQueue Was Full)
     Signal(Condition_variable)
Unlock(guarding_mutex)
```

As Chapter 8 discusses, the call to event_receive is a blocking call. The calling task is blocked if the event register is empty when the call is made. Remember that the event register is a synchronous signal mechanism. The task might not run immediately when events are signaled to it, if a higher priority task is currently executing. Events from different sources are accumulated until the associated task resumes execution. At that point, the call returns with a snapshot of the state of the event register. The task operates on this returned value to determine which events have occurred.

Problematically, however, the event register cannot accumulate event occurrences of the same type before processing begins. The task would have missed all but one timer tick event if multiple timer ticks had occurred before the task resumed execution. Introducing a counting semaphore into the circuit can solve this problem. Soft timers, as Chapter 11 discusses, do not have stringent deadlines. It is important to track how many ticks have occurred. This way, the task can perform recovery actions, such as fast-forwarding time to reduce the drift.

The data buffer in this design pattern is different from an RTOS-supplied message queue. Typically, a message queue has a built-in flow control mechanism. Assume that this message buffer is a custom data transfer mechanism that is not supplied by the RTOS.

Listing 15.6   Pseudo code for writer tasks.

```
Lock(guarding_mutex)
While (msgQueue is Full)
    Wait(Condition_variable)
Produce message into message queue
Unlock(guarding_mutex)
```

Note that the lock call on the guarding mutex is a blocking call. Either a writer task or a reader task is blocked if it tries to lock the mutex while in the locked state. This feature guarantees serialized access to the shared message queue. The wait operation and the signal operation are both atomic operations with respect to the predicate and the guarding mutex, as Chapter 8 discusses.

In this example, the reader tasks create the condition for the writer tasks to proceed producing messages. The one-way condition creation of this design implies that either there are more writer tasks than there are reader tasks, or that the production of messages is faster than the consumption of these messages.

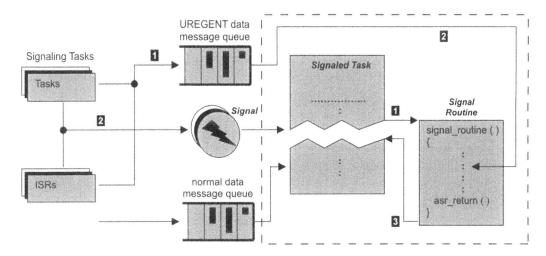

Figure 15.21   Using signals for urgent data communication.

15.7.5 Sending High Priority Data between Tasks

In many situations, the communication between tasks can carry urgent data. Urgent data must be processed in a timely fashion and must be distinguished from normal data. This process is accomplished by using signals and an urgent data message queue, as shown in Figure 15.21. For the sake of this example, the reader should assume the message queues shown in Figure 15.21 do not support a priority message delivery mechanism.

As Chapter 8 describes, one task uses a signal to notify another of the arrival of urgent data. When the signal arrives, the receiving task diverts from its normal execution and goes directly to the urgent data message queue. The task processes messages from this queue ahead of messages from other queues because the urgent data queue has the highest priority. This task must install an asynchronous signal handler for the urgent data signal in order to receive it. The reason the signal for urgent data notification is deploying is because the task does not know of the arrival of urgent data unless the task is already waiting on the message queue.

The producer of the urgent data, which can be either a task or an ISR, inserts the urgent messages into the predefined urgent data message queue. The source signals the recipient of the urgent data. The signal interrupts the normal execution path of the recipient task, and the installed signal handler is invoked. Inside this signal handler, urgent messages are read and processed.

In this design pattern, urgent data is maintained in a separate message queue although most RTOS-supplied message queues support priority messages. With a separate message queue for urgent data, the receiver can control how much urgent data it is willing to accept and process, i.e., a flow control mechanism.

15.7.6 Implementing Reader-Writer Locks Using Condition Variables

This section presents another example of the usage of condition variables. The code shown in Listings 15.7, 15.8, and 15.9 are written in C programming language.

Consider a shared memory region that both readers and writers can access. The example reader-writer lock design has the following properties: multiple readers can simultaneously read the memory content, but only one writer is allowed to write data into the shared memory at any one time. The writer can begin writing to the shared memory when that memory region is not accessed by a task (readers or writers). Readers precede writers because readers have priority over writers in term of accessing the shared memory region.

The implementation that follows can be adapted to other types of synchronization scenarios when prioritized access to shared resources is desired, as shown in Listings 15.7, 15.8, and 15.9.

The following assumptions are made in the program listings:

1. The `mutex_t` data type represents a mutex object and `condvar_t` represents a condition variable object; both are provided by the RTOS.
2. `lock_mutex`, `unlock_mutex`, `wait_cond`, `signal_cond`, and `broadcast_cond` are functions provided by the RTOS. `lock_mutex` and `unlock_mutex` operate on the mutex object. `wait_cond`, `signal_cond`, and `broadcast_cond` operate on the condition variable object.

Listing 15.7 shows the data structure needed to implement the reader-writer lock.

Listing 15.7   Data structure for implementing reader-writer locks.

```
typedef struct {
        mutex_t        guard_mutex;
        condvar_t      read_condvar;
        condvar_t      write_condvar;
        int            rw_count;
        int            read_waiting;
} rwlock_t;


rw_count == -1 indicates a writer is active
```

Listing 15.8 shows the code that the writer task invokesto acquire and to release the lock.

Listing 15.8   Code called by the writer task to acquire and release locks.

```
acquire_write(rwlock_t  *rwlock)
{
        lock_mutex(&rwlock->guard_mutex);
        while (rwlock->rw_count != 0)
                wait_cond(&rwlock->write_condvar, &rwlock->guard_mutex);
        rwlock->rw_count = -1;
        unlock_mutex(&rwlock->guard_mutex);
}


release_write(rwlock_t  *rwlock)
{
        lock_mutex(&rwlock->guard_mutex);
        rwlock->rw_count = 0;
        if (rwlock->r_waiting)
                broadcast_cond(&rwlock->read_condvar, &rwlock->guard_mutex);
        else
                signal_cond(&rwlock->write_condvar, &rwlock->guard_mutex);
        unlock_mutex(&rwlock->guard_mutex);
}
```

Listing 15.9 shows the code that the reader task invokes to acquire and release the lock.

Listing 15.9   Code called by the reader task to acquire and release locks.

```
acquire_read(rwlock_t  *rwlock)
{
        lock_mutex(&rwlock->guard_mutex);
        rwlock->r_waiting++;
        while (rwlock->rw_count < 0)
                wait_cond(&rwlock->read_condvar, &rwlock->guard_mutex);
        rwlock->r_waiting = 0;
        rwlock->rw_count++;
        unlock_mutex(&rwlock->guard_mutex);
}
```

Listing 15.9   Code called by the reader task to acquire and release locks. (Continued)

```
release_read(rwlock_t *rwlock)
{
        lock_mutex(&rwlock->guard_mutex);
        rwlock->rw_count --;
        if (rwlock->rw_count == 0)
                signal_cond(&rwlock->write_condvar, &rwlock->guard_mutex);
        unlock_mutex(&rwlock->guard_mutex);
}
```

In case `broadcast_cond` does not exist, use a `for` loop as follows

```
for (i = rwlock->read_waiting; i > 0; i--)
    signal_cond(&rwlock->read_condvar, &rwlock->guard_mutex);
```

15.8 Points to Remember

Some points to remember include the following:

- Synchronization is classified into resource and activity synchronization.
- Resource synchronization is closely related to critical sections and mutual exclusion.
- Activity synchronization is also called condition synchronization or sequence control.
- Barrier synchronization can be used to perform activity synchronization for a group of tasks.
- Rendezvous synchronization is used to perform activity synchronization between two tasks.
- Tasks communicate with each other to transfer data, to signal event occurrences, to allow one task to control other tasks, to synchronize activities, and to implement custom resource synchronization protocols.
- Interrupt locks should be used only when necessary to synchronize access to shared resources between a task and an ISR.
- Preemption locks can cause priority inversion.

In this chapter...

- Resource Classification 260
- Deadlocks. 260
- Priority Inversion. 273
- Points to Remember 280

CHAPTER 16

COMMON DESIGN PROBLEMS

16.1 Introduction

Most embedded RTOSes facilitate a multitasking- or multithreading-capable environment. Many challenging design problems arise when developing embedded applications in multitasking systems.

The nature of this environment is that multiple threads of execution share and contend for the same set of resources. As such, resource sharing requires careful coordination to ensure that each task can eventually acquire the needed resource or resources to continue execution.

In a preemptive multitasking environment, resource sharing is a function of task priority. The higher the priority of a task, the more important the task is. Higher priority tasks have precedence over lower priority tasks when accessing shared resources. Therefore, resource sharing cannot violate this rule. On the other hand, if higher priority tasks always take resources from lower priority tasks, this sharing scheme is not fair and can prevent lower priority tasks from ever completing. This condition is called *starvation*. Maximization of resource utilization is yet another conflicting requirement.

Two of the most common design problems facing embedded developers are the deadlock and the priority inversion problem.

Specifically, this chapter focuses on:

- resource classification,
- resource request models,
- definition of deadlocks,

- deadlock detection, recovery, avoidance and prevention,
- definition of priority inversion, and
- solutions to priority inversion.

16.2 Resource Classification

In embedded systems, resources are shared among various concurrently executing tasks. Examples of these shared resources include I/O devices, machine registers, and memory regions. These shared resources are categorized as either *preemptible* or *non-preemptible*.

A preemptible resource can be involuntarily and temporarily removed from a task without affecting the task's execution state or result. The machine registers set that is shared among multiple tasks is an example. When kernel scheduling preempts a current task, the content of the machine registers, including the execution state of the current task, is saved into main memory. The registers are reinitialized to execute another task. When that other task completes, the execution state is restored to the register set, and the preempted task is resumed. The scheduler guarantees that the register set contains the execution state from a single task even though the registers are shared among multiple tasks throughout the system's lifetime.

A non-preemptible shared resource must be voluntarily relinquished by the owning task, or unpredictable results can occur. A shared memory region belongs to this category. For example, one task should not be allowed to write to a shared memory region before another task completes its read or write operation.

The types of resources a task holds are important when deciding on what solutions to take when the task is involved in deadlock situations. Section 16.3.3 discusses the relationship between the resource types and deadlock recovery mechanisms in detail.

16.3 Deadlocks

Deadlock is the situation in which multiple concurrent threads of execution in a system are blocked permanently because of resource requirements that can never be satisfied.

A typical real-time system has multiple types of resources and multiple concurrent threads of execution contending for these resources. Each thread of execution can acquire multiple resources of various types throughout its lifetime. Potential for deadlocks exist in a system in which the underlying RTOS permits resource sharing among multiple threads of execution. Deadlock occurs when the following four conditions are present:

Mutual exclusion—A resource can be accessed by only one task at a time, i.e., exclusive access mode.

No preemption—A non-preemptible resource cannot be forcibly removed from its holding task. A resource becomes available only when its holder voluntarily relinquishes claim to the resource.

Hold and wait—A task holds already-acquired resources, while waiting for additional resources to become available.

Circular wait—A circular chain of two or more tasks exists, in which each task holds one or more resources being requested by a task next in the chain.

Given that each resource is non-preemptible and supports only exclusive access mode, Figure 16.1 depicts a deadlock situation between two tasks.

Figure 16.1 is a *resource graph*. An arrow labeled *holds* going from a resource to a task indicates that the task currently holds (or owns) the resource. An arrow labeled *wants* going from a task to a resource indicates that the task currently needs this resource to resume execution.

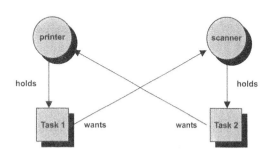

Figure 16.1   Deadlock situation between two tasks.

In this example, task #1 wants the scanner while holding the printer. Task #1 cannot proceed until both the printer and the scanner are in its possession. Task #2 wants the printer while holding the scanner. Task #2 cannot continue until it has the printer and the scanner. Because neither task #1 nor task #2 is willing to give up what it already has, the two tasks are now deadlocked because neither can continue execution.

Deadlocks can involve more than two tasks.

As shown in Figure 16.2, task T1 currently holds resource R1 (a printer), and T1 wants resource R2 (a scanner). Task T2 holds resource R2 and wants resource R3 (a memory buffer). Similarly, task T3 holds resource R3 and wants resource R1. It is easy to see the cycle, i.e., the circular-wait condition in this system. Tasks T1, T2, and T3, and resources R1, R2, and R3 comprise the *deadlocked set*. Note that in the system in Figure 16.2, one instance per resource type exists, i.e., there is one

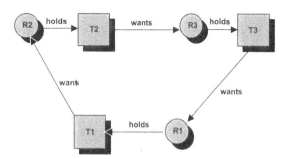

Figure 16.2   Deadlock situation among three tasks.

instance of R1, one instance of R2, and one instance of R3. A later section, "Multi-Instance Resource Deadlock Detection" on page 266, discusses deadlock situations that involve multiple instances of a resource type.

In this example, each task requires a single instance of a single resource type at any given time. Many situations exist in which a task might require multiple instances of multiple types of resources. The formation of deadlocks depends on how a task requests resources (formally known as a *resource request model*). The deadlock detection algorithms are constructed according to the resource request models.

16.3.1 Resource Request Models

When tasks ask for resources, the way the task makes the requests can be classified into these request models:

- the Single resource request model,
- the AND resource request model,
- the OR resource request model, and
- the AND-OR resource request model.

In the Single resource request model, exemplified in both Figure 16.1 and Figure 16.2, a task can have at most one outstanding resource request at any given time. In the request model, a task asks for resources as in "wants a printer."

In the AND resource request model, a task can have multiple simultaneous requests outstanding at any given time. For example, a task can request resources as (R1 *and* R2) or (R1 *and* R2 *and* R3). A task is blocked until all of the requested resources are granted. In this request model, a task asks for resources as in "wants both a printer and a scanner." The task resumes execution only when it successfully acquires both the printer and the scanner.

In the OR resource request model, a task can request a set of resources, but the task can resume execution as soon as any one of the resources from the request set becomes available. For example, a task can request resources as (R1 *or* R2) or (R1 *or* R2 *or* R3). In this request model, a task asks for resources as in "wants either a printer or a scanner." The task resumes execution when it acquires either the printer or the scanner.

In the AND-OR resource request model, a task can make resource requests in any combination of the AND and OR models. For example, a task can request a set of resources as (R1 *or* R2 *and* (R3 *or* R4)). In this request model, the task asks for resources as in "wants either a printer or a scanner, and wants either a memory buffer or a message queue." The task can resume execution when it acquires both the printer and the memory buffer, when it acquires both the printer and the message queue, or when it acquires the scanner and the memory buffer, or when it acquires the scanner and the message queue. A generalization of the AND-OR model is the $C(n,k)$ model. In this model, a task can make n resource requests and can resume execution as soon as k resources are granted, where $k \leq n$.

16.3.2 Deadlock Detection

A deadlock condition is called a *stable deadlock* when no task in the deadlocked set expects a timeout or an abort that can eliminate the deadlock. A stable deadlock is permanent and requires external influence to eliminate. The external influence is the deadlock detection and recovery by the underlying RTOS.

Deadlock detection is the periodic deployment of an algorithm by the RTOS. The algorithm examines the current resource allocation state and pending resource requests to determine whether deadlock exists in the system, and if so, which tasks and resources are involved.

The deadlock detection algorithm that the RTOS deploys is a global algorithm because it is used to detect deadlocks in the entire system. In general, each task of the deadlocked set is not aware of the deadlock condition. As a result, the recovery algorithm is more intrusive on the normal execution of the tasks belonging to the deadlocked set. The recovery algorithms and reasons why these algorithms are intrusive on the execution of the tasks involved in the deadlock are discussed shortly.

A *temporal deadlock* is a temporary deadlock situation in which one or more tasks of the deadlocked set either times out or aborts abnormally due to timing constraints. When the task times out or aborts, it frees the resources that might have caused the deadlock in the first place, thus eliminating the deadlock. This form of detection and recovery is localized to an individual task, and the task has deadlock awareness.

A system that is capable of deadlock detection is more efficient in terms of resource utilization when compared to a system without deadlock detection. A system capable of deadlock detection is not conservative when granting resource allocation requests if deadlock is allowed to occur. Therefore, resources are highly utilized. A system without deadlock detection is conservative when granting resource allocation requests. A resource request is denied if the system believes there is a potential for deadlock, which may never occur. The conservatism of the system results in idle resources even when these resources could be used.

Deadlock detection does not solve the problem; instead, the detection algorithm informs the recovery algorithm when the existence of deadlock is discovered.

For deadlock in the Single resource request model, a cycle in the resource graph is a necessary and sufficient condition.

For deadlock in the AND resource request model, a cycle in the resource graph is a necessary and sufficient condition. It is possible for a task to be involved in multiple deadlocked sets.

For deadlock in the OR request model, a knot is a necessary and sufficient condition.

Therefore, deadlock detection involves finding the presence of a cycle in the resource graph for both the Single and the AND resource request models. Deadlock detection involves finding the presence of a knot in the resource graph for the OR resource request model.

> For node *A* in the resource graph, the reachable set of *A* is the set of all nodes *B*, such that a directed path exists from *A* to *B*. A *knot* is the request set *K*, such that the reachable set of each node of *K* is exactly *K*.

For deadlock in the AND-OR model, no simple way exists of describing it. Generally, the presence of a knot after applying the algorithm to the OR model first and then subsequently applying the algorithm to the AND model and finding a cycle is an indication that deadlock is present.

The following sections present two deadlock detection algorithms—one for the single resource request model and one for the AND resource request model—to illustrate deadlock detection in practice.

Single-Instance Resource Deadlock Detection

The deadlock detection algorithm for systems with a single instance of each resource type, and tasks making resource requests following the single resource request model, is based on the graph theory. The idea is to find cycles in the resource allocation graph, which represents the circular-wait condition, indicating the existence of deadlocks.

Figure 16.3 shows the resource allocation graph. The graph represents the following:

- a circle represents a resource,
- a square represents a task or thread of execution,
- an arrow going from a task to a resource indicates that the task wants the resource, and
- an arrow going from a resource to a task indicates that the task currently holds the resource.

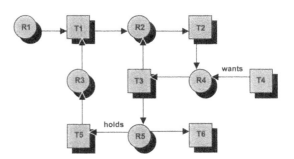

Figure 16.3 Current state of resource allocations and requests.

In the following discussions, *node* refers either to the circle (resource) or the square (task) in Figure 16.3. *Arc* refers to the arrow. The deadlock detection algorithm can be stated in these seven steps:

1. Make a list of all the nodes, *N*, from the graph.

2. Pick a node from *N*. Create another list, *L*, initially empty, which is used for the graph traversal.

3. Insert the node into *L* and check if this node already exists in *L*. If so, a cycle exists; therefore, a deadlock is detected, and the algorithm terminates. Otherwise, remove the node from *N*.

4. Check whether any un-traversed outgoing arcs from this node exist. If all of the arcs are traversed, go to step 6.

5. Choose an un-traversed outgoing arc originating from the node and mark the arc as traversed. Follow the chosen arc to the new node and return to step 3.

6. At this stage, a path in the graph terminates, and no deadlocks exist. If more than one entry is in *L*, remove the last entry from *L*. If more than one entry remains in *L*, make the last entry of *L* the current node and go to step 4.

7. If the list *N* is not empty, go to step 2. Otherwise, the algorithm terminates, and no deadlocks exist in the system.

The actual implementation from step 3 to step 6 translates into a depth first search of the directed graph.

Applying this algorithm to the system depicted in Figure 16.3 provides the following:

Step 1: *N* = { R1, T1, R2, T2, R3, T3, R4, T4, T5, R5, T6 }

Step 2: *L* = { *<empty>* }; pick node R1

Step 3: *L* = { R1 }; no cycles are in *L*; *N* = { T1, R2, T2, R3, T3, R4, T4, T5, R5, T6 }

Step 4: R1 has one outgoing arc

Step 5: Mark the arc; reaches node T1; go back to step 3

Step 3: *L* = { R1, T1 }; *N* = { R2, T2, R3, T3, R4, T4, T5, R5, T6 }; no cycles are in *L*

The algorithm continues from step 3 to step 5 and reiterates until it reaches node T3, in which the list *L* = { R1, T1, R2, T2, R4, T3 } and the list *N* = { R3, T4, T5, R5, T6 }. Two outgoing arcs are at node T3. When the downward arc is picked, *L* = { R1, T1, R2, T2, R4, T3, R5 }. Two outgoing arcs are at node R5. When the rightward arc is picked, *L* = { R1, T1, R2, T2, R4, T3, R5, T6 }.

Step 4: T6 does not have any outgoing arcs; continue to step 6

Step 6: Remove T6 from the list *L*; *L* = { R1, T1, R2, T2, R4, T3, R5 }; return to step 4

Step 4: Pick the unmarked leftward arc at R5

Step 5: Mark the arc; reaches node T5; return to step 3

Step 3: *L* = { R1, T1, R2, T2, R4, T3, R5, T5 }; *N* = { R3, T4 }; no cycles are in *L*

Step 4: Pick the only outgoing arc at T5

Step 5: Mark the arc; reaches node R3; go back to step 3

Step 3: $L = \{$ R1, T1, R2, T2, R4, T3, R5, T5, R3 $\}$; $N = \{$ T4 $\}$; still no cycles are in L

Step 4: Pick the only outgoing arc at R3

Step 5: Mark the arc; reaches node T1; go back to step 3

Step 3: $L = \{$ R1, T1, R2, T2, R4, T3, R5, T5, R3, T1 $\}$; Node T1 already exists in L. A cycle is found in the graph, and a deadlock exists. The algorithm terminates.

The deadlock set is comprised of the entire nodes enclosed by the two occurrences of node T1 inclusively. Therefore, the discovered deadlock set is {T1, R2, T2, R4, T3, R5, T5, R3}. One thing worth noting is that the algorithm detects deadlocks if any exist. Which deadlock is detected first depends on the structure of the graph. Closer examination of the resource graph reveals that another deadlock exists. That deadlock set is {R2, T2, R4, T3}. At node T3 if the upward arc is chosen first instead of the downward arc, this later deadlock occurrence would be discovered, and the algorithm would terminate much sooner.

Multi-Instance Resource Deadlock Detection

The deadlock detection algorithm takes a different approach for systems with multiple instances of each resource type, and tasks make resource requests following the AND model. An underlying assumption is that a resource allocation system is present. The *resource allocation system* is comprised of a set of different types of resources, R1, R2, R3, ..., Rn. Each type of resource has a fixed number of units. The resource allocation system maintains a resource allocation table and a resource demand table.

Each row of tables C and D represents a task T. Each column of tables C and D is associated with a resource type. C is the resource allocation table representing resources already allocated. D is the resource demand table representing additional resources required by the tasks.

N = Total System Resources Table	N_1	N_2	N_3	...	N_k

where N_i is the number of units of resource type R_i for all i where $\{\ 1 \le i \le k\ \}$.

A = Available System Resources Table	A_1	A_2	A_3	...	A_k

where A_i the number of units remaining for resource type R_i available for allocation.

C = Tasks Resources Assigned Table	C_{11}	C_{12}	C_{13}	...	C_{1k}
	C_{21}	C_{22}		...	C_{2k}
	...			...	
	C_{m1}			...	C_{mk}

D = Tasks Resources Demand Table	D_{11}	D_{12}	D_{13}	...	D_{1k}
	D_{21}	D_{22}		...	D_{2k}
	...			...	
	D_{m1}			...	D_{mk}

For example in table C, there are C_{11} units of resource R1, C_{12} units of resource R2, and so on, which are allocated to task T1. Similarly, there are C_{21} units of resource R1, C_{22} units of resource R2, and so on, which are allocated to task T2. For example in table D, task T1 demands additional D_{11} units of resource R1, additional D_{12} units of resource R2, and so on, in order to complete execution.

The deadlock detection algorithm is as follows:

1. Find a row i in table D, where $D_{ij} < A_j$ for all $1 \leq j \leq k$. If no such row exists, the system is deadlocked, and the algorithm terminates.
2. Mark the row i as complete and assign $A_j = A_j + D_{ij}$ for all $1 \leq j \leq k$.
3. If an incomplete row is present, return to step 1. Otherwise, no deadlock is in the system, and the algorithm terminates.

Step 1 of the algorithm looks for a task whose resource requirements can be satisfied. If such a task exists, the task can run to completion. Resources from the completed task are freed back into the resource pool, which step 2 does. The newly available resources can be used to meet the requirements of other tasks, which allow them to resume execution and run to completion.

When the algorithm terminates, the system is deadlocked if table T has incomplete rows. The incomplete rows represent the tasks belonging to the deadlocked set. The algorithm is illustrated in the following example.

N =	4	6	2	
A =	1	2	0	
C =	0	2	0	Task 1
	1	1	0	Task 2
	1	1	1	Task 3
	1	0	1	Task 4
D =	2	2	2	Task 1
	1	1	0	Task 2
	0	1	0	Task 3
	1	1	1	Task 4

Step 1: Task 1 cannot continue because the available resources do not satisfy its requirements.

Task 2 can continue because what it needs can be met.

Step 2: A = 2   3   0

Step 3: Task 1, task 3, and task 4 remain. Return to step 1.

Step 1: Task 1 still cannot continue. The requirement from task 3 can be met.

Step 2: A = 3   4   1

Step 3: Task 1 and task 4 remain. Return to step 1.

Step 1: Task 1 still cannot continue, but task 4 can.

Step 2: A = 4   4   2

Step 3: Task 1 remains. Return to step 1.

Step 1: Task 1 can continue.

Step 2: A = 4   6   2

Step 3: No more tasks remain, and the algorithm terminates. No deadlock is in the system.

Now if the resource requirement for task 3 were [0 1 1] instead of [0 1 0], task 1, task 3, and task 4 cannot resume execution due to lack of resources. In this case, these three tasks are deadlocked.

It is worth noting that executing a deadlock detection algorithm takes time and can be non-deterministic.

16.3.3 Deadlock Recovery

After deadlock is detected, the next step is to recover from it and find ways to break the deadlock. No one magic solution exists to recover from deadlocks. Sometimes it is necessary to execute multiple recovery methods before resolving a deadlock, as illustrated later.

For preemptible resources, resource preemption is one way to recover from a deadlock. The deadlocked set is transferred to the recovery algorithm after the detection algorithm has constructed the set. The recovery algorithm can then exercise preemption by taking resources away from a task and giving these resources to another task. This process temporarily breaks the deadlock. The latter task can complete execution and free its resources. These resources are used in turn to satisfy the first task for its completion. Resource preemption on preemptible resources does not directly affect the task's execution state or result, but resource preemption can affect a task's timing constraints. The duration of resource preemption can cause the preempted task to abort, which results in an incomplete execution and indirectly affects the result of a task.

For non-preemptible resources, resource preemption can be detrimental to the preempted task and can possibly affect the results of other tasks as well. For example, consider the situation in which one task is in the midst of writing data into a shared memory region, while at the same time a second task requests read access from the same memory region. The write operation is invalidated, when another task causes a deadlock, and the system recovers from the deadlock by preempting the resource from the writing task. When the second task gets the resource and begins accessing the shared memory, the data read is incoherent and inconsistent. For this reason, a shared memory region is classified as a non-preemptible resource. The preempted task writes the remaining data when the access to the shared memory is returned. The data is no longer useful, and the write operation is wasted effort. Sometimes this type of resource preemption is as good as eliminating the preempted task from the system altogether.

On the other hand, the effects of non-preemptible resource preemption can be minimized if a task has a built-in, self-recovery mechanism. A task can achieve self-recovery by defining checkpoints along its execution path. As soon as the task reaches a checkpoint, the task changes a global state to reflect this transition. In addition, the task must define a specific entry point to be invoked by the deadlock recovery algorithm after the task is allowed to resume execution. The entry point is nothing more than the beginning of the task's built-in, self-recovery routine. In general, the recovery involves rolling back and restarting execution from the beginning of the previous checkpoint. The concept is illustrated in Listing 16.1.

Listing 16.1   Checkpoints and recovery routine.

```
<code>                              recovery_entry()

...                                 {

<code>                                  switch (state)

...                                     {

/* reached checkpoint #1 */                 case CHECKPOINT_1:
state = CHECKPOINT_1;                           recovery_method_1();

...                                             break;

<code>                                      case CHECKPOINT_2:

...                                             recovery_method_2();

/* reached checkpoint #2 */                     break;
state = CHECKPOINT_2;
                                            ...

...                                     }

...                                 }
```

In Listing 16.1, a resource preemption is performed on a writer task and the preempted resource is given to the reader task. The writer task's self-recovery involves returning to the previous checkpoint and perhaps repeating the write operation, followed by a broadcast notification to all other tasks that the shared memory region has just been updated. This process can reduce the impact on other tasks.

The reassignment target of the preempted resource plays an important role in breaking the deadlock. For example, assume the deadlocked set {T1, R2, T2, R4, T3, R5, T5, R3} has been discovered, as shown in Figure 16.3. In addition, suppose resource R2 is preempted from T2 as the first recovery step. Figure 16.4 shows the resource graph if R2 were reassigned to T3.

The problem is not solved because a new deadlock is formed by this resource assignment. Instead, if R2 were given to T1 first, the deadlock is broken as shown in Figure 16.5.

Consequently, T1 can complete and then frees R1, R2, and R3. This process in term enables T5 to complete and releases R5. Now, both R2 and R5 are available to T2, which allows it to run to completion. Finally, T2 is given a second chance to execute, and the deadlock is eliminated by proper resource reassignment.

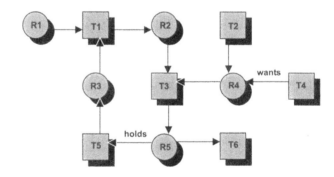

Figure 16.4   Resource preemption with a new deadlock.

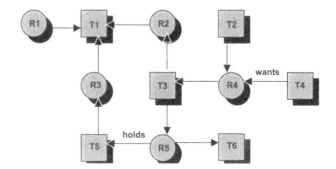

Figure 16.5   Deadlock eliminated by proper resource reassignment.

16.3.4 Deadlock Avoidance

Deadlock avoidance is an algorithm that the resource allocation system deploys. The algorithm predicts whether the current allocation request, if granted, can eventually lead to deadlock in the future.

Deadlock avoidance is similar to the deadlock detection algorithm outlined in the "Multi-Instance Resource Deadlock Detection" on page 266. Each time a resource request is made, the system tests whether granting such a request might allow the remaining resources to be given to different tasks in subsequent allocations so that all tasks can run to completion. Revisiting the example given in "Multi-Instance Resource Deadlock Detection" provides the following:

N =	4	6	2	
A =	1	2	0	
C =	0	2	0	Task 1
	1	1	0	Task 2
	1	1	1	Task 3
	1	0	1	Task 4
D =	2	2	2	Task 1
	1	1	0	Task 2
	0	1	0	Task 3
	1	1	1	Task 4

If task 2 requests one unit of resource R1, granting such a request does not lead to deadlock because a sequence of resource allocations exists, i.e., giving the remaining resources to task 2, to task 3, followed by allocation to task 4, and finally to task 1, which allows all tasks to complete. This request from task 2 is safe and is allowed. If task 4 were to make the same request for R1 and if such a request were granted, this process would prevent task 2 from completing, which would result in a deadlock such that no task could resume execution. The request from task 4 is an unsafe request, and the deadlock avoidance algorithm would reject the request and put task 4 on hold while allowing other tasks to continue.

In order for deadlock avoidance to work, each task must estimate in advance its maximum resource requirement per resource type. This estimation is often difficult to predict in a dynamic system. For more static embedded systems or for systems with predictable operating environments, however, deadlock avoidance can be achieved. The estimations from all tasks are used to construct the demand table, D. This resource estimation only identifies the potential maximum resource requirement through certain execution paths. In the majority of cases, there would be overestimation. Overestimation by each task can lead to inefficient resource utilization in a heavily loaded system. This problem is caused because the system might be running with most of the resources in use, and the algorithm might predict more requests as being unsafe. This issue could result in many tasks being blocked, while holding resources that were already allocated to them.

16.3.5 Deadlock Prevention

Deadlock prevention is a set of constraints and requirements constructed into a system so that resource requests that might lead to deadlocks are not made. Deadlock prevention differs from deadlock avoidance in that no run-time validation of resource allocation requests occurs. Deadlock prevention focuses on structuring a system to ensure that one or more of the four conditions for deadlock i.e., mutual exclusion, no preemption, hold-and-wait, and circular wait is not satisfied.

This set of constraints and requirements placed on resource allocation requests is as follows:

- **Eliminating the hold-and-wait deadlock condition.** A task requests at one time all resources that it will need. The task can begin execution only when every resource from the request set is granted.

  This requirement addresses the hold-and-wait condition for deadlock. A task that obtains all required resources before execution avoids the need to wait for anything during execution. This approach, however, has limited practicality and several drawbacks. In a dynamic system, tasks have difficulty predicting in advance what resources will be required. Even if all possible resource requirements could be accurately predicted, this prediction does not guarantee that every resource in this predicted set would be used. Execution paths, which external factors affect, determine which resources are used.

  One major drawbacks to this approach is the implicit requirement that all resources must be freed at the same time. This requirement is important because a resource can be needed in multiple code paths; it can be used and later be reused. So, the resource must be kept until the end of task execution. Some of the resources, however, might be used once or used only briefly. It is inefficient for these resources to be kept for a long time because they cannot be reassigned to other tasks.

- **Eliminating the no-preemption deadlock condition.** A task must release already acquired resources if a new request is denied. The task must then initiate a new request including both the new resource and all previously held resources.

This requirement addresses the no-preemption condition for deadlock. This approach is slightly more dynamic than the previous method in that resources are acquired on an as-needed basis and only those resources needed for a particular execution path, instead of all possible resources, are acquired.

This approach, however, is not much better than the previous one. For tasks holding non-preemptible resources, this requirement means that each task must restart execution either from the beginning or from well-defined checkpoints. This process nullifies partially complete work. Potentially, a task might never complete, depending on the average number of tasks existing in the system at a given time and depending on the overall system scheduling behavior.

- **Eliminating the circular-wait deadlock condition.** An ordering on the resources must be imposed so that if a task currently holds resource R_i, a subsequent request must be for resource R_j where $j > i$. The next request must be for resource R_k where $k > j$, and so on.

This imposition addresses the circular-wait condition for deadlock. Resources are organized into a hierarchical structure. A task is allowed to acquire additional resources while holding other resources, but these new resources must be higher in the hierarchy than any currently held resources.

16.4 Priority Inversion

Priority inversion is a situation in which a low-priority task executes while a higher priority task waits on it due to resource contentions.

A high task priority implies a more stringent deadline. In a priority-based, preemptive scheduling system, the kernel schedules higher priority tasks first and postpones lower priority tasks until either all of the higher priority tasks are completed or the higher priority tasks voluntarily relinquish the CPU. In real-time embedded systems, the kernel strives to make the schedulability of the highest priority task deterministic. To do this, the kernel must preempt the currently running task and switch the context to run the higher priority task that has just become eligible, all within a known time interval. This system scheduling behavior is the norm when these tasks are independent of each other. Task interdependency is inevitable when tasks share resources and synchronizing activities. Priority inversion occurs when task interdependency exists among tasks with different priorities.

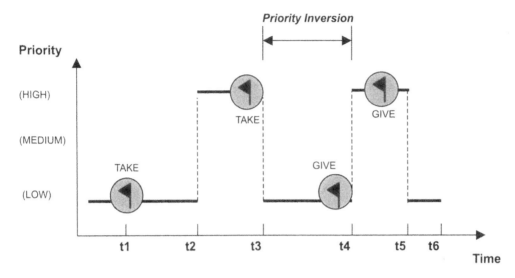

Figure 16.6   Priority inversion example.

Consider the situation shown in Figure 16.6, in which a higher priority task shares a resource with a lower priority task. The higher priority task must wait when the lower priority task has locked the resource, even though the higher priority task is eligible to run.

As shown in Figure 16.6, at time t1 the low-priority task (LP-task) locks the shared resource. The LP-task continues until time t2 when the high-priority task (HP-task) becomes eligible to run. The scheduler immediately preempts the LP-task and context-switches to the HP-task. The HP-task runs until time t3 when it requires the shared resource. Because the resource is in the locked state, the HP-task must block and wait for its release. At this point, the scheduler context-switches back to the LP-task. Priority inversion begins at time t3. At time t4, the LP-task releases the shared resource, which triggers preemption and allows the HP-task to resume execution. Priority inversion ends at time t4. The HP-task completes at time t5, which allows the LP-task to resume execution and finally complete at time t6.

The priority inversion shown in Figure 16.6 is a *bounded priority inversion*. The duration of the low-priority task's holding time on the shared resource is known. It is possible for a medium-priority task to preempt the low-priority task for an undetermined amount of time, which would cause the high-priority task to wait indefinitely. This priority inversion scenario is called *unbounded priority inversion* and is shown in Figure 16.7.

As in the previous example, priority inversion takes place at time t3. The low-priority task (LP-task) executes until time t4 when an unrelated medium-priority task (MP-task)

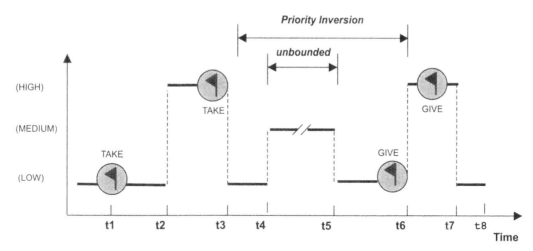

Figure 16.7   Unbounded priority inversion example.

preempts it. Because the MP-task does not share resources with either the HP-task or the LP-task, the MP-task continues execution until it completes at time t5. The duration between t4 and t5 is unknown because the duration depends on the nature of the MP-task. In addition, any number of unrelated medium-priority tasks can execute during this period. These unknown factors affect the interval and translate into unbounded priority inversion.

When priority inversion occurs, the execution times for some tasks are reduced, while others are elongated. In Figure 16.7, consider the case in which the high-priority task (HP-task) takes the guarding semaphore before the low-priority task (LP-task). The medium-priority task (MP-task) must wait until the HP-task completes. However, when the MP-task executes first, it is preempted by the HP-task. Again, the MP-task resumes execution after the HP-task completes. In both cases, the overall execution times for the MP-task are longer than the execution time to complete the MP-task during the priority inversion. Although some tasks are completed early, other tasks, such as the HP-task, might miss their deadlines. This issue is called *timing anomaly* introduced by priority inversion.

Priority inversion results from resource synchronization among tasks of differing priorities. Priority inversion cannot be avoided, but it can be minimized using resource access control protocols.

A *resource access control protocol* is a set of rules that defines the conditions under which a resource can be granted to a requesting task and governs the execution scheduling property of the task holding the resource.

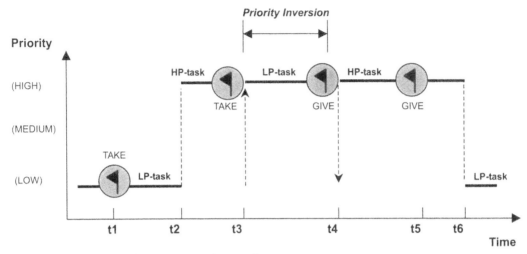

Figure 16.8   Priority inheritance protocol example.

Access control protocols are discussed in the following sections. These access control protocols eliminate the unbound priority inversion, and two of these protocols reduce the inversion time.

16.4.1 Priority Inheritance Protocol

The Priority Inheritance Protocol is a resource access control protocol that raises the priority of a task, if that task holds a resource being requested by a higher priority task, to the same priority level as the higher priority task. This access control protocol follows the rules in Table 16.1 when a task T requests a resource R.

Table 16.1   Priority Inheritance Protocol rules.

Rule #	Description
1	If R is in use, T is blocked.
2	If R is free, R is allocated to T.
3	When a task of a higher priority requests the same resource, T's execution priority is raised to the requesting task's priority level.
4	The task returns to its previous priority when it releases R.

This access control protocol is shown in Figure 16.8.

With the priority inheritance protocol, when the LP-task blocks the HP-task at time t3, the execution priority is raised to that of the HP-task. This process ensures that unrelated medium-priority tasks cannot interfere while the LP-task executes, which results in the elimination of the unbounded priority inversion. When the LP-task releases control

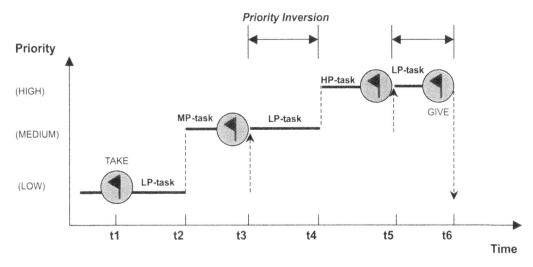

Figure 16.9   Transitive priority promotion example.

of the shared resource, the priority is immediately lowered to its previous level, which allows the HP-task to preempt its execution. This action ends the priority inversion at time t4. The HP-task continues its execution, however, even when it releases the resource at t5. This is the nature of the priority-based, preemptive scheduling scheme. The HP-task runs because it has the highest priority in the system.

The priority inheritance protocol is dynamic because a task does not have its priority raised until a higher-priority task makes a request on the shared resource. An unrelated higher-priority task can still preempt the task, which is the nature of the priority-based, preemptive scheduling scheme. The priority promotion for a task during priority inversion is transitive, which means the priority of a promoted task continues to rise even if higher-priority tasks make requests on the same shared resource while priority inversion is taking place, as shown in Figure 16.9.

In this example, three tasks with differing priorities share a resource. The LP-task acquires the resource first at time t1. At time t2, the MP-task preempts the LP-task and executes until t3 when it needs the resource. The MP-task is blocked. At that point, the LP-task inherits the priority from the MP-task and resumes execution at that level. The HP-task preempts the LP-task when it readies at t4. The HP-task is blocked at t5 when it also needs access to the shared resource. Once more, the LP-task inherits its priority from HP-task and resumes execution at the highest level. As soon as the LP-task completes at time t6, its priority is immediately lowered to the level originally assigned.

In this example, the MP-task can hold some additional resource required by the HP-task. The HP-task can also acquire some other resources needed by the MP-task before the HP-task blocks. When the LP-task releases the resource and the HP-task immediately gets to run, it is deadlocked with the MP-task. Therefore, priority inheritance protocol does not eliminate deadlock.

16.4.2 Ceiling Priority Protocol

In the ceiling priority protocol, the priority of every task is known, as are the resources required by every task. For a given resource, the *priority ceiling* is the highest priority of all possible tasks that might require the resource.

For example, if a resource R is required by four tasks (T1 of priority 4, T2 of priority 9, T3 of priority 10, and T4 of priority 8), the priority ceiling of R is 10, which is the highest priority of the four tasks.

This access control protocol follows the rules in Table 16.2 when a task T requests a resource R.

Table 16.2   Ceiling priority protocol rules.

Rule #	Description
1	If R is in use, T is blocked.
2	If R is free, R is allocated to T. T's execution priority is raised to the priority ceiling of R if that is higher. At any given time, T's execution priority equals the highest priority ceiling of all its held resources.
3	T's priority is assigned the next-highest priority ceiling of another resource when the resource with the highest priority ceiling is released.
4	The task returns to its assigned priority after it has released all resources.

This access control protocol is shown in Figure 16.10.

With the ceiling priority protocol, the task inherits the priority ceiling of the resource as soon as the task acquires the resource even when no other higher priority tasks contend for the same resource. This rule implies that all critical sections from every sharing task have the same criticality level. The idea is to finish the critical section as soon as possible to avoid possible conflicts.

16.4.3 Priority Ceiling Protocol

Similarly to the ceiling priority protocol, the priority of every task is known in the priority ceiling protocol. The resources that every task requires are also known before execution. The *current priority ceiling* for a running system at any time is the highest priority ceiling of all resources in use at that time.

For example, if four resources are in use and if R1 has a priority ceiling of 4, R2 has a priority ceiling of 9, R3 of a priority ceiling 10, and R4 of a priority ceiling 8, the current priority ceiling of the system is 10. Note that different tasks can hold these resources.

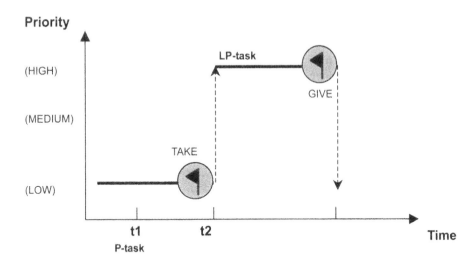

Figure 16.10 Ceiling priority protocol example.

This access control protocol follows the rules in Table 16.3 when a task T requests a resource R.

Table 16.3   Priority ceiling protocol rules.

Rule #	Description
1	If R is in use, T is blocked.
2	If R is free and if the priority of T is higher than the current priority ceiling, R is allocated to T.
3	If the current priority ceiling belongs to one of the resources that T currently holds, R is allocated to T, and otherwise T is blocked
4	The task that blocks T inherits T's priority if it is higher and executes at this priority until it releases every resource whose priority ceiling is higher than or equal to T's priority. The task then returns to its previous priority.

In the priority ceiling protocol, a requesting task can be blocked for one of three causes. The first cause is when the resource is current in use, which is *direct resource contention blocking*, and is the result of rule #1. The second cause is when the blocking task has inherited a higher priority and its current execution priority is higher than that of the requesting task. This cause is *priority inheritance blocking* and is the result of rule #4. A task can be blocked when its priority is lower than the current priority ceiling even when the requested resource is free. This cause is *priority ceiling blocking* and is a direct consequence of the "otherwise" clause of rule #3. Rule #3 prevents a task from blocking itself if it holds a resource that has defined the current priority ceiling.

One of the deadlock prevention strategies in the "Deadlock Prevention" on page 272, section 16.3.5, is to impose ordering on the resources. The resource ordering can be realized by using the priority ceilings of the resources. Rule #2 says if the priority of T is higher than the current priority ceiling, T does not require any resources that are in use. This issue occurs because otherwise the current priority ceiling would be either equal to or higher than the priority of T, which implies that tasks with a priority higher than T's do not require the resources currently in use. Consequently, none of the tasks that are holding resources in use can inherit a higher priority, preempt task T, and then request a resource that T holds. This feature prevents the circular-wait condition. This feature is also why deadlock cannot occur when using the priority ceiling protocol as an access control protocol. The same induction process shows that the condition in which a task blocks another task but is in turn blocked by a third task, transitive blocking, does not occur under the priority ceiling protocol.

The priority ceiling protocol has these characteristics:

- A requesting task can be blocked by only one task; therefore, the blocking interval is at most the duration of one critical section.
- Transitive blocking never occurs under the priority ceiling protocol.
- Deadlock never occurs under the priority ceiling protocol.

16.5 Points to Remember

Some points to remember include the following:

- Resources can be classified as either preemptible or non-preemptible resources.
- Deadlock occurs when all four of these conditions are true: mutual exclusion, no preemption, hold-and-wait, and circular wait.
- Resource requests can be classified into Single, AND, OR, and AND-OR request models.
- Strategies exist for dealing with deadlocks: deadlock detection and recovery, deadlock avoidance, and deadlock prevention.
- Access control protocols exist for dealing with priority inversion: priority inheritance protocol, ceiling priority protocol, and priority ceiling protocol.
- Deadlock never occurs under the priority ceiling protocol.

Appendix A

References

Almasi, George S., and Allan Gottlieb. 1994. *Highly Parallel Computing*. 2nd ed. Redwood City, CA: The Benjamin/Cummings Publishing Company, Inc.

Association of Computing Machinery. "Source of Unbounded Priority Inversions in Real-Time Systems and a Comparative Study of Possible Solutions." *ACM Operating Systems Review* 26, no. 2 (April 1992): 110–20.

Barr, Michael. 1999. *Programming Embedded Systems in C and C++*. Sebastopol, CA: O'Reilly & Associates, Inc.

Coffman, E.G., Jr., M.J. Elphick, and A. Shoshani. "System Deadlocks." *Computing Surveys* 3, no. 2 (June 1971).

Douglass, Bruce Powel. 1999. *Doing Hard Time*. Reading, MA: Addison-Wesley.

Fontao, Rafael O. "A Concurrent Algorithm for Avoiding Deadlocks in Multiprocess Multiple Resource Systems." *Tech Report No. 70-5*, Department of Computer Science, Cornell University, Ithaca, NY (January 1970).

Frailery, Dennis J. "A Practical Approach to Managing Resources and Avoiding Deadlocks." *Communications of ACM* 16, no. 5 (May 1973).

Gomaa, Hassan. 1996. *Designing Concurrent, Distributed, and Real-Time Applications with UML*. Boston, MA: Addison-Wesley.

Goodenough, John B. and Lui Sha. "The Priority Ceiling Protocol: A method of minimizing the blocking of high priority Ada tasks." *Ada Letters, Special Issues: Proc. 2nd Int'l Workshop on Real-Time Ada Issues* VIII, Vol. 7, (Fall 1988): 20–31.

Holt, Richard C. "Some Deadlock Properties of Computer Systems." *Computing Surveys* 4, no. 3 (September 1972).

Howard, John H., Jr. "Mixed Solutions for the Deadlock Problem." *Communications of ACM* 16, no. 7 (July 1973).

Institute of Electrical and Electronics Engineers. "Priority Inheritance Protocols: An approach to real-time synchronization." *IEEE Transactions on Computers* 39, 1990.

Knotothanassis, Leonidas I., Robert W. Wisneiwski, and Michael L. Scott. "Scheduler-Conscious Synchronization." *ACM Transactions on Computer Systems* 15, no. 1 (February 1997): 3–40.

Kopetz, Herman. 1997. *Real-Time Systems: Design Principles for Distributed Embedded Applications*. Norwell, MA: Kluwer Academic Publishers.

Kopetz, H., and G. Gruensteidi. "TTP—A Protocol for Fault-Tolerant Real-Time Systems." *IEEE Computer* 24, no. 1 (1994): 14–23.

Kopetz, H., and T. Thurner. "TTP—A New Approach to Solving the Interoperability Problem of Independently Developed ECUs." *SAE World Congress 1998 (Detroit, Michigan)*, Warrendale, PA: SAE Press.

Klein, M.H., T. Ralya, B. Pollak, R. Obenza, and M.G. Harbour. 1993. *A Practitioner's Handbook for Real-Time Analysis: Guide to Rate Monotonic Analysis for Real-Time Systems*. Boston, MA: Kluwer Academic Publishers, ISBN 0-7923-9361-9.

Labrosse, Jean J. 2002. *Embedded Systems Building Blocks*, 2nd ed. Lawrence, KS: CMP Books.

Lamport, Leslie. "The Mutual Exclusion Problem: Part I—The Theory of Interprocess Communication." *Journal of the Association for Computing Machinery* 33, no. 2 (April 1986): 313–326.

Lamport, Leslie. "The Mutual Exclusion Problem: Part II—Statement and Solutions." *Journal of the Association for Computing Machinery* 33, no. 2 (April 1986).

Lander, Leslie C., Sandeep Mitra, and Thomas F. Piatkowski. "Priority Inversion in Ada Programs During Elaboration." *Washington Ada Symposium Proceedings* (June 1990): 133.

Lehoczky, J.P., L. Sha, J.K. Strosnider, and H. Tokuda. 1991. "Fixed Priority Scheduling Theory for Hard Real-Time Systems." *Foundations of Real-Time Computing, Scheduling, and Resource Management*. Andre M. Van Tilborg, Gary M. Koob, editors. Boston, MA: Kluwer Academic Publishers, ISBN 0-7923-9166-7.

Locke, Douglass. "Priority Inversion and Its Control: An experimental investigation." IBM FSD, *Ada Letters*. Special Edition 8, no. 7 (1988): 39.

Lui, C.L. and J.W. Layland. "Scheduling Algorithms for Multiprogramming in a Hard Real-Time Environment." *Journal of Association for Computing Machinery* 20, no. 1 (January 1973): 46–61.

Motorola, Inc. *PowerPC*^{*a*}*Microprocessor Family: The Programming Environments*, 1994. Motorola, Inc., pages 6–10, Table 6-3.

Nissanke, Nimal. 1997. *Real-time Systems*. Hertfordshire, England: Prentice Hall Series in Computer Science, ISBN 0-13-651274-7

Poledna, S. 1996. *Fault-Tolerant Real-Time Systems: The Problem of Replica Determinism*. Boston, MA: Kluwer Academic Publishers.

Sha, L., M.H. Klein, and J.B. Goodenough. 1991. "Rate Monotonic Analysis for Real-Time Systems." *Foundations of Real-Time Computing, Scheduling, and Resource Management*. Andre M. Van Tilborg, Gary M. Koob, editors. Boston, MA: Kluwer Academic Publishers, ISBN 0-7923-9166-7. Simon, David E. 2000. *An Embedded Software Primer*. Boston, MA: Addison-Wesley.

Shih, Chia-Shiang, and John A. Stankovic. 1990. *Distributed Deadlock Detection in Ada Runtime Environments*. ACM.

Simon, David E. 2000. *An Embedded Software Primer*. Boston, MA: Addison-Wesley.

Singhal, Mukesh and Niranjan G. Shivaratri. 1994. *Advanced Concepts in Operating Systems*. McGraw-Hill, Inc.

Sprunt, B., L. Sha, and J.P. Lehoczky. "Aperiodic Task Scheduling for Hard Real-Time Systems." *The Journal of Real-Time Systems* (1989): pages 27–60.

Stankovic, John A. and Krithi Ramamritham. 1998. *Tutorial Hard Real-Time Systems*. Washington, D.C.: Computer Society Press of the IEEE, ISBN 0-8186-4819-8

Tanenbaum, Andrew S. 1992. *Modern Operating Systems*. Englewood Cliffs, NJ: Prentice-Hall, Inc.

Tzeng, Nian-Feng, and Angkul Kongmunvattana. 1997. "Distributed Shared Memory Systems with Improved Barrier Synchronization and Data Transfer." In *SIGARCH—ACM Transactions on Computer Architecture*. ISBN 0-89791-902-5.

Vahalia, Uresh. 1996. *Unix Internals*. Upper Saddle River, NJ: Prentice-Hall, Inc.

.

ABOUT THE AUTHORS

Qing Li is currently a senior architect at Wind River systems and has four patents pending in the embedded kernel and networking protocol design areas. His 12+ years in engineering include expertise as a principal engineer designing and developing protocol stacks and embedded applications for the telecommunications and networks arena. Qing is the lead architect of Wind River's embedded IPv6 products and is at the forefront of various IPv6 initiatives. In the past, Qing owned his own company developing commercial software for the telecommunications industry. Additionally, he was one of a four-member Silicon Valley startup that designed and developed proprietary algorithms and applications for embedded biometric devices in the security industry.

Qing holds a Bachelor of Science degree with Specialization in Computing Science from the University of Alberta in Edmonton, Alberta, Canada. Qing has a Masters of Science degree with Distinction in Computer Engineering, with focus in Advanced High Performance Computing from Santa Clara University, Santa Clara, CA, USA. Qing is a member of Association for Computing Machinery and a member of IEEE Computer Society.

Caroline Yao has 15+ years in technology and the commercial software arena with six years in the embedded market. She has expertise ranging from product development, product management, product marketing, business development, and strategic alliances. She is also a co-inventor and co-US patent pending (June 12, 2001) holder for "System and Method for Providing Cross-Development Application Design Tools and Services Via a Network."

Caroline holds a Bachelor of Arts in Statistics from the University of California Berkeley.

INDEX

Symbols

.const 41
.data 26, 30–31, 33–34, 41, 43
.sbss 26, 33–34, 41
.sdata 26, 33–34, 41
.section 27
.strtab 27
.symtab 27
.text 26, 30–31, 33–34, 43

A

A/V decoder 5
acknowledgement 38, 106–107, 109, 117
acquire 73–75, 79–95, 126–127, 129, 205, 210, 236, 245–246, 248, 257, 259–262, 273, 277–278
active I/O device 218–222
activity synchronization 61, 97, 120, 231–258
alignment exception 144
allocation table 200–201, 203, 207, 266
aperiodic 11–12, 16, 219–223, 226, 229
archive utility 20
Arshad, Nauman xii
assembler 20, 23, 26, 30
asynchronous 10, 117, 121, 125, 144, 149–150, 174, 219–221, 233, 236, 239–240, 242–244, 248, 255
    event handler 122
    exception 144, 149–150, 155, 160, 165
    signal routine 122
asynchronous exception 158
ATM 134
atomic operation 127–129, 160, 163, 241, 254
atomicity 128
audio/video decoder 5

B

Background Debug Mod
    See BDM.
backtrack 209
barrier 233–236, 238
BDM 36–37, 51–52
binary semaphore 81, 83, 87–88, 90–91, 93, 95, 107, 235, 241–242, 246, 249
blocked state 67–74, 80, 83–85, 87–91, 93, 102, 110–111, 116, 123–125, 128, 149, 174, 209–211, 227–228, 234, 236, 239, 252, 260, 262, 272, 276–280
blocking call 69–71, 76, 89, 102, 239–240, 254
block-mode device 190–192
board support package
    See BSP
boot image 37–39, 43, 48
booting 8, 35–36, 41, 43–44, 46, 49
bootstrap 40
bounded priority inversion 274
bounded timer inaccuracy 172
broadcast communication 105, 109
BSP 46, 50, 62, 182
    initialization phase 50
bus error 202
byte stream 111, 115

C

C&D system 12
caches 41, 49
catch 124–125
ceiling priority protocol 278
character-mode device 190, 192
checkpoint 209, 269–270, 273
checksum 44
clock drift 239
COFF 24

command interpreter 136
command shell 134, 136–137, 139
Common Object File Format
    See COFF
communication 234, 236–238, 247–258
compactness 62, 64
competing critical section 232, 240
component configuration 139, 141
    table 140
component description file 139
compression 44
computationally bound 218, 225
concurrency 61, 65, 77, 145–146, 163, 213, 217–229, 231
concurrent 61, 65–66, 79, 90, 231–232, 260
condition synchronization 233
condition variable 111, 128–130, 233, 235, 258
context 58, 60, 71, 75, 152, 156, 158, 161–162, 171, 174, 214–215, 217, 239, 273
    switch 57–59, 69, 73, 153, 156, 163, 274
controlled system 11–13
controlling system 11–12
counting semaphore 81–84, 86, 89–90, 93, 95, 209–211, 241, 244–248, 251, 254
critical section 74–75, 85, 123, 232, 239–241, 278, 280
criticality 224, 226, 229, 241, 278
cross compiler 8, 20
cross-platform development 7–8, 19–20

D

data communication 61, 97, 105–108, 110, 237, 245, 248, 255
deadlock 60, 83, 92, 259–273, 278, 280
    avoidance 271–272
    detection 262–268, 271
    prevention 272–273, 280
    recovery 263, 269–270
deadlocked set 261, 263, 266, 270
debouncing 164
debug agent 20, 36, 39, 46, 67, 137–139, 146

debugger 20, 23–24, 39, 41, 46, 52, 67, 137–138, 141, 146
decompression 44
default action 124, 131, 152, 165
default handler 123–124, 152
delayed 68, 74, 191, 239
descriptor 111, 113–114, 116
destructive read 104
detection recovery 268
deterministic 14–15, 63, 199, 209, 273
device
    control 188
    table 196–197
device table 198
digital set-top box
    See DST.
digital signal processor
    See DSP
Direct Memory Access
    See DMA
direct resource contention blocking 279
dispatcher 57, 59
DMA 7, 170, 188, 190–191
DRAM 9, 32, 34, 170
driver table 196–198
DSP 6, 17
DST 5
dynamic linking 22–23, 26
Dynamic RAM
    See DRAM

E

E2PROM*See EEPROM*
edge triggering 164
EEPROM 8–9, 36, 43
Electrically Erasable Programmable ROM
    See EEPROM
ELF 24, 36, 38, 43, 45
embedded processor 5–7, 39, 51, 143, 145–146, 149, 154, 169, 202
embedding system 5

entry 22, 27, 67, 152, 175–177, 183, 196–197, 203, 207, 265, 269
   in rendezvous synchronization 234
EPROM 8–9
Erasable Programmable ROM
   See EPROM 8
Ethernet 7, 134, 138, 209
event register 118–121, 241, 243, 250–251, 254
exception 143–165
   facility 143, 146
   frame 151, 158
   service routine 145, 152, 158
Executable and Linking Format
   See ELF
executable image 20–25, 27–32, 34–36, 41, 140
External Data Representation
   See XDR 136
external fragmentation 201

F

FAT 135
Fiddler, Jerry ix
Field Programmable ROM
   See PROM
FIFO 80, 99, 102–103, 105, 111–113, 128
Figure 8.15 130
File Transfer Protocol
   See FTP
filtering 164
finite state machine 68
first in/first out
   See FIFO
flash memory 8–9, 29, 31–32, 36, 38, 40–41, 134
floating point 149
flow of control 59
frequency 12, 147, 157, 160–161, 163, 170, 177, 182–183, 220, 228
FTP 38
functional cohesion 218, 225
functional correctness 13, 16

G

general exception table 152
general-purpose operating system 5, 54
general-purpose processor 6, 8
global symbol 22

H

handshake 107
hard real-time system 14–16
hard timer 167
heap 200, 205, 207, 209
   array 206–207
   data structure 205–206
hierarchical timing wheel 180–181
hook 73
host system 8, 19–20, 27, 35–37, 39, 42, 46–47, 137

I

I/O 42, 47, 62, 86, 90, 138, 183–192, 215, 217–218, 225, 227, 233, 236, 238, 240, 251, 260
   active device 219–222
   isolated 189
   passive device 219, 223–224
   port 189–190
   subsystem 187–198
   uniform 192, 195–197
idle task 67, 69
IEEE 1149.1 52
imprecise exception 149
IN 189
in-circuit emulator 51
indeterminism 239–240
industrial automation 2
input and output
   See I/O
instruction pointer
   See IP
interleaving 57, 206, 217
interlocked 105, 107
internal error 145–146

internal fragmentation 200, 209
interrupt 143–165
    latency 161, 168
    lock 238–240, 245–246, 248, 250
    mask register 160
    nested 147, 155–156, 246
    overhead 168
    request line
        See IRQ
    response time 161, 163
    service routine 58–59, 86, 90, 97, 102, 106, 124, 147, 149, 152, 160–161, 168, 170–171, 182, 240, 246
    software 121–126
    stack 151, 158
    table 147–148, 152
interrupt request line 147
IP 43, 183, 217
IRQ 147, 159, 193
ISDN 134
ISO 9660 135

J

Joint Test Action Group
    See JTAG
JTAG 36–37, 51–52

K

kernel 20, 42, 55–62, 65–75, 79–80, 82–83, 86, 97–99, 101–102, 104–105, 111, 133, 153, 165, 171, 174, 183, 188, 200, 239, 250, 273, 285
    scheduling 74, 160, 171, 260, 273
knot 264

L

label 43
last-in/first-out
    See LIFO
level triggering 164
library 21–22, 138, 158, 163, 184

LIFO 102–103
link loader 20, 24
linker 20–24, 27, 41, 43, 140
    command file 20–21, 27, 29–31
    directive 27
load address 24, 27, 38, 41, 43
loader 20, 24–25, 27, 30, 32–33, 36–41, 44, 136
lock 82
logical correctness 17
logical expression 126
loosely coupled communication 236

M

mailbox 107
makefile 20
Mask Programmed ROM 9
maskable exception 149
mass storage device 134, 139
MEMORY 28–29
memory 199–212
    alignment 31
    compaction 199, 201–202
    fragmentation 199–202
    leak 73–74
    map 28–29, 40–41, 50
    mapped I/O 189
memory management unit
    See MMU 211
message
    length 98, 100
    queue 56–57, 61, 72, 77, 97, 105, 110, 112, 115–116, 138, 234, 237–238, 244, 247–249, 251–252, 254–255, 262
    sink 105
    source 105
micro-kernel 133, 141
MMU 5, 211
monitor 20, 32–33, 36, 38–39, 44, 46, 51
monolithic 54, 133
MS-DOS 135
multitasking 5, 54, 57–58, 65, 211, 217

mutex 80, 82–87, 91–94, 126–129, 209–211, 233, 235–236, 245–246, 254
mutual exclusion 232–233, 240–241, 260
mutually exclusive access 79, 86, 90

N

named pipe 113–114
native development 20
nested interrupt 147, 155–156, 246
Network File System
    See NFS
network protocol stacks 134
NFS 134–135
NMI 149–150
non-destructive read 104
non-deterministic 125, 179, 268
non-interlocked 105–106
non-maskable exception 149
non-maskable interrupt
    See NMI
non-preemptible resource 260–261, 269, 273
non-privileged state 153
Nonvolatile RAM
    See NVRAM
NVRAM 8–9

O

object file 20–23, 38
    format 20, 23, 38, 45
    relocatable 21–22
objects 56, 61, 65
OCD 51–52
on-chip debugging
    See OCD
on-chip timer 169
OUT 189

P

passive I/O device 218–219, 223–224
PC
    See program counter
PDA 6, 187, 199

penalty 14–15, 17
pending 119–120, 123, 125–126, 154
performance 6–7, 41, 55, 57–59, 62–63, 65, 100–101, 149, 173, 192, 199, 217, 220
periodic 9, 11–12, 16, 169–171, 177, 218–224, 226–227, 229, 251, 263
peripheral 6–7, 38, 188
personal digital assistant
    See PDA
personality module 52
pervasive computer 1
pipe 111–112
    control block 112–113
PIT 169, 171
platform 8, 52, 136
polling 74, 220, 223–224
port number 189
power conservation 67
precise exception 149–150
predicate 126–128, 252, 254
predictability 62–63
preemptible resource 260
preemption lock 75, 238–240, 246
preemptive scheduling 56, 61, 66, 69, 77, 226, 239, 273, 277
priority 59–61, 66–72, 74–76, 87–91, 103, 109, 115, 126–129, 147–165, 174–175, 222, 224–226, 239, 259
    ceiling blocking 279
    ceiling protocol 278–280
    inheritance blocking 279
    inheritance protocol 84, 276–278
    inversion 75, 82, 84–85, 87, 211, 259–280
        bounded 274
priority inversion ix, 60, 273
privileged instruction set 145
privileged state 144
process
    control 238
program counter 67, 149–152, 217
program header table 24–25, 43
programmable interval timer
    See PIT

programmable interval timer chip 146
PROM 8–9
protocol 37, 39

Q

queue
    control block 98
    length 98, 100

R

raise 84, 144–145, 151, 154, 160–161, 164,
    276–278
RAM 9, 42
random access memory
    See RAM
Rate Monotonic Analysis
    See RMA
rate monotonic scheduling
    See RMS
read only memory
    see ROM
ready state 67–73, 80
real 13
real-time clock 147–148, 168–169, 182, 184
real-time embedded system 1, 3, 10, 54–56,
    61, 67, 101, 208–209, 214, 217
real-time operating system
    See RTOS
real-time system 10–13, 63, 65, 71, 97, 125,
    213–214, 219, 225–227, 229, 260
    hard 14, 16
    hard vs. soft 14
    soft 14
recursive access 82–83
recursive mutex 83
refresh rate 170
release 72, 74, 79–87, 89–91, 93, 124, 127,
    129, 174, 211, 245–246, 257, 270, 273–
    274
reliability 62
relocatable object file 21–22

relocation
    entry 22, 26
    table 22–23
remote procedure call
    See RPC
rendezvous 86, 234
reset vector 39, 43, 48
resource
    graph 261, 263–264, 266, 270
    leak 73–74
    request model 262–264
    server 233
    synchronization 231–240, 275
resource access control protocol 275
resource request model 262
resource synchronization 47, 231–258
restart 74–75, 209, 269, 273
RMA 214, 226–228
    schedulability test 226
RMS 226
ROM 9, 42
round-robin scheduling 56, 59–61, 175
RPC 135–136
RTOS 53–64
run address 24, 41
running state 67–73, 80

S

scalability 62
schedulability 226–229
schedulable entity 57
scheduler 46, 56–61, 69, 133, 160, 171, 175,
    182, 217, 239–240, 260, 274
scheduling
    algorithm 56, 59–61, 69, 226
    delay 163, 174–175
    policy 55, 59
schematic 28, 170
SDRAM 32, 34
SECTION 28–30, 33
section 24–28
    header table 24–25, 43
select 112, 114, 116–117

semaphore 57, 61, 79–95, 138, 234
    control block 79
    counting 81, 209–210, 246
    mutex 82–87, 91–94, 126–129, 209–211, 233, 235–236, 245–246, 254
sequence control 233
sequential 65, 222
    cohesion 219, 225, 229
services 56, 62, 133–141, 150–163, 167–185
signal 121–126
    control block 122–123
    facility 125, 244
    glitch 163
    handler 122, 124–125, 255
Simple Network Management Protocol
    See SNMP
SNMP 134
SoC 7
soft real-time system 14
soft timer 171
soft-timer facility
    See timer facility
software interrupt 121–126
sporadic 158, 164
spurious interrupt 163–165
SRAM 9
stable deadlock 263
stack overflow 156–158
stack pointer 40, 43–44, 153, 158
starvation 71, 259
Static RAM
    See SRAM
status register 152, 160
stray pointer 145
stubs 135
supervisor stack 153
suspended 67–68, 73, 75
symbol
    relocation 22–23
    resolution 22, 24, 28
    table 23
symbol resolution 22

synchronization 57, 61, 77, 79, 87–94, 107, 111, 117, 120, 125, 133, 209, 211, 213, 225, 227, 231–236
synchronous 10, 149–150, 219–221
    exception 144, 149–150, 155, 160
system call 59, 63, 137
system clock 168–169, 171, 182, 184
system reset exception 144
system-on-a-chip
    See SoC

T

target system 8, 20–21, 27–29, 32, 34–52, 137–139
task 61, 65–78, 138
    control block 58, 66, 119, 122, 152, 250
    deletion lock 74, 83
    routine 66–67
    state 67
    structure 76
task-ready list 69–70
TCP/IP 51, 133–134, 139–140
Telnet 134
temporal
    cohesion 218, 225, 229
    deadlock 263
TFTP 38
thread 46, 57–58, 61, 65, 77, 79, 90, 217, 231, 259–260, 264
throughput 63
tick 170–171, 174–175, 177–178, 182–183, 238, 251, 254
tightly coupled communication 107, 236–237
time slicing 60–61
timer
    See Chapter 11
timer chip 169
timer facility 171–176
timer interrupt 170
    rate register 170
timer services
    See Chapter 11

timing
    anomaly 275
    correctness 13, 15–16
    wheel 176, 179–182
        hierarchical 180
TRAP 145
triggering mechanism 160, 164
Trivial File Transfer Protocol
    See TFTP

U

UDP 134
unbounded priority inversion 274–276
uniform I/O 192, 195–197
uniprocessor 57, 233
universal processor 5
unlock 74, 82–83, 85–86, 91, 94, 128–129,
    210, 236, 254, 257
unnamed pipe 113–114
unresolved external symbol 22
updates to book xii

urgency 218, 223–224, 244–245, 255
user stack 153
utilization
    bound 226
    factor 226

V

vector 149, 155
    address 148, 152, 155
    control 147
    reset 39, 43, 48
    system exception 41
    table 124, 149, 152, 155, 182

W

web tablet 4

X

XDR 136

Printed and bound by CPI Group (UK) Ltd, Croydon, CR0 4YY

22/10/2024

01777636-0005